THE CASE OF THE PERSEVERING MALTESE:
COLLECTED ESSAYS

Works by Harry Mathews

FICTION
The Conversions
Tlooth
Country Cooking and Other Stories
The Sinking of the Odradek Stadium
Cigarettes
Singular Pleasures
The American Experience
The Journalist
Sainte Catherine
The Human Country: New and Collected Stories

POETRY
The Ring: Poems 1956-1969
The Planisphere
Trial Impressions
Le Savoir des rois
Armenian Papers: Poems 1954-1984
Out of Bounds
A Mid-Season Sky: Poems 1954-1991
Alphabet Gourmand (with Paul Fournel)

MISCELLANIES
Selected Declarations of Dependence
The Way Home
Écrits Français

NONFICTION AND CRITICISM
The Orchard: A Remembrance of Georges Perec
20 Lines a Day
Immeasurable Distances
Giandomenico Tiepolo
Oulipo Compendium (with Alastair Brotchie)
The Case of the Persevering Maltese: Collected Essays

The Case of the Persevering Maltese: Collected Essays

HARRY MATHEWS

Dalkey Archive Press

Portions of this volume have previously appeared in *Immeasurable Distances* (Lapis Press), and *Onward: Contemporary Poetry & Poetics* (Peter Lang Publishing). Original places and dates of publication appear at the end of each essay.

Library of Congress Cataloging-in-Publication Data

Mathews, Harry, 1930-
   The case of the persevering Maltese : collected essays / Harry Mathews.— 1st ed.
      p. cm.
   ISBN 1-56478-288-3 (pbk. : alk. paper)
   I. Title.

PS3563.A8359C37 2003
814'.54—dc21

2002041511

Partially funded by a grant from the Illinois Arts Council, a state agency.

Dalkey Archive Press books are published by the Center for Book Culture, a nonprofit organization.

www.centerforbookculture.org

Printed on permanent/durable acid-free paper and bound in the United States of America.

TABLE OF CONTENTS

IV

APPENDIX: PRACTICAL ILLUSTRATIONS

PREFACE

A majority of these pieces were written in response to newspapers and reviews that had invited me to contribute to their pages. Given the diversity of audiences and the many years covered, the collection cannot pretend to develop a unified theory of writing, reading, or language, even if the essays all touch on these topics (sometimes, it should be said, autobiographically rather than critically). But running through them there may, as I suggested in the foreword to an earlier collection, run "a tacit working assumption": a belief in the lasting relevance of the modernist view in literature. I said that (among other things) this presumed written language to be "a predetermined, autonomous system" within which subject matter plays a secondary role; and in support of my claim I cited a writer hardly associated with modernism whose words for me still ring true. Near the end of a short work called "A Humble Remonstrance," Robert Louis Stevenson writes:

> The novel, which is a work of art, exists, not by its resemblances to life, which are forced and material, as a shoe must still consist of leather, but by its immeasurable difference from life, which is designed and significant, and is both the method and the meaning of the work.

New York, November 25, 2002

vii

I

FOR PRIZEWINNERS

to Joseph McElroy

I intend to talk to you seriously.

Before coming here today, I considered several possibilities of what to say to you, especially to the prizewinning writers who are being honored on this occasion. I first thought of warning all of you who plan to write professionally what a bleak future lies ahead of you, in the manner of Virgil Thomson, whom I once heard address the commencement audience at a music school so eloquently that each new graduate must have left in search of a plain steady job—anything rather than a musical career. I then told myself that, after all, the world gives writers an easier time than musicians: they do not require organized performances to make themselves heard, and their audience can be reached in bedrooms and subways rather than in public halls. I next turned to the possibility of entertaining you, of cheering you with funny and edifying tales of the writing life, so that you could go home warmed by the prospect of a delightful as well as worthwhile future. Conscientiousness nipped that idea. I had gradually been coming to recognize this occasion as too large for mere entertainment: I felt that I would be remiss in not taking advantage of the opportunity it was offering to make myself genuinely useful, which I have since decided means this: to make available to you as appropriately as possible what I have learned from my own experience as a writer. So I intend to talk to you seriously, perhaps at times even thornily.

Even if you are not musicians, I shall start with a warning: If any of you expects that being a writer will give you a better or happier life than you would otherwise have, forget it. "Being a writer"—proclaiming writing as your livelihood, thinking of yourself as "being a writer" when you go to bed at night and get up in the morning—will make no difference in your life; at least, none that matters. Being a writer will bring you some minor privileges. Out of either respect or mistrust or both, most people will keep a distance from you when they find out what you are: you will thus acquire a certain safety. (When someone asks me what I do, I usually say that I sell insurance. This sets both of us at ease.) Being a writer will also cloak you in a rather spurious authority. You may be asked to express yourself publicly on the fate of the snail darter more often than other citizens, not because you know anything, simply because you're a writer; you will also from time to time be offered the pleasure of lecturing captive audiences. Finally, you may get occasional recognition: "See that guy? He's a writer." "A writer? A *real* writer?" ("Help! I'm an insurance salesman!") This will sometimes enable you to make money. I'm actually being paid to tell you what I think because I "am a writer."

Being a writer intermittently and unreliably brings you safety, authority, and recognition—values oriented toward the public world and that, perhaps because of this, give little private satisfaction. No one will deny that their satisfaction is small, that this kind of safety, authority, and recognition add little to our capacity for happiness or liveliness or wisdom. I do not call these values bad, merely disappointing. If you are to spend several hours each day with pencil, pen, typewriter, or word processor, you will want more satisfaction than these values can give—you will want satisfaction in fact. Otherwise the effort looks pointless. And I—someone who enjoys society at least as much as solitude, who persistently daydreams of finding occasions for working with others—I spend several hours every day closeted with pencil and typewriter. What satisfaction do I expect? Do I get it?

First of all, I assert that satisfaction in every activity can be accurately defined as residing in the private counterparts of safety, authority, and recognition: that is, in power, knowledge, and love. For convenience, let's think of power as the ability to create energy over and over; of knowledge as the awareness of things as they exactly are (neither information nor theory), of love as whatever you say it is.

If you cannot find power, knowledge, and love in the condition of "being a writer" (only their public substitutes), the one place you can then look for them must be in the act of writing itself. The act of writing: taking words and setting them down, reading what you have written, and then of course rewriting that, and rereading and rewriting it again and again. Here our questions begin to look interesting—they begin to look like questions: because, leaving writing for the moment aside, I have always—almost always—found the power, knowledge, and love that bring satisfaction to be made available through participation. Participation means engaging in collaborative activity with others, whether in work, play, conversation, lovemaking. I wish right now that instead of me speaking and you listening we were having a discussion. That would satisfy me more; and if I haven't proposed it to you, that is only because we would then need a day or two to work our way through our subject. All of you doubtless have experienced satisfaction through participation in work, in sports, in performing with others whether on stage, playing musical instruments, or singing together; you know what I'm talking about. If we can agree that satisfaction finds expression in participation, we are faced with the inevitable question: How can you be satisfied in the act of writing, sitting alone at your desk? How can you participate? What can you participate in? Whom do you participate with?

To the last of these questions the answer must take the shape of that legendary beast, The Reader. Let me remind you of something you have probably found out for yourselves: the writer has no communication with his actual readers (aside from himself). To elaborate the point: for a number of reasons, we cling to the notion that the writer communicates with the reader the way a speaker communicates with a listener, or a letter writer with a correspondent. These analogies can only mislead us. When I speak to you in conversation, I can tell I am communicating with you by your response (or by your lack of response, which is only another kind of response). I can expect an answer to a letter I write; the answer will validate my communication. A writer never receives this validation from his readers, no matter how strongly they feel about what he has written. They provide no feedback, without which direct communication, since it depends on a two-way relationship, disappears. You may point out that readers can tell me about what I have written in conversation, letters, reviews. These apparent exceptions only confirm the rule, because they always come hopelessly late—weeks, months, or years after the moment when I was writing my poem or story or essay. These comments have lost all relevance, and they almost always embarrass more than they please me. My reader is discussing an event that lies dead and buried in the past. I invariably feel that I'm being told how beautiful my ex-wife is.

The question of how to participate with your reader therefore remains an urgent one. Solving it—and understanding how it may be solved—means replacing our intuitive notion that the writer is "saying something" to the reader with a new conception of their relationship. I suggest that in order to guarantee his participation with the reader, a writer does two things. First, he gives up his claim to be the one in the relationship who creates. Second, to establish a space in which participation can take place, he chooses as the innermost substance of what he is writing a terrain unfamiliar to both the reader and himself. You may find these two points obscure; I mean to spend the rest of this talk making them clearer.

The first of the points—the relinquishing by the writer of his role as creator—is the easier to grasp. A simple analogy can indicate why this needs to happen. Imagine that I am a victim of multiple disasters and in utter despair because of them. I now decide to communicate my feelings to the young lady in the first row, whose name is? Sharon. If I rush up to her, grasp her hands, squeeze them furiously, burst into tears, and start screaming, I'll certainly be expressing my feelings; and no less certainly I shall destroy in her all interest in finding out what they are. The only thing Sharon will want to do is get out of the room. If on the other hand I supply her dispassionately with the facts—that the IRS has just confiscated my house, my car, and my savings; that my wife and children died this morning in a horrible accident; that tomorrow I must enter the hospital to have my head amputated—if I supply her with these facts and give her a chance to add them up, she can start imagining what my feelings may be: she can recreate my feelings and eventually respond to them. (She may head for the nearest exit all the same; that's life.) Similarly, if in writing I do all the work on my reader's behalf, explaining everything, painting a picture in which nothing is left out, the reader, having nothing to do, will not even read what I have written. Like Sharon, he will go elsewhere. The writer must take care to do no more than supply the reader with the materials and (as we often say nowadays) the space to create an experience. That is all the creating that takes place: of writer and reader, the reader is the only creator. This is how reading can be defined: an act of creation for which the writer provides the means. The writer's privileges are restricted to choosing the means and, more important, to becoming his own first reader. He becomes a creator to the same extent as any of his other readers. This is the first way writer and reader participate with one another: in creating the experience for which the writer has provided the means.

The second thing a writer does to open up the possibility of participation is harder to explain. As I said before, the writer chooses, as the substance of his writing, matter unfamiliar both to his reader and to himself. What I say now may appear to contradict that first assertion almost absurdly: the unfamiliar matter the writer chooses is nothing else than his own story.

How can someone's own story be unfamiliar to him? Proust's remarks on the subject may help. He writes that the true, essential book does not need to be "invented by a great writer—it exists already inside him—but it has to be translated by him." He goes on to compare the writer's task of translating the symbols within him to the deciphering of hieroglyphs. Proust thus sees the story within not as readily available but as something to be decoded. Our own stories belong to us, but we cannot easily read them.

I suggest that the apparent contradiction between "one's own story" and "something unfamiliar" comes from confusing our real stories with the stories we tell *about* ourselves (and not only to others: each to himself): publicity stories, explanations of ourselves. Such explanations generally assume one of two forms: either, "My parents are awful to me, my boss (or my teacher) is a jerk, nobody understands me, I don't stand a chance, no wonder I feel so bad," or, "My parents are wonderful to me, I'm successful at what I do, I have nothing to complain about, how come I feel so bad?" Have you noticed how rarely anyone tells you how much he enjoys life? If the person doesn't feel bad about himself, he will point out the near and distant disasters rampant in our world—if nothing else, he will remind you that the forces of evil are once again ganging up on the snail darter. Stories such as these can never escape the category of versions or interpretations of what is happening. And all the while we know that something quite different is going on inside and around us, and the difference, we also know, amounts to the difference that separates life from the pretense of life, from the renunciation of life.

How can we win access to our real stories, to what is truly happening in our lives? We have three places where we can look for the decipherable hieroglyphs Proust refers to. First, we have our personal history, the sum of inner and outer events that have made up our lives. Even as we plunder this domain for our publicity stories, we realize how much of it we neglect; this material can be explored at length and in depth. Second, we have our bodies, which are packed (in case you didn't know it) with meanings and indeed with words. Your shoulders are bursting with nouns, your knees with verbs. An insatiable "but" is locked into your right wrist. All these words are held there by force and are waiting to be released. The third place we have to look for our stories I shall call our consciousness; let me define my use of this word straight off. By consciousness I do not mean your feelings, or your ideas, or your imagination; I mean what you feel *with*, what you have ideas *with*, what you imagine *with*. Not the voice chattering in the back of your head telling you what's right and wrong, rather what enables you to hear that voice, and also what enables you to hear yourself listening to that voice. Not your experience: your awareness of experience.

A new question arises: How does a writer go about looking for his story in these three places? In regard to our personal history, the answer is simple enough. The act of writing itself works the necessary wonders. As far as each of us is concerned, personal history means what we can remember; and it so happens that because language is inextricably bound up with the act of remembering, a deliberate use of language inevitably fishes up memories.

To explore your history, you need only begin writing about it. As you write, you will discover things about yourself that you did not know you knew. Don't take my word for it: try it. I recently asked my mother to write down all she could remember about certain people she had known as a child. Before starting, she told me that with luck she might fill a few pages. She now expects to be busy for months, at least.

Next, what of the body? How can the body be persuaded to release those words it holds in store? Although we might exploit a number of techniques—for instance, those practiced by actors—to unlock our muscles and bones, I propose for a start resorting to a rather ordinary notion: words are commonly released from our bodies through our breath; that is, if words are to emerge they have to be spoken; so writers should make a point of keeping what they write in touch with how they speak. Here lies a clue to why so many writers find it useful to read what they have written out loud: it gives the body a chance to show up what is phony in their writing. As a second valuable habit, I recommend taking your actual everyday speech as the starting point for what you write. A minute of reflection will convince you that when you talk to your friends there is nothing you know that you cannot communicate to them. (Although you may have to repeat and re-phrase, sooner or later you will get your meaning across.) Even if such direct communication is impossible with a reader, that ability to communicate looks like a good place in which to begin writing. Here is a way to do just that. Before setting down a sentence on paper, imagine yourself sitting in a coffee shop with a friend. How would you tell him what you have to say in that next sentence? Write it down. What you have to write down may strike you as chaotic, vulgar, and undignified. This makes no difference—you can clean it up later; in the meantime you will not have resorted for words to the information dump inside your head; you won't be running away from yourself in order to hide behind the not-so-impressive bastions of culture; and you will have started down the path to discovering your own voice in writing. Let me give you one small example of what such a procedure can produce. Last year I asked my students to translate a passage from *Brideshead Revisited* into their own speech. One sentence in the passage read: "The evening passed." How would you tell your friend in the coffee shop that "the evening passed"? One student rendered it perfectly: "It got late." The translation of course evoked another world: his world.

Finally, what about the third place where we can look for our stories, the domain of consciousness? Like the body, consciousness—what you think and feel *with*—generates a profusion of words and meanings. Unlike the body, however, it does not contain or withhold meaning; and consciousness itself has no meaning at all. More accurately, we might say that consciousness generates not meaning but the power to create meaning. It does not produce a particular meaning—it produces no conclusions. Instead, it has the capacity of creating meaning again and again, one meaning after another. We could also describe it as an infinite potentiality of meaning.

Let me once again use an analogy to suggest the way consciousness works. My analogy is the night sky, the star-filled sky. From the first Babylonian shepherd down to our own age, the night sky has been looked on as a vision that must be deciphered, as if it were a text so fascinating that we feel obliged to read it, so obviously significant that it inspires us with a passion for understanding it. While interpretations of the sky have changed many times and are still changing, what has not changed is this desire to understand. Every explanation of the sky, from mythical constellations to present-day theories of the creation of the universe, turns out to be inadequate. Whatever formulations the long process of explanation may have yielded strike me as not mattering much when they are confronted with the overwhelming desire for knowledge that the night sky never fails to inspire. This desire is expressed as speculation—a word that etymologically signifies mirroring. What the night sky mirrors is ourselves, and it will serve as a mirror of what I have called our consciousness. What we long to know in our speculations about the stars surpasses merely something: We long to know everything. And in fact the consciousness is capable of exactly that: of knowing not only anything but everything.

How can this capacity for engendering infinite meaning, this capacity for absolute knowledge, be drawn upon in writing? What must the reader do so that this domain can be made accessible to writer and reader?

The writer cannot content himself, as he does with his history and his body, with providing something—he cannot provide "things" at all. Somethings are what consciousness produces—its residue—and so consciousness must never be equated with particular things: Although consciousness generates particularities, it is never limited to them. Doesn't the answer to our last question stare us in the face? If providing somethings will not do, the writer must provide nothings. I am not playing with words. A little observation will show you that writers do nothing else. They make the experience of consciousness available through nothings—absences, negations, voids. To put it another way, writing works exclusively by what the writer leaves out.

(Let me return in passing to an earlier point. The nothingness the writer offers the reader opens up space—a space that acknowledges that the reader, not the writer, is the sole creator. Providing emptiness, leaving things out, gives the reader exactly the space he needs to perform his act of creation.)

To show you that I am not babbling about an idea that I happen to be fond of, let me read you parts of the opening pages of a classic realistic English novel, Jane Austen's *Northanger Abbey*. The book begins:

> No one who had ever seen Catherine Morland in her infancy would have supposed her born to be an heroine. Her situation in life, the character of her father and mother, her own person and disposition, were all equally against her.

The rest of the long first paragraph lists all the qualities Catherine Morland does not possess: she is declared to be not an orphan, not poor, not mistreated, not misunderstood, not beleaguered by ill health, not beautiful, not feminine (i.e., not physically weak), not sensitive, not exceptionally gifted, not stupid, not pathetically submissive, not artistic, not particularly good, and not particularly bad. With one exception, to which I shall return presently, what we learn about Catherine is all the things she isn't; as a result of having her introduced to us in this fashion, we, the readers, are invited to think up what she is. The opening sentence—"No one who had ever seen Catherine . . . would have supposed her born to be an heroine"—of course obliges us to think, "There's our heroine." The method resembles that of telling someone "Don't think of a white horse" when you want to make them think of a white horse. We are less insistently encouraged to imagine Catherine through the description of what she is not; we nevertheless inescapably find ourselves creating her, or at least creating what she may be. (For those of you who know the book, I cannot resist pointing out that its climactic scene—Henry Tilney's visit to Catherine at her parents' house, one of the most affecting scenes I have read—is also narrated by not describing it: in place of what happens between Henry and Catherine, we are told about Mrs. Morland's search for the volume entitled *The Mirror.*)

I hope that this example has persuaded you to accept, at least provisionally, the possibility that the first step a writer takes to ensure participation in the domain of consciousness is to supply the reader with negations and absences. As you might guess, he must do more than that. The reason he must do more can be expressed in the question: So then what? The writer provides a void, the reader fills it up, and now you have a something. As soon as a particular meaning (a something) is produced, consciousness wants to move on. So the writer provides a new emptiness, the reader creates a new something to fill it, and this process must be maintained to the end of the work (and perhaps beyond). In other words, the second step a writer takes to engage consciousness is to initiate and maintain movement. You may think of this as a kind of action, but you should realize that such movement or action bears no resemblance to narrative action. The movement I am discussing sustains narrative (or the progression of the poem or essay); it does not manifest itself as a feature of narrative.

To understand this kind of movement better, let's return to Jane Austen. I mentioned that in the opening paragraph of *Northanger Abbey* one attribute of Catherine Morland was presented in positive rather than negative terms. That item reads:

> . . . [The Morlands] were in general very plain, and Catherine, for many years of her life, as plain as any. She had a thin awkward figure, a sallow skin without colour, dark lank hair, and strong features;—so much for her person . . .

Remember, this is virtually the only one of her qualities that we are not allowed and invited to imagine for ourselves, the one thing we are *told*. It is also the last thing we want to hear. We have been happily concocting a heroine of our own; we had no intention of giving her "a thin awkward figure," and so forth. The fact sticks in our craw; for my own part, I simply pretended it had never been said (it still stuck in my craw). Then, in the next paragraph, something remarkable happens. First we read:

> Such was Catherine Morland at ten. At fifteen, appearances were mending: she began to curl her hair . . . ; her complexion improved; her features were softened by plumpness and colour, her eyes gained more animation, and her figure more consequence.

What a relief! We can at last begin to swallow those earlier remarks about her plainness. And *then* . . . Listen:

> . . . she had now the pleasure of sometimes hearing her father and mother remark on her personal improvement. "Catherine grows quite a good-looking girl,—she is almost pretty today," were words which caught her ears now and then; and how welcome were the sounds! To look *almost* pretty, is an acquisition of higher delight to a girl who has been looking plain the first fifteen years of her life, than a beauty from her cradle can ever receive.

Catherine feels exactly the way we do. The fact of her plainness has been sticking in her craw, and when that plainness goes she experiences a relief like our own. For a moment, without warning, and of course *without* being told, we become Catherine. She and I are briefly the same person. As a result, I am propelled head- and heartlong into her story. How can I help feeling concerned about Catherine? She is me: naturally I want to know how my own story turns out. Since, moreover, I can usually manage to forgive myself for anything, I shall follow Catherine through thick and thin, and no stupidity or injustice on her part will dent my loyalty to her.

The movement of consciousness illustrated in this example occurs precisely at the moment in which I identify myself with Catherine. I invite you to notice that this extraordinary moment is woven out of the purest illusion. We are in this moment thoroughly, beautifully conned. Catherine does not exist (we have barely started inventing her) or, if you prefer, she need not exist. The effect of the moment in no way depends on Catherine, on this particular story, on this scene. The effect could belong to a story about Eskimos; Catherine could be a middle-aged man called Schwarzenberg, or a dog named Minnie—why not? The effect is produced by a formal device (so sure that one is tempted to find a place for it among the tropes of rhetoric) that precedes and remains independent of any specific material assigned to it. The effect belongs to the realm of what might be called form; however, since that word raises the eyebrows, dander, and hackles of many sincere people, I shall call the special aspect of form that engages the movement of consciousness—not *process*, although I might use that word, or *procedure*, or *progression*, or *prosody*—I shall call it syntax. Clearly the ordinary sense of the word *syntax* has to be stretched slightly to accommodate the meaning I am now giving it; but only slightly. To the sense "the way in which words are put together to form phrases and sentences" must be added the sense of "the way in which sentences are put together to form stanzas and paragraphs." With that modification, I think I can claim that syntax is what engages my consciousness in an action of shifting, of discovery, at the moment when I recognize that Catherine and I are one and the same person.

To show how truly syntactic the operation of this expanded syntax can be, I have prepared a demonstration for you using as material a complete and unabridged work by a modern master: a very short short story by Franz Kafka. My demonstration demands a certain patience, since you must listen to and reflect on three texts: that of the short story itself and, in addition, those of two revisions or rewritings of the story. Here, first of all, the story. It is entitled "The Truth about Sancho Panza":

> Without making any boast of it Sancho Panza succeeded in the course
> of years, by feeding him a great number of romances of chivalry in the
> evening and night hours, in so diverting from himself his demon, whom
> he later called Don Quixote, that this demon thereupon set out, unin-

hibited, on the maddest exploits, which, however, for lack of a pre-ordained object, which should have been Sancho Panza himself, harmed nobody. A free man, Sancho Panza philosophically followed Don Quixote on his crusades, perhaps out of a sense of responsibility, and had of them a great and edifying entertainment to the end of his days.

(Translation by Willa and Edwin Muir)

Let me interrupt my argument to say a few words about the matter of the story, not to define or limit it, only to indicate its general scope and give those of you who have never read it a chance to become aware of the topics involved. As you noticed, the two characters in this very short story are taken from another very long work of fiction. We might suspect from this fact alone that "The Truth about Sancho Panza" involves fiction as its subject in some way or other; and our suspicion is corroborated by what takes place—by the "plot." The narrative, quantitatively minimal, presents us with the original and, in its implications, vast proposition that Sancho Panza, the skeptical, realistic servant of Don Quixote, was his master's creator—that he was, in other words, responsible for the invention of one of the most extravagant characters in the history of literature. Sancho Panza's act of creation is presented, however, as anything but an extravagance, rather as the sober means by which he preserved himself from terrible suffering, by which he actually transformed that suffering into an "edifying entertainment." We can reasonably deduce that Sancho Panza is to be identified with Cervantes; more interestingly, we can guess that this story of Kafka's proposes a general view of fiction: that, at least on occasion, fiction can serve to make the most oppressive aspects of reality bearable, even entertaining, not by describing them "realistically," not by denying or running away from them, but by "masking" them—by pretending that one has made them up, or by making something else up to take their place. Kafka makes his point clear by following the precepts implicit in his view in this very story, which is thus transformed into an elegantly economical metaphor illuminating both itself and the practice of the art of which it is an example.

I shall now read you my two rewritings of "The Truth about Sancho Panza," which I shall henceforth refer to as translations. In my first translation, while I

have kept the vocabulary and phrasing of the original, I have divided the two
sentences of the original—the first long, the second much shorter—into five
sentences of less disproportionate length:

> Without making any boast of it, Sancho Panza succeeded in diverting
> his demon from himself—the demon he later called Don Quixote. What
> he did was feed him a great number of romances of chivalry and adven-
> ture in the evening and night hours. As a result, this demon set out,
> uninhibited, on the maddest exploits; but since they lacked a preor-
> dained object, which should have been Sancho Panza himself, they
> harmed nobody. Sancho Panza thus became a free man. Perhaps out of
> a sense of responsibility, he philosophically followed Don Quixote on
> his crusades and had of them a great and edifying entertainment to the
> end of his days.

In the second translation, I have kept the two sentences of Kafka's story
intact; on the other hand, I have replaced all its nouns with other nouns
chosen with no consideration for the meanings of the original ones (this
choice has been made in a way that I need not explain to you except to say
that it leaves virtually nothing either to personal fancy or to chance*):

"The Tub about Sancho Panza"

> Without making any bobbin of it Sancho Panza succeeded, in the court-
> ship of yellowness, by feeding him a great numskull of romantics of
> chloroform and advertisement in the evil and nil housings, in so divert-
> ing from himself his demonstrative, whom he later called Don Quixote,
> that this demonstrative thereupon set out, uninhibited, on the maddest
> exports, which, however, for lack of a preordained objurgation, which
> should have been Sancho Panza himself, harmed nobody. A free man-
> ager, Sancho Panza philosophically followed Don Quixote on his cruxes,
> perhaps out of a sensitiveness of restaurants, and had of them a great
> and edifying enticement to the endlessness of his dead.

---

*The method followed, known as S + 7 or N + 7, was invented by Jean Lescure
for the Oulipo; see the entry N + 7 in *Oulipo Compendium* (editors: Harry Mathews
and Alastair Brotchie; London: Atlas Press, 1998), 198 ff. The *Concise Oxford Dictionary* was the dictionary used in this instance.

Putting it simply, one can describe what has been done in the two translations by saying that in the first the sense of the original is kept and its structure altered, in the second the sense is altered and the structure kept. If you agree to this description, it may strike you as a waste of time if I ask you which of the two translations best preserves the meaning of the original. Obviously, you have already concluded—who wouldn't?—that the translation that keeps the sense of the original must best preserve the original's meaning. (Let me add that I am making only the most ordinary kind of distinction between sense and meaning.) If, furthermore, the little story is indeed a metaphor, the second translation has without doubt destroyed—in addition to the literal sense of each phrase and sentence—any possibility of engendering the metaphorical content that I found so enlightening. How, you may wonder, can the second translation even begin to be taken seriously?

Let me reread the original and the two translations—the translations twice each.

Two developments, you will notice (and I observe that you *are* noticing), have begun taking place. The first translation (unlike the original) is growing steadily more boring; the second translation is making more and more sense—or, at least, we seem more and more to be expecting it to make sense; and much of the sense we are persuading ourselves to discover sounds, while in no way replicating that of the original, like a kind of commentary on it. "A great numskull of romantics of chloroform and advertisement" can certainly be read as a respectable gloss on the character of Don Quixote; calling one's demon a "demonstrative" fits—our demons, alas, compel us to demonstrate ourselves; exploits are often for export (cf. "advertisements" above); Sancho Panza most definitely becomes the "manager" of the situation. (As for the "sensitiveness of restaurants": imagine what most of us would be thinking about if *we* were traveling through Spain. . . .)

Little by little, the "meaningless" second translation is accumulating an appearance of meaning. I suggest that this is no accident, and that the meaning of the second translation has its source in the original. I suggest that this meaning can certainly not be found in what the translation has changed—its vocabulary—but in what it has left intact: the structure and rhythm of Kafka's story. I claim that the essential meaning of the story is produced by the contrast between the long, complex, almost teeteringly clumsy first sentence (so exquisitely preserved by the Muirs in *their* translation) and the short, forthright, satisfyingly balanced concluding sentence. That contrast embodies the moment of discovery, the moment in which confusion gives way to clarity, the moment in which Sancho Panza learns how to exorcise his demon, in which whoever is telling this story perceives the usefulness of writing fiction, perhaps the moment in which Franz Kafka sees the possibility of truth in writing a story called "The Truth about Sancho Panza." This movement of discovery and resolution irresistibly survives the travesty of sense perpetrated by the second translation, just as it irresistibly succumbs to the "faithful" rendering of the translation in five sentences. You should notice in conclusion that this embodiment, in the contrast between the two sentences, of what I called action empowers the reader to create, using the sense of the words made available to him, the experience of discovery that is the substance of the story. Syntax makes the metaphor work; and we may conclude that meaning is to be equated not with content but with what makes content produce its effect. Here, as so often in Kafka, the nominal sense of the words gives only indirect clues as to what is really going on. Syntax and syntax alone delivers the goods.

To those of us who write, the consequences of this demonstration offer one notable advantage. Once you accept that the movement or action embodied in syntax provides the *essential* meaning of what you write, you will find it easier to get off the hook on which most of us so painfully dangle—the notion that subject matter gives writing its significance. If you can even hypothetically entertain the possibility that the meaning of what you write does not depend on what you write about, you will be spared needless hours and days of frustration. I suggest, incidentally, that this possibility corresponds to the experience of our nonwriting lives. Don't you already know that to get into an argument, any subject will do? That to express love for someone, almost no words will do? You may argue with murderous violence about politics or the superiority of Babe Ruth over Hank Aaron. In every case your meaning remains: I want to argue with you. As for telling someone you love them, the difficulties often look insurmountable. For instance: "You never tell me you love me!" "Oh, sure—uh—I love you." At such a moment, neither party experiences very much satisfaction. The moment might nevertheless be redeemed by a bout of dancing.

You are free to write about anything—whatever you find necessary to tell your story. You are free to pick material that you are drawn to, remembering that you may be drawn to what is strange or frankly appalling. Do not resist that appeal, no matter how disgraceful or unreasonable it may look. In a talk a few weeks ago Italo Calvino said that all his books began with problems that he knew he never could solve. Plainly he is attracted to insoluble problems. Why? They allow him to make discoveries. Choose your subjects so that you can discover what you didn't know you knew. You cannot, after all, *start* with syntax. When you sit down to write, you will probably have no more than an inkling of where your syntactical strength is to be found; it will be part of what you discover in the process of working. Perhaps that is why rewriting is always so crucial a part of writing; why reading must be the locus of participation. There, where you have become a reader among readers, you at last begin to *know:* The community of your readers participates in an act of discovery that you have made accessible, to yourself no less freshly than to any of your fellows.

I realize that you think the world is a mess and that you have a responsibility to do something about it. The world *is* a mess, one of our very own making. Two points, nevertheless. First, all the solutions to the world's problems have already been written down, and this fact continues to make very little difference—the problems do not go away. We might even say that the problems are so mired in words that we can rarely manage to approach them directly, and that most of the time writing about them only stirs up other people's mud. Perhaps you may deal with them more usefully, if less obviously, by writing a romance about a butterfly and a lollipop—if that is what you feel like doing. Second, no one yet knows who you are—not the you whose secret story can be recreated in the medium of the written word. There lies the extraordinary contribution you can make to the world, and I recommend that you give yourself the chance to make it. Write about the things that attract you. Choose your subjects the way you used to choose your toys: out of desire. You have the universe for your toy shop now. The time has come for you to go out and play.

An address delivered in May 1982 at Queens College, New York. First published in *Review of Contemporary Fiction,* 1987.

NOTES ON THE THRESHOLD OF A BOOK

In 1983 I attended the Action Workshop created by Fernando Flores and Werner Erhard. The workshop demonstrated the proposition that "performative speech"—speech capable of guaranteeing material results—necessarily uses only four kinds of statement: questions, promises, assertions, and declarations. In order to see what consequences this notion might have in written language, I decided to translate the beginning of Ruskin's The Stones of Venice *as an experiment in "performative writing." These pages constitute a prelude to the experiment and a rehearsal of it.*

I declare that "I" is the name I shall assign myself as I write these exploratory pages. I declare that "you" is the name I shall assign myself as I read these pages.

I declare that writing these pages means a recording of the conversation I am having with you.

I request you read these exploratory pages.

I assert that in its form a book is a request: an unopened book is asking to be opened; an open book is asking to be read. (I point out to you that right now *The Stones of Venice* is lying beside your pad, opened, not being read.)

I ask you, why does a book have particular names attached to it (title, author, publisher, at least)? I ask you to consider my answer to the question. I suggest that the names attached to a book are meant to conceal the uniformity of the experience of reading. (I point out to you that the names people have conceal their likeness in a similar way—except that in our case, I must also point out that since *our* names refer to the same object, they reveal our likeness. I suggest this may be less apparent to readers other than yourself.)

I admit to you that we are not on an equal footing: you never have a chance to speak. Only I can speak—I can declare that absolutely. I realize that I could "let you speak" by attributing words to you, which would conventionally appear in quotation marks to show that a character (a not-I) is doing the talking. But I maintain that the quotation marks and the rest of my procedure will fool nobody, that as soon as you begin speaking you will become I, I talking to you—just what is happening now.

I suggest, as a consolation, that if I alone can speak, you alone can listen: as soon as I begin to listen I become, by definition, you.

I point out again to you that *The Stones of Venice* is lying open next to your pad, asking to be read.

Now, as I begin to read, or rather to look at the page that I am planning to read, I ask you another question: Do the opening sentences of a nonfiction book constitute a request or an assertion? Are the opening sentences inviting you to accept what you are going to read or telling us that such-and-such is so?

I suggest the following answer: An essay is a request that pretends to be an assertion. I therefore accuse nonfiction by virtue of this lie to be fiction.

But wait: I make a further suggestion to you, in the form of another question: Are assertions a false category altogether, being essentially requests inviting listeners to give their assent, agreement, or belief? I propose that every assertion can be rephrased as a request. Example: "Apples are often red" means "I request you to accept the proposition that apples are often red, since you can probably provide evidence to that effect or, if not, you can count on me to provide ample testimony for it."

I conjecture that this proposition, if it turns out to be true, will not affect my assertion that nonfiction is fiction. (I also point out that this assertion is consistent with my earlier one that the experience of reading is uniform).

Now, another question: If a book is a request to you to read it, what do you ask of the book? I assume that when you begin reading, you are expecting—therefore requesting—something, which I have so far only called the experience of reading. What do you think that means?

I maintain that what you ask of a book is the possibility of learning—of knowing, in thought or feeling, something new; or something that if not new in substance will be made available in an unfamiliar way and so will be made new for you (be renewed). I suggest furthermore that since there is almost nothing that is truly new (and what there is will as soon as it is known become part of what is old), what you ask of a book is not learning as the acquisition of thoughts or feelings that you don't yet possess but learning as a process. I suggest that what you ask of a book, whether it be a book of poetry or a manual for the repair of air conditioners, is to be given the satisfaction of experiencing the process of learning—that without this satisfaction any book you read you will reject as a waste of time. I assert that this is what is *common* to all books, common to your expectation of any book; I admit, too, that particular books must satisfy particular expectations as well—so that the air conditioner will keep working on this stifling Saturday afternoon; so that I can know what happens when Wallace Stevens uses the word *orange*.

I can now say that when you open *The Stones of Venice* you have the primary expectation of learning in itself, as a process, and perhaps another, particular expectation. So I ask you, is there a particular expectation?

Is there something in particular you want to learn *about?*

You want to learn about Venice and more particularly the Stones of Venice, *stones* here standing for *building stones,* or architecture.

I suggest, however, that what you have already started learning about (having read no more than the title, having just opened the book) has nothing to do with Venice or architecture and everything to do with a way of using language:

See above, "*stones* standing, for . . ."

"Standing for" instead of naming. (I immediately add a more extended interpretation: *stones* stands for not only architecture but architecture considered as an important subject—stones being durable, heavy, and grave in sound; no doubt *stones* stands for much more than this.) I suggest to you that you already know that Ruskin's subject will not be architecture but its significance. Is this what you want to read about? I suggest that you already know that you will not get what you think you expect; or that by now you expect words to tell you something they are not saying—words will be standing in for other words. I insist you recognize that as soon as words stand in for other words nominal subjects dissolve, and what is written can be "about" everything and anything.

I propose that in the matter of Ruskin's success, which led him to complain that no one listened to what he was saying and everyone praised him for the way he said it, he was wrong and his readers were right: Ruskin spoke himself in every sentence, and what his readers loved was him, not his ideas.

A question: How can Ruskin have spoken himself in every sentence? Is this a subject open to stylistic analysis, or does the question demand bringing in matters beyond the test itself?

I advance the possibility that this alternative is a false one: Stylistic analysis can discover the intentions of the writer as he wrote, and at the same time I suggest that these intentions were not necessarily confined to being expressed through writing, that they did not require writing to exist (even if they required language), that they could have been given other forms, such as the designing of a garden or an engineering project. I consider the style of Ruskin to be the way he speaks himself in that it manifests his commitment to the possibilities peculiar to written language. That is why his subject matter and his message do not matter, and his style does. I contend that the real subject of *The Stones of Venice* is not Venice or architecture but the written word. I emphasize that in saying this I do not mean to portray Ruskin as ignorant of what he was doing, because I find that the results—the effects—of his writing are close to his explicit ideas; but while he demonstrated those ideas undeniably in the way he arranges words, the points he makes about architecture are always subject to argument.

Because I'm giving up the idea of using *The Stones of Venice* as a text for translation into performative speech, and because stylistic analysis is fun and worthwhile but irrelevant to my preoccupations at this moment, I conclude my comments on Ruskin's book with the first words you read after the book's title, which form the title of the opening chapter: "The Quarry." I point out that whereas *stones* stood in a particular, clear way for architecture, *quarry* remains to the end of the chapter it heads definitely ambiguous. You never learn whether it means the place from which stones are extracted, or if it means the writer's (and reader's) prey. I deduce that you are then not in a world of stones at all, but one purely of words.

I confess that today (9/6/83) I cannot be sure whether there is or is not a speaker present in written language. I admit that for years I have been telling you that there isn't; now I ask you, is there any more of one when the speaker is physically in front of you (since then, if you hear him, you are doing the speaking yourself)? If in written language there is a speaker, is he created by the reader, by you—is one of the writer's tasks to give you materials and space to create a speaker as well as all the rest? When the American Express bill thanks you for sending money, and you imagine a printing machine doing the thanking—why not?

I suggest to you that this question (still unanswered) casts light on the nature of characters in fictitious works—which means in all written works. This morning I read of Unamuno's remark that "Don Quixote is no less real than Cervantes"; to make the point even more obvious, I add that Sherlock Holmes is much more real than Conan Doyle. I can deduce at once that in these explorations I am a character who by speaking according to certain rules enables you to imagine me as *a* person, the emphasis being on the *a* as signifying unity and coherence, what I could also call personality. Then "I" am that person, and what I-Harry Mathews think about who I really am has no connection with, or at least no effect on, the me whom you are creating out of the way I express myself in these lines you are reading. Can I not now assert that in written language there is always a speaker, who is a character created by the reader out of the materials at his disposal? I can furthermore insist that this speaker does not correspond to and therefore cannot be expected to represent the individual to whom the speaking voice nominally refers—Harry Mathews here, Benjamin Franklin in his autobiography, James Reston in the articles he signs in the *New York Times*. I suggest that not only must you the reader make up the speaker for him to exist, you cannot help doing so. You use the telephone book: Who is reading you that list of names and numbers? I suggest someone—or something—is.

I speculate that the genius of writing is to know how to let you imagine me as the speaker I assert myself to be, at that particular point, for my present purpose. I infer that the genius of autobiographical writing (I remind you that I find all successful writing to be autobiographical; here I mean what is overtly so) is to provide you with materials and space to create me in a way identifiable with my historical reality and with the way I assert that that historical reality should be read.

In any writing that alleges to speak in the first-person mode, I suspect that you are always what you were defined as being at the start of these explorations (the name I give myself reading) and that I am always what I was defined as being (the name I give myself writing).

Review of Contemporary Fiction, 1988

THE MONKEY AT THE WHEEL

W ords and music—or should it be music and words?

The first prose I ever wrote and saw published touched on this question. It was a chapter (in the middle of my first novel) that described an imaginary renaissance "motto" mass: the motto, consisting of three notes, was supposed to encode a secret verbal message. What the code and message were is not relevant here; but it occurs to me that writing the chapter may have betrayed a chronic desire—perhaps a nostalgic one—to see the sense of music and the sense of words made one, more emphatically, a desire to annex music's mysterious power to the more familiar coherence of speech.

This desire certainly accompanied and conditioned my first enthusiasm for classical music. At the age of nine or ten I was smitten with a passion for Wagner's *Ring* operas. I made my way into them via two seventy-eight RPM records on which their leitmotifs were announced and played in the order of their appearance. I learned these records by heart; so that when I began listening to the works themselves, I was equipped with a kind of lexicon that allowed me to read what I heard: I could label musical events with the names of the leitmotifs. I felt that with this knowledge I could safely start journeying across the forbidding expanses of the operas. As I listened, I would hang on to a familiar motif until the next appeared, then leap across the intervening fog, like a fearful sailor dashing from the cover of one island to the next. I think it was the mere existence of the names that reassured me—at ten, it was hard to know what a phrase like "Redemption through Love" was supposed to mean. I simply memorized the phrase and told myself: that is the proper term for Sieglinde's ecstatic wail, it sounds important, and I can let myself succumb to the wail itself. (Later, the German libretto worked for me in a similar way: not understanding most of it did not matter).

But if the leitmotifs were a comforting introduction to *The Ring*, my faith in them was shortlived. Safe islands soon became mirages. According to Wagner, leitmotifs were musical phrases that could be lifted from their original context and reintroduced wherever that context might be relevantly invoked. They were a means of recollection and anticipation. Wagner is supposed to have been faithful to this definition until *Siegfried;* but the trouble starts much earlier. Leitmotifs make appearances that require elaborate explanations by defenders of the faith. Even a credulous ten year old begins wondering if he hasn't been conned.

One glaring inconsistency concerns a leitmotif called the Renunciation of Love *(Entsagungsmotiv)*. It is first met early in *Das Rheingold,* where it is sung by one of the Rhine Maidens to Alberich, the dwarf blacksmith who is pursuing them. The rising sun has lighted up the Rhine gold, a lump embedded in an underwater rock. From this gold, we learn, an all-powerful ring can be fashioned, but only at a price:

> Nur wer der Minne Macht entsagt,
> nur wer der Liebe Lust verjagt,
> nur der erziehlt sich den Zauber
> zum Reif zu zwingen das Gold

(He alone who renounces love, he alone who rejects love's joys will obtain the magic power to force the ring from the gold).

The motif returns after Alberich has indeed renounced love and ripped the gold from its bed; and we hear it twice more in late scenes when this renunciation is mentioned.

The phrase appears next at the end of the first act of *Die Walküre*. Siegmund, the anonymous, involuntary, and unarmed guest of his worst enemy, is told by his host's wife, Sieglinde, that a sword meant for a hero has been sunk into the ash tree by which they are sitting. At the end of a long exchange, during which the two fall in love, Sieglinde identifies Siegmund, calling him by his rightful name. As he approaches the tree and grasps the sword, Siegmund sings the Renunciation of Love motif to these words:

> Heiligste Minne höchste Noth,
> sehnender Liebe sehrende Noth
> brennt mir hell in der Brust,
> drängt zu Tat und Tod

(Holiest love and highest destiny burn brightly in my breast and compel me to high deeds and death . . .).

Siegmund is hardly renouncing love: he is invoking it. Words and action are the opposites of those in *Das Rheingold*. What can this mean? Max Friedlander says* that if one considers all the motif's appearances in the

---

*See Robert W. Gutman, *Richard Wagner: The Man, His Mind, and His Music* (New York, 1968), p. 368.

Ring operas, it can be interpreted as standing for relinquishment and demission in general; here Wotan, by yielding the sword to his son Siegmund, is initiating a series of events that will cost him his daughter Brünnhilde, who is the apple of his eye. Maybe so; when this passage is heard no one is thinking of Wotan or Brünnhilde. And even if Max Friedlander is right, other, more immediate explanations of the anomaly are available. These do not, however, restore the Renunciation theme to its role as leitmotif.

Between the scenes in *Das Rheingold* and *Die Walküre* there is, first of all, a striking gestural analogy: a man reaches up to pluck a magical object from the mass in which it is lodged. Doing so, each man chooses his destiny—Alberich goes after power, Siegmund romantic doom. A second, obvious link is the key of C minor in which the motif is heard in both instances. Third, and most curiously, the two sets of words sung to the motif have, in spite of their different content, a conspicuous material feature in common. The words for love, *Minne* and *Liebe,* stand in identical metrical positions: *Nur wer der* Minne . . . and *Heiligste* Minne; *Nur wer der* Liebe . . . and *sehnender* Liebe. In both passages the words are, for opposite reasons, crucial, and the upward leap of a minor sixth sets them in relief.

These shared characteristics suggest that Wagner in the first act of *Die Walküre* reused the Renunciation theme for specific rhetorical effect—an effect that has nothing to do with its signification as leitmotif: gesture, dramatic situation, tonality, and word pattern determined its use, not its name tag. One can describe the feeling of this effect—solemn aspiration? love in a cold climate?—but wouldn't a better description be something like: a minor sixth up, two major thirds down, over the dominant and tonic chords of C minor? Isn't the best description the music itself (whatever it may mean)? To explain the music in terms of the story seems not only superfluous but perplexing, because it makes problematic what is otherwise clear. The music works; the scene works. Only defenders of Wagner's theories find cause for worry. To others, the music speaks for itself.

My point is not to attack Wagner (or his hard-working defenders) but to suggest, first, that the apparently inconsistent use of the Renunciation motif is musically normal; second, that the anxiety it has provoked in many people (not all of them ten year olds) points to a mistake in our assumptions about what happens when music is combined with words.

When I say "our" assumptions I mean particularly my own. I have always been an assiduous reader of librettos and song texts, and when I have to listen to an opera or a lieder recital without knowing in detail what is being sung, I have an uneasy feeling that I'm missing something essential. I expect words to give me access not only to the feelings expressed in the work, but to its purpose, its intention, its very meaning. It is as if the precise power of music could not *have* meaning unless a name were given to it; so that in vocal music, where words abound, the multitude of "names" can marvelously increase my ability to understand the music and make it my own. Assumptions such as these are, I think, shared by many. It is because of this that I thought it would be useful to summarize what I have learned in practice from listening to vocal music. Experience has not confirmed my assumptions; my examples will show why. They are not meant to exhaust the topic, but they all seem to me, by their typical or peculiar qualities, justly pertinent to it.

A second interesting example of "inconsistency" in text setting is found in two songs by Josquin Des Prez (ca. 1445-1521). Compare these passages from "Basiez moy" and "La Déploration de Johan Okeghem" (see figure A).

The passages differ in a number of ways, but harmonically they have a great deal in common. This can be outlined schematically (see figure B).

This descending sequence of interlocking thirds accompanies startlingly different poems. "Basiez moy" is a lighthearted erotic dialogue; the "Déploration" commemorates the death of Josquin's beloved teacher. Sense

Figure A

Figure B

and mood differ even more than in the examples from Wagner. To explain this we might, à la Friedlander, point to the presence of a common theme— the theme of loss (of love, of life). In the "Déploration" a disciple has lost his master; in "Basiez moy" the lover fails in his suit (and one might add that sexual desire, which emanates from the piece like fragrance from flowering thyme, is in any case condemned to eventual "death"). But this would be an unsatisfactory explanation. So much poetry is about loss (all the examples in this essay, which were chosen for quite other reasons, evoke it directly or indirectly): why associate the theme with these two poems in particular? Why did Josquin use the descending sequence here and not on other equally melancholy occasions? Musically, the answer is tautological: the sequence is appropriate and effective in both cases. The only inconsistency exists between the sets of words. The music's consistency is what "makes sense."

Obviously, the examples from Wagner and Josquin can be considered special cases. Since we all know music that illustrates the words it sets less problematically, it is such music we should look at next. For our first case, let us turn to Bach's cantatas: specifically, the tenor aria from Cantata No. 92 ("Ich hab in Gott Herz und Sinn"). The text of the da capo section goes:

> Seht, seht wie reisst, wie bricht, wie fällt,
> Was Gottes starker Arm nicht hält!
> Seht aber fest und unbeweglich prangen,
> Was unser Held mit seiner Macht umfangen!

(See, see how everything tears, breaks, and collapses that is not upheld by God's strong arm! Yet see how what our Hero wraps in His might shines firm and unshakable!).

The setting of the opening line is typical of the whole (see figure C).

Figure C

As he so often does, Bach has here let words suggest musical texture. The combination of quick up-beat runs, wide melodic leaps, and dotted rhythm clearly "tears" and "breaks" (and, even more, *reisst* and *bricht:* the sound of the German words contributes to the texture). The illustration is so successful that we might be tempted to conclude that here at least the correspondence between text and music is a forthright one. But it becomes clear after a moment's reflection that the correspondence is of a peculiar sort. It applies to only one facet of the text—its violent and spectacular side. What is the main point of these lines? Not breaking and tearing, but firmness and unshakeability. From a hopeful text, Bach has chosen for his musical illustration only what is disastrous. He ignores what God sustains; he turns instead to the vivid consequences of faithlessness.

The total effect, however, is anything but one of disaster. What we feel in this aria is immense rejoicing. And the instance is a typical one: again and again in the sacred cantatas, we are told of pain, grief, and loss and are left in joy; and usually, as here, what is plainly described is the pain while the joy is manifested in some other, less overt manner. This should not be taken as a personal perversity of Bach's: the method seems to correspond to the way Lutherans in general look at the world. All that is human is sinful and hopeless; our only hope lies in divine grace, which can redeem anything—even us. The surface, the "appearance," of Bach's music illustrates the purely human anguish announced by the text. It is the music's "invisible" elements that redeem this appearance. (I would suggest that these elements amount to no more than the very fact that the text is being sung. The act of putting music to words is itself a celebration—think of Brecht's complaint that no matter how gloomily Kurt Weill set his pessimistic poems, they always left people cheered up. There is, furthermore, nothing specifically religious about much of Bach's cantata music in style or form.) The power of music to "redeem" its mere appearance through its totality gives it a role analogous to that of divine grace, and it explains Bach's predilection for illustrating sin and gloom. It also once again shows us music creating a meaning independent of the words it sets: "redemption" clearly cannot depend on any particular text (or texts), which is part of what it is redeeming. . . . Theology aside, is this not the effect of Bach's music as we listen to it?

As another example of clear musical illustration let us take the "Romance" from Schubert's music to *Rosamunde*. This is a translation of the poem (see figure D):

> "The full moon shines on the mountain peaks. How much have I missed you! Ah, tender heart, how sweet when a faithful kiss is faithfully given!
>
> "What use is the loveliness of May? You were my sun. Light of my night, smile on me once again in death."
>
> She steps forward in moonlight, looks toward the sky—"Apart in life, yours in death!"—and heart softly breaks on heart.

Figure D

Schubert's setting seems to render the stillness, the solitude, and the poignancy of the scene perfectly. The perfection is of a kind reserved, apparently, for strophic songs—songs in which the same music is repeated for each stanza. It is worth asking how a strophic setting works in the case of the "Romance" since the poem moves through such extraordinary changes of mood. The opening stanza's placid rapture gives no hint of the fatality to come, and not until the eighth line, with the words ". . . again in death," can we suspect that what began as a love song will end as a dirge. How can the same music not only mirror such different moods but give us a satisfaction rarely achieved in songs where the music varies with the text?

An analogy can help us: the use of the mask in theater. Whether in a puppet show or a Nō play, we have all seen masks on stage and noticed more or less consciously that here, too, an apparent miracle took place. A character with an unvarying expression experiences joy, grief, and rage, and his face somehow accords itself to these dissimilar emotions, not merely adequately but with uncanny intensity. A "realistic" actor would be hard put to affect us so consistently.

The "magical" unchangingness shared by mask and strophic song might be called their abstractness: mask and music have *no* defined meaning at the outset; they can thus accommodate whatever words or situations are assigned to them. Then, when they reappear in new circumstances, their original indefiniteness is restored and immediately readapted. It is as though mask and strophic music contained the meanings of *all* potential words and situations; and isn't this (once again) in fact what we feel as we listen to the "Romance"—that a universe of meaning lies behind this particular text? The poem's words and situations, we sense, are only one reading of this potentiality, which belongs to the music, not to them; indeed, it seems to us that the potentiality of meaning precedes their appearance, just as it survives their mutability.

It can be objected that all the examples presented so far favor music unfairly—Wagner's poetry would be unknown without his operas, and we do not much care who wrote the texts set by Josquin, Bach, and Schubert. What happens when the words set are as fine as the setting? Here are two such cases.

The first is from the High Middle Ages: Guillaume de Machaut's motet "Qui es promesses." In his time, Machaut was as famous for his poetry as for his music. Here, furthermore, he is setting his own words. Not one but two poems: the top voice, or *triplum*, sings:

Qui es promesses
de fortune se fie
et de richesses
de ses dons s'asseure
ou cilz qui croit
qu'elle soit tant s'amie
que pour li soil
en riens ferme ou seure,
   est non seure,
c'est fiens couvers de
   riche couverture,
qui dehors luist et
   dedens est ordure. . . .

The man who trusts the
promises of Fortune and
counts on the wealth of
her gifts, or who believes
that she is such a friend
that she can be relied
on in anything firmly or
with certainty, is hope-
lessly insane; for she is
uncertain—dung over-
laid with rich covering,
gleaming without, filth
within. . . .

The middle voice, or *motetus*, sings:

Ha! Fortune, trop me suis
   mis loing de port,
quant en la mer m'as mis
   sans aviron
en un bastel petit, plat et
   sans bort,
foible, porri, sans voile,
   et environ
sont tuit li vent contraire. . . .

Ah, Fortune, I find my-
self far from shore,where
you have led me: at sea,
without oars, in a small,
shallow boat with no
gunnel, a frail, rotten,
sailless boat, and all
around me the winds are
contrary. . . .

The poems are obviously related: both treat the same subject—the inconstancy of Fortune—in complementary modes, didactic in the *triplum*, personal in the *motetus*.

It is as if Machaut wanted to treat his poetic material as he does that of his music: extracting two strains from a common source, he sets them contrapuntally against one another. His two poems about fickle Fortune are not only different in point of view: "Ha! Fortune" can also be read as a particular consequence of the generality of "Qui es promesses." An individual is describing the painful consequences of not knowing what the didactic poem proclaims. We are given the moral of the lesson simultaneously with the lesson itself—an intriguing and ambitious undertaking. The motet begins like this:

Our second example is the trio at the end of the third act of *Der Rosenkavalier.* Strauss's librettist is Hugo von Hofmannsthal, a remarkable poet and dramatist and a prose writer of genius. The long collaboration between Strauss and Hofmannsthal was marked by patience, commitment, and respect on both sides; and if Hofmannsthal today looks the more interesting and original of the two, he himself was more than satisfied with the way Strauss treated his work: "In your music," he wrote, "my words have achieved a fullness that they never would otherwise have found." He also took his libretto writing seriously. In the case of the final pages of *Der Rosenkavalier*, for instance, he kept an eager Strauss waiting for weeks. He at last explained the delay:

> I would have done the end of the opera ages ago if only weeks of the vilest weather hadn't darkened my mood. The ending must be *exceptionally* good—otherwise it will be terrible. It must be right psychologically and at the same time lose nothing in delicacy and subtlety. . . . It must express the relief of the young couple without being cruel toward the Marschallin. In a word, there must be happiness and vivacity: and to manage that, I must be sitting in my garden in sunshine, not under glacial downpours.

The trio is sung by the Marschallin, Sophie, and Octavian (a mezzosoprano). The Marschallin, who is Octavian's mistress, has arrived at a moment when she was not expected. For different reasons, Octavian and Sophie, who have just fallen in love, are mortally embarrassed. In spite of her pain at giving up Octavian, the Marschallin brings him and Sophie definitively together. The three then sing:

> *The Marschallin:* I had sworn to love him so perfectly that I would even love the love he gave another. How could I know I'd have the chance so soon? There are things in this world one cannot give credence to, even after learning they have happened. But the person they happen to has to believe them, even if they cannot be understood. There he is, my little boy, and here I am, and over there is the unfamiliar girl who will teach him happiness—or what with men passes for happiness.

> *Octavian:* Something has happened, something has come to pass. . . . I long to ask the Marschallin, must this be? It is the one question forbidden me. I long to ask her, why is something inside me trembling so? Is what has happened a great injustice? This is a question I have no right to ask. And then, Sophie, I look at you, and you are the one thing I see, you are the one thing I feel, Sophie, and the one thing I know is: I love you.

> *Sophie:* I feel as though I were in church. Something holy has penetrated me, making me afraid, and something that isn't holy at all. I can't tell what's happening. I long to go down on my knees to this woman, and I long to hurt her—I feel she's giving him to me, and she's keeping a part

of him that will never be mine. I just can't tell what's happening to me. I long to understand everything, and nothing at all. I long to ask questions and not ask questions. I feel hot, I feel cold. And what I feel above all is you, and the one thing I know is: I love you.

The Marschallin sings a few measures alone, then Sophie and Octavian join her. There is also a small orchestra playing (see figure E).

Figure E

What has happened to the intelligent, serious, carefully written lines of Machaut and Hofmannsthal? They have been annihilated. If one reads them ahead of time, one may catch a phrase here and there; but most of the time, because the parts are sung simultaneously, the words obliterate each other into incomprehensible sound. For all we hear, the singers might be comparing laundry prices in Tucson and Macao. Remember, Machaut is doing this to his own poetry, and Hofmannsthal never complained. . . . We don't complain, either. The words have been sacrificed to that elemental and delicious musical texture, vocal counterpoint, here heightened by a particular formal complexity. The complexity is considerable in Machaut—he uses highly "abstract" isorhythmic patterns (that is—oversimply—the repetition of long rhythmic patterns unconnected with the melodic and poetic phrasing); it is a lesser but still determining factor in Strauss—he loosely builds his trio on the opening motif of a deliberately dopey waltz that has appeared earlier in the act, here transformed, with seeming irrelevance and even impudence, into the main tune of this pathetic scene. The transformation *is* impudent: it puts words in their place. It shows us who's really powering the car we're riding in. *And* no one is complaining. Perhaps that's where words belong—sitting behind the steering wheel and pretending to be smart?

Needless to say, wherever vocal counterpoint has been practiced, instances abound of words canceling each other out. In some cases, such as settings of the mass, the familiarity of the text renders the destruction innocuous; in other cases the result can be ascribed to indifference or the conventions of the style; but in almost every period it would not be difficult to find examples of composers sacrificing words they know to be "significant." This sacrifice, furthermore, is not always performed for the sake of counterpoint: the sacred texts of the organa of Léonin and Pérotin, of the twelfth-century School of Notre-Dame, have their syllables stretched out to lengths defying normal powers of recall. More recently, Pierre Boulez has systematically disrupted the integrity of sung words not by prolonging but by isolating and fragmenting their syllables. His treatment of Mallarmé's poems in particular is very pertinent to our subject.

Boulez's admiration of Mallarmé was his declared reason for taking his poems as texts. The results (see figure F) are illustrated with the setting of a line taken from the sonnet (in *Pli selon pli No. 2: Improvisation sur Mallarmé I*) that begins:

> Le vierge, le vivace, et le bel aujourd'hui
> Va-t-il nous déchirer avec un coup d'aile ivre . . .

(Will today—virgin, vigorous and fair—sunder with a drunken wrench of its wing . . .).

Figure F

The words have here become as incomprehensible as in the examples from Machaut and Strauss. The leaping intervals tear syllables so thoroughly from their context as to make them unrecognizable. The composer has decomposed his text. We can, as before, grasp bits of it, especially if we know it well; and Boulez's listeners are in truth expected to be familiar with the words—the composer has told us as much *("je suppose acquis par la lecture le sens direct du poème").* In such circumstances music does not have to present or interpret a text: it can quite openly adopt it as a pretext for generating its own forms. These forms may be related to those of the text, but it is worth noting that they do not need it except as an idea (as a memory). Léonin expands and extends the notes of the Gregorian melody with which the text is associated to the point that we can no longer hear melody or text, just as we may forget, looking at the elaborate carvings on a Romanesque column, that we are moving along the aisle of a church. Boulez's intentions are made clear in his comments on *Pli selon pli.* He wanted to derive his music from Mallarmé's poetry. How could this be done? "The transposition thus imposed requires the invention of equivalences. . . ." After considering several possibilities, Boulez says: "the marriage of poem and music . . . tries to plumb the very depths of invention, which are structure." Thus "each piece strictly follows the sonnet form." What Boulez undertook was not to set Mallarmé's words but to replicate in music the process that created them. The process necessarily preceded the particular words, so it is hardly surprising if, once more, they are—in the heard meaning of the work—relegated to a minor role.

I think that Mallarmé, like Hofmannsthal, would have approved. And not only of the composer's procedure: these exquisite, opaque, ambiguous sounds—so complex in their scoring, so simple in their effect—are wonderfully Mallarméan. And yet . . . and yet would that notion ever occur to us if we were ignorant of Boulez's methods? Does music need this kind of comment to be complete?

If Boulez's reverence for the art of Mallarmé cannot be questioned, *Pli selon pli* may nevertheless strike us as something of a case apart. There is,

---

*The quotations are from the liner notes of the composer's recording of the work. Here as elsewhere, the translations are mine.

however, a category of musical settings where the supremacy of the text is at least as great and is in addition universally accepted by its practitioners: that of sacred music.

The relation of music to words is here a special one. The first fact about it to remember is that until recent times the "sacredness" of sacred music was rarely a problem for the composer. What was sacred was the word itself. Music for religious use was automatically sanctified by what it set, or by the ritual use to which it was put. There was no religious style—virtually any style could be made to work. Even our liberal, hypocritical ears are not bothered by the absence of demarcations between the sacred and profane works of Bach and Handel, not to mention composers preceding them. In the classical period we begin feeling uneasy. Haydn's and Mozart's masses are so plainly operatic—we must get to know them before we recognize their appropriateness. (Even in Austria they are rarely performed in church.) After that, what is or isn't religious becomes a matter of opinion. Some approve of the *Missa Solemnis* and Brahms's *Requiem* but not of Bruckner's masses. For some, *Parsifal* is a sublimely spiritual work, for others a pathological fraud. Function, subject, even the presence of the holy word no longer guarantee sacredness. It has become a question of effect.

How can a post-enlightenment composer set a sacred text? Can it properly be done at all? For an answer, let us consult a master at word setting whose piety is beyond question: What does Verdi do?

The final movement of his stupendous *Requiem* is the Responsory of Absolution:

> *Libera me, Domine, de morte aeterna, in die illa tremenda . . .*
> Deliver me, O Lord, from everlasting death, on that fearful day when heaven and earth shall tremble and Thou shalt come to judge the age with fire. Shaking overcomes me, and I am terrified at the approach of judgment and of the wrath to come. A day of wrath shall that day be, of ruin and wretchedness, a day both great and very bitter.
> Give them eternal rest, O Lord, and may perpetual light shine on them.
> Deliver me, O Lord, from everlasting death . . .

The movement contains the only music that, rather than informing me about fear, actually frightens me; rightly enough, since the fear invoked is of "everlasting death," which doesn't mean being dead a long time but experiencing death over and over with no hope of remission. The first words are given to the soprano soloist, who sings unaccompanied:

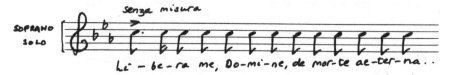

This monotone is as close to not setting words as music can manage. After that, "all Hell breaks loose"—there follows a prodigious variety of textures and tempi. Two formal procedures are worth mentioning: the recapitulation at "A day of wrath . . ." of the music that opens the second movement *(Dies irae),* and the four-part fugue that is the longest of several settings of "Deliver me, O Lord. . . ." These textures do not merely thicken the sauce. They make us aware, as we confront prospects of "everlasting death" or "eternal rest," that for the moment we are very much stuck in time. The recapitulation invokes time on a grand scale by reminding us how much has happened since the *Dies irae.* The fugue invokes time as a one-instant-to-the-next medium, a scurrying of "did" and "will do" that depicts confusion and disarray as explicitly as the Bach aria. Then something different happens. The fugue has been sung by the chorus. Its first subject begins:

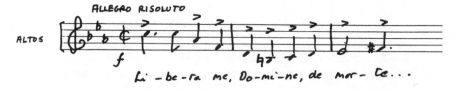

The choral scurrying lasts several minutes. Suddenly the soprano soloist, who has been silent, sings "out of the blue" (her voice does seem to sail down from the last sky short of invisible heaven):

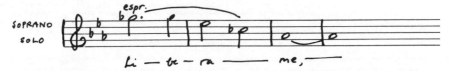

She is singing the opening notes of the fugue subject, but doubled in length—an ancient device called augmentation, here given new point: she is catching hold of scurrying time and stopping it in its tracks. Her entrance thus becomes the culmination of this prayer for deliverance. She is making time last longer. This side of eternity, what more can be done? It is as if she were singing, through the words: I can go no farther, music can go no farther.

Music can go no farther. The movement continues in textures less complex. At the very end, this is what we hear (see figure G). It is the same near monotone with which the *Libera me* began ("deflated" to a lower octave). Nothing has changed. There has been no deliverance. Twenty minutes of heart-rending, glorious music have made no difference in this ultimate prayer, which Verdi at last relinquishes to its proper nature as a particular kind of speech. The sacred word is beyond music.

Figure G

Verdi's answer to the question, How can a modern composer set a sacred text? is, enact the question itself. It's the impossibility of setting such a text that provides the drama of the *Libera me;* and it is the drama that Verdi sets, not the words. More broadly considered, it is the drama of prayer. Someone praying speaks words that "make no sense," because their reality depends entirely on the will of Christ (and, for Roman Catholics, on His church), over which he has no control. The words of a prayer do not belong to their speaker: they can be vouchers for his unreasonable—that is, hopeless—faith, but they can hardly express the anguish of his position, on whose surge (so powerfully embodied by the music) they ride like froth.

It would be facile to claim that, here as in our earlier examples, meaning is produced entirely by the music without regard to the text. More accurately, it can be said that meaning is produced entirely by the music *in the presence of a text.* It isn't music that accompanies words but the other way round. Words accompany music; music is set to words. When a composer picks a text to set, he is giving himself an excuse to invent an autonomous musical work that will eventually devour it. Perhaps not devour—half swallow: the tail of the excuse will be left hanging out, visibly wagging in time to the bites that consume it. And the tail serves a purpose. It is something we can identify, like a flag. That is the text's function: it is the music's emblem. We are comforted by recognizing it. But it cannot tell us more than any other emblem: it can only name and categorize. Furthermore, since cheating in art is a virtue (see some of the preceding examples), one should remember to beware of flags of convenience.

The point may become clearer if we reverse our approach. What happens to a purely instrumental piece of music when words are added to it? For our experiment, here is the opening of Mendelssohn's "Song without Words," Opus 53, No. 3 (see figure H). As to the words to set: avoiding musicological controversy, let's assume that Mendelssohn sometimes had specific poems in mind when writing the "Songs without Words," and that in this case, the poem was "Versenkung," one of Klopstock's lost unrhymed lyrics—the very one supposedly translated by the young Shelley (and his lines do fit the irregular phrasing exactly).

Figure H

The first stanza reads:

> Pale pours the light of melancholy heaven,
> The ministers of autumn winds are guiding us to darkness,
> Away fade the beams beneath profoundest ocean—
> No respite is there in the shadows' gathering cold,
> No music is there in their mood,
> No resting is there in their deep
> But turbulence and solitude
> In dereliction's sad appointed home.

Now we have words to sing, or to pretend to hear sung (whatever gives us an idea of the false work's performance):

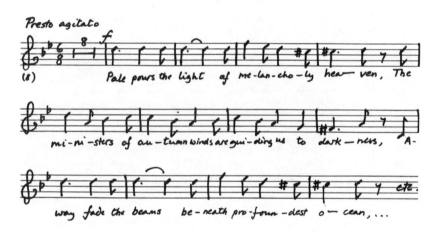

This is obviously a different work. First of all, many more people are to be considered. Where before there was only the composer and pianist, there are now, in addition, a singer, a poet, and the character who is uttering the poem (he may be the poet, or someone else, like a shepherd). This increase in humanity gives us more to react to. ("A shepherd?" "Klopstock—poor man." "His voice is nice, but those teeth!") More pertinently, we can now be sure that the song is about something. And what is it about? ". . . Melancholy . . . turbulence and solitude . . .

dereliction. . . ." Uh-oh—serious stuff. We begin listening accordingly, with long faces, and longer ears. We notice how skillfully the composer has caught the sweep of paleo-Romantic passion. We notice subtle reflections of the text in the music, like the peaking A flats for "turbulence" and "dereliction," those beacons of *Sturmunddrang*ishness. Gosh, maybe we were wrong about the gilded Mendelssohn. . . . His "tragic sense." . . .

Words breed words to pile on top of music, to familiarize and obscure it. If it is nonsensical to talk this way about a trumped-up song, it is no less so when we discuss real vocal settings. Once we look to words for the meaning of a musical work, they will lead us away from the act of listening to it. Setting words to the Mendelssohn piece certainly changed it; the presence of text and voice makes a difference. But what they do is add something to the music, and what they do not do is reveal anything about it. If only they did! That's our temptation. We want what we're hearing explained. So we look to the words—and soon there are more words, bigger and bigger ones, that give us more room to think and not hear. They indulge our longing to know, not to let things simply happen, but to be sure of what's happening—

> So runs my dream; but what am I?
> An infant crying in the night,
> An infant crying for the light,
> And with no language but a cry.

And to hear and understand a cry—like the soprano's *"Libera me . . ."*—no one needs the word "cry."

Geoffrey Grigson has written, "To a good tune you can still sing words—as long as they fit—which have turned half or absolutely into nonsense." Giving up the tempting illusion that what the composer sets indicates what he is really doing provides a welcome stillness in which to freshly listen—listen to music that, of course, *includes* words.

We have looked at nine examples of vocal music, each chosen to illustrate the priority of music in creating meaning. Other conclusions might have been drawn from them. We might have used them to start compiling a lexicon of musical rhetoric: What are the effects and affects of descending sequences of major and minor thirds and sixths? of the voice as an element in musical texture? The question then arises, Can we deal with such questions in words at all? Won't that make for more irrelevant comment? Probably. Still, what else can we do? No matter how faulty words may be, what else can we use when we want to communicate? One answer is that musicians solve musical problems with a minimum of speech. When they put their heads together, they use the music itself.

Here is a last object for reflection. It is drawn from an interesting kind of "vocal" music in which there is no singing and words are only implicitly present. We are all familiar with instances of such music—Leporello's mute appearance in the Diabelli variations, Ives quoting "Turkey in the Straw" in his second string quartet. In the theme and variations of Haydn's "Emperor" Quartet in C major (Opus 76, No. 3), the quotation is the theme itself: a song, "Gott erhalte Franz den Kaiser," written by Haydn shortly before to honor the Austrian emperor. The tune became the national anthem of the Austrian empire and, later, of Germany, to the well-known words "Deutschland, Deutschland über alles" (words made ominous not only by history but by their being commonly misunderstood); in English-speaking countries, it became a Protestant hymn, "Glorious things of thee are spoken, Sion, city of our God." That is to say, to a great many people in the Western world Haydn's melody is charged with political or religious significance. It is impossible, furthermore, to ignore the melody at any point in the quartet movement—it is repeated intact in each of the four variations. There is no denying that on first hearing the theme one is startled or shocked or distracted; and we might expect that music that repeatedly invokes the weighty words of anthem or hymn would sink beneath them, so that we would have to write it off as an unfortunate historical casualty. But this is not what happens. I have German, English, and French witnesses: by the end of the second variation, it becomes almost impossible to *remember* those words. By then we are in another world, one of musical celebration of the most delicate and demanding sort, so that if we are listening at all, we are incapable of thinking about anything else. And who would want to? Who needs to think of soup in a garden? Here, again, it is music that has the last word.

Parnassus, 1982

FEARFUL SYMMETRIES

The subject of these pages, translating American English into French, is plainly one I cannot claim to know much about. I am in fact familiar with only one small body of work that involves the process—my own. That the work is mine is largely irrelevant. What has led me to set down these remarks is that two of my translators, Georges Perec and Marie Chaix, have been highly gifted writers; that they produced translations of exceptional quality; and that I collaborated with them routinely in the process of translation. Thanks to these collaborations, I became familiar with many ordinary problems facing translators of American English, as well as with the exceptional ones due to my own eccentricities; and as any translator knows, it is often the plainest statements that produce the biggest headaches.

I have pointed out elsewhere[1] that one disparity in American and French ways of thinking can de demonstrated by two of the plainest statements of all: the way citizens of the two countries declare their national identities: *"Je suis français"*; "I'm American." Translating these words by "I'm French" and *"Je suis américain"* brings to light differences rather than similarities. In the language of a Frenchman, nationality basically means a complex cultural history; in the language of an American it basically means the fact of citizenship, often coupled with a disrespect for history. While it would be fatuous to translate these statements in any other way, we can see how the translations leave out what is vividly implicit in each language.

Curiously, the same statements can with slight modification be turned into much closer equivalents of one another. With some emphasis, the Frenchman now says, *"Je suis français, monsieur!"* The American responds, "I'm American, and you better believe it!" The effective meaning of both statements is the same: not so much an assertion of nationality as of membership in one's very own community. What makes the equivalence interesting is that it depends not on the sense of the words used (where the French/American difference remains entire) but on other linguistic factors, whatever they may be. And it should be said at once that, whatever they may be, they have nothing to do with style: stylistically, there is still an ocean of difference between *"Je suis français, monsieur!,"* and "I'm American, ard you better believe it."

This example of what we may call efficient translation suggests that one thing a translator should look for is a means of letting non-nominal meaning pass into the target language; and this in turn implies that fidelity in translation should apply not only to nominal meaning but to what may be provisionally called effect. A further implication is that reinvention rather than replication can best realize this aim. Let me cite some examples of my own experience in support of this view.

My first work with a French translator provided me with a basic apprenticeship in the practicalities of converting written English into French. (The work being translated was a novel appropriately called *The Conversions*.) At the start, whenever a difficulty arose, I would soon find a solution for it, only to be reluctantly but accurately informed that *"c'est une chose qu'on ne peut pas dire en français."*[2] I thus discovered that there are numerous rules of French compositon not to be found in grammars, that in order to learn them it is advisable to attend twelve years in a French primary school and lycée, and that I would be well advised to restrict my own writing of French to such easily imitated forms as official letters. As for the actual rendering of- the book, Claude Portail, my translator, was knowledgeable, sensitive, and talented enough; she was also, unfortunately, all too modest when confronted with a demanding author; and since I was stupidly obsessed with preserving the rhythm of my sentences and paragraphs (that is, their shape and phrasing), she did her utmost to oblige my usually unreasonable insistence, with results that were inevitably flawed.

How unreasonable my insistence was became glaringly evident on the very title page of my second novel, the first of two translated by Georges Perec. In English the book was called *Tlooth*, a meaningless, made-up word suggesting both a "tooth" and the word "truth" as a Chinaman or a Thai might pronounce it. Perec and I spent much time concocting analogous French words. Of his many ingenious inventions, I particularly remember *Dentité*;[3] like the rest, it was discarded as being too literary, *too* clever. (The word *tlooth*, after all, sounds like nothing so much as a grunt.) One day Perec suggested as a title *Les verts champs de moutarde de l'Afghanistan*, words that end a chapter more or less half way through the novel; I did not approve; so he waited until I was safely on the the other side of the Atlantic before announcing, after the book had been sent to the printer, that he and Geneviève Serreau had agreed that *Les verts champs de moutarde de l'Afghanistan*[4] was indeed the best possible title for the French edition.

Now Georges had understood that, aside from its semantic implications, the title of the book performs a specific function: *tlooth* is an undefined something that hovers over the novel, page after page, until—at a moment when it has become both familiar and forgotten—the word surfaces in the text itself. Its unheralded appearance then interrupts the normal progress of reading; and for a moment the book is transformed from a distanced narrative into a physically present object. As a means of achieving this effect, the title *Les verts champs de moutarde de l'Afghanistan* works every bit as well as the original *Tlooth:* its significance is no less mysterious, its emergence in the text no less abrupt. Here we have a perfect example of efficient translation—one where, need I point out, nominal meaning is completely abandoned, and form no less so: a grotesquely short title has been replaced with a grotesquely long one.

In both *Tlooth* and *The Sinking of the Odradek Stadium,* Perec performed innumerable and prodigious feats of translation; like the title of *Tlooth*, most of them were provoked by linguistic peculiarities of my own making and are

therefore not pertinent to our subject today; but one of his less spectacular
contributions is worth mentioning, that is, his handling of the terms of the
Great American Pastime, the game of baseball. At that time—perhaps still
today—French baseball devotees called the pitcher *le lanceur,* the catcher
l'attrapeur, the infielders *les basemen,* and the outfielders *les fielders,* terms
that, appearing at a narrative's outset, might very well convince a reader to
proceed no further—a possibility that Perec felt it was imperative to avoid.
Here are his own terms for the nine positions of a baseball team, as they
appear on the first page of *Les verts champs* :

left field	*aile gauche* (left wing—a soccer term)
center field	*demi-centre* (center half)
pitcher	*pointeur* (from French game of *boules:* one who pitches the ball accurately to a particular spot)
1st base	*1ère base*
shortstop	*arrière* (back)
2nd base	*2ème base*
right field	*aile droite* (right wing)
catcher	*catcheur* (wrestler—making no sense: but the term in undeniably French)
3rd base	*3ème base.*

(In *Le Naufrage du Stade Odradek, aile gauche* and *aile droite* became *ailiers
gauche et droite,* and the shortstop changed—a definite improvement—from
l'arrière to *le volant.*) In similar fashion, a single is translated as *un solo,* a
double as *un doublé* (a doublet); a walk is *un fauteuil* (*arriver dans un fauteuil*
means to win in a walkover); to strike or foul out is *se faire forclore* (to be
shut out), to hit safely is *marquer* (when used transitively, it means to score
a point).

   In terms of fidelity to nominal meaning, *pointeur, ailiers, catcheur, volant,
solo,* and *fauteuil* are "mistakes"; in terms of efficient translation, they work
admirably, using as they do terms from other sports well-known in France.
Once again, Perec gave primary consideration to the text's effect on the
reader: in both novels, the details of the baseball games are of little narrative

importance, and to an American reader the terms associated with the sport would pass unnoticed; so Perec decided to replace them with words that, no matter how vague their correspondance to their originals, would be acceptable to French readers—words both appropriate and ordinary enough to allow the flow of reading to proceed normally. Efficient translation here demanded that inconspicuous familiarity replace canonical fidelity as a rule of procedure.

Perec used a similar if less arbitrary approach to solve another problem in *The Sinking of the Odradek Stadium*. The novel consists of an exchange of letters between a husband and wife. As the plot evolves, the husband falls into the hands of con artists (more formally known as confidence men—*des arnaqueurs*); at the end of the book he is convinced that his wife is working with them and against him. In frequenting these criminals, he has gradually picked up their jargon, and in his last letter to his wife he denounces her in terms drawn entirely from that jargon:

> This chump never blowed you were turned out to hopscotch. You let him find the leather, and he copped you for the pure quill, when you're nothing but a crow. It took a long time to bobble him but now you've knocked him good and he feels like a heavy gee had slipped him a shiv. Well, no twist will ever beat this savage again, not if she hands over her bottom bumblebee—it's cheaper loaning cush to Pogy O'Brien. Don't you play the hinge but stick to the big con. You're a class raggle with a grand future, even if this mark knows you're snider.

Perec would have been happy to find a repertory of *l'argot des arnaqueurs*; but since this proved impossible, and knowing that in translating this letter what mattered was the presence on the page of a compact mass of exotic slang, he put together an effective vocabulary compounded of standard French argot and ordinary language. He knew that its impact here was intended above all to reflect the letter-writer's state of mind, that of one who has taken bitter refuge in the speech of those who have duped him:

> Ce chapon n'avait jamais reniflé que tu t'alignais à la marelle. Tu lui as fait la cornanche et il t'a chopée pour une moelleuse alors que tu n'es

rien d'autre qu'une corbaque. Ça a pris du temps pour l'empiler mais tu l'as bien démarqué et il a l'impression qu'un sueur l'a tailladé au surin. Eh bien, aucune chouquette ne lui refilera plus le coton, même si elle lui donne sa dernière dentelle—ça coûte moins cher de prêter ses arjoncs à Pierrot-la-Torpille. Ne pivote pas des bernicles, mais reste dans la grosse carotte. Tu es une catiche badour avec un avenir maousse même si ce miquel sait que tu es un bide.[5]

Marie Chaix faced a similar challenge in translating certain passages of my novel *Cigarettes.* They occur in a chapter that relates a sadomasochistic relationship between two men. At each of their intimate encounters, the normally well-spoken sadist plays his role by (among other things) systematically denigrating his sensitive lover in appalling terms taken entirely from gay slang—an extraordinarily rich and ingenious dialect based on the ironic attitude known as "camp." After Chaix had started translating *Cigarettes*, both she and I began asking our many gay friends for French equivalents of the sadist's words: but the only responses we received were either medical terms or crude vulgarities. After persisting for weeks in our quest, we were forced to conclude that in a language so much richer than English in erotic nuances gay slang does not exist and that the notion of camp is quite unknown. By the time we abandoned our research, time was running out, so Chaix simply decided to make up what she needed. (Like Perec, she adapted words wherever she could, although relatively more from the language of the original than from her own.) Here is the sadist's last harangue:

> "Even if I don't like reading you the stations, I won't spread jam. So please, Louisa, get it and go. You're a mess, a reject, a patient—I could go on for days. And don't tell me—I have your nose wide open. I'm sorry. Spare me the wet lashes, it's all summer stock. Because the only one you've ever been really strung out on is your own smart self, and you always will be. Think I'm going to stick around and watch the buns drop? And for what—to keep catching my rakes in your zits? Forget it, Dorothy. This is goodbye. Remember one thing, though. No matter what I've said to you, no matter how I've turned you out, the truth is, and I'm singing it out: I lo— . . ."

In Marie Chaix's translation:

> "Même si je je n'aime pas déplier mon Golgotha, je ne vais pas faire dans
> la marmelade. Alors, s'il te plaît, Louisa, c'est ça et pas autre chose : T'es
> qu'une foire, un défaut, un invalide . . . et ainsi de suite à perpète. Et ne
> me dis pas que tu bats des naseaux. Excuse-moi! Pas besoin d'éponger
> tes faux-cils, ce n'est que la tournée de province. Le seul pour qui tu
> pinces le banjo, c'est ton self à la con et ça changera jamais. Tu t'imagines
> pas que je vais me carier à attendre que tes meringues dévissent ? Et
> pourquoi ? Pour continuer à ratisser tes bourgeons ? Tu peux courir
> Berthe. Bonjour et bonsoir. Souviens-toi d'une chose pourtant. Peu
> importe ce que je t'ai dit, peu importe comment je t'ai décapé, la vérité,
> c'est . . . La vérité c'est, j'te la chante sur trois notes : je t'a— . . ."[6]

What all these examples suggest is that efficient translation requires a
fidelity to aesthetic function at least as great as the conventional fidelity to
nominal meaning. In some of my examples, admittedly exceptional ones,
fidelity to meaning has even been dispensed with altogether; but a more
useful point to make is that when fidelity to meaning is given undisputed
priority, distortion often follows, and sometimes outright disaster. Let me
provide a short sample of what I mean.

When I worked with the Italian and Spanish translators of *Cigarettes*, I
was often frustrated by *in*efficient translations. They took one of two forms:
they were either bulky, descriptive elaborations of concise English expressions or reductive formulations of explicit statements. Both kinds were invariably justified by the same assertion: there is no other way of saying this
in our language. One instance concerned a very ordinary sentence describing the influence of Oliver, a man in his twenties, on Pauline, a somewhat
younger woman who had been a virgin when Oliver artfully seduced her.
The disputed sentence reads in English: "He invented the ways she felt." In
Italian this became, "*Inventò la sessualità di Pauline*" ("He invented Pauline's
sexuality"). An argument lasting a good half hour did little to reduce the
total lack of agreement between the two sides—in the end, all I achieved
was to have *sessualità* replaced with *sensualità,* and this hardly mattered.
What mattered to me was that "the way she felt" is an indefinite phrase

where the verb acts as a dynamic agent of possibility; whereas *"inventò la sessualità di Pauline"* describes a circumscribed and completed fact. Yes, my translator would reply, but doesn't the sentence ultimately mean that Oliver taught Pauline about sex? Maybe, I would counter, but that's not how it works. In that case, came the conclusive response, this is the way you say that in good Italian. The discussion went round and round in this pointless circle. The only thing I gained from it was the knowledge that Italians are not only addicted to nominal meaning but that they prefer nouns to verbs, and abstract nouns at that.

At this point it would clearly be easy to classify a translator's options, in some such way as: translation where nominal meaning is identified and defended at all costs; translation where, as in Perec's treatment of baseball terms, adapting convenient substitutes can replace literal replication; translation where wholly new terms are introduced to recreate the function of the original, as was done for the French title of *Tlooth* and the gay slang passages in *Cigarettes*. I think, however, that there are other comments to be made, ones more interesting and certainly more relevant to the topic of this discussion.

One inference of the battle with my Italian translator is that Americans and Italians—and for Italians, read Europeans, *de la petite Europe*—hold knowledge in very different ways. To put it in broad terms, Americans look on knowledge as something to be invented or discovered; Europeans look on knowledge as something to be recognized and identified, that is, placed within a preexisting order of ideas. This does *not* mean that Americans are more original than Europeans or that Europeans are more reductive than Americans, rather that in their approach to knowledge Americans tend to start from a point of uncertainty and Europeans from one of certainty.

This distinction makes itself notably apparent in the domain of written language. Unless I am hopelessly mistaken, it seems to me perfectly possible to write well in French simply by writing correctly—by writing well I obviously do not necessarily mean elegantly or brilliantly; I mean only that there exists a normative written language available to anyone who takes the trouble to learn it that will enable its user to write prose that can be universally read without objection. Such a "correct" language does not exist in America (or in England, for that matter). Left to itself, merely correct American English tends to go flat. American writing of any kind has an *ad hoc* quality about it, a quality of having been improvised for the occasion; and good writing invariably involves the admixture of a particular individual manner. This difference manifests itself conspicuously in literary translations. French translations of the Greek and Roman classics strike me as pure marvels, because the normative language in which they are written allows me a familiar access to the substance of the text uncluttered by special stylistic effects (I believe Chateaubriand's *Paradise Lost* to be the only exception to the general rule); whereas much as I enjoy Lang's Homer or Dryden and Clough's Plutarch, they are, as in English they must be, "worked up" stylistically so as to attain not only weight but a significant presence on the page. For the same reason many French translators of atrociously written contemporary American works produce versions of them that are far better and more readable than the originals. They have, of course, no choice in the matter; but I know of no analogous examples in English, even if, as with the classics, translators often dress up the original work, as Scott Montcrief did in poeticizing Proust.

The reason for my bringing in these generalities will no doubt be obvious. In translating from an American author—someone who will, if she is gifted, *necessarily* have an idiosyncratic language of her own—Europeans schooled in their admirably normative languages may find themselves at a disadvantage whenever efficient translation is required; and the more professionally skilled they are as translators, the greater that disadvantage will be. Idiosyncratic inventiveness cannot yield its sense to the exercise of systematic recognition and identification, no matter how perceptive: within any normative language, the pitfalls of reductiveness will always remain an imminent danger. My own experience certainly confirms this view. The professional translators I have had, all highly qualified, have generally aimed at producing faithful renderings that broke no rules. Where efficient translation is desirable, that is not enough. Whenever Perec and Chaix, who were anything but experts in English, started translating something I had written, they always began by asking, usually in an irritated grumble, "How can I possibly say that in French?," meaning: "If I were the one saying the crazy things this man has thought up, what might they be?" In other words, they set out to recreate the original text as if it were their very own work. That is, of course, a huge commitment to take on; but it is sometimes the only way to get the job properly done.

The Literary Review, 2002

NOTES

1. "Translation and the Oulipo: The Case of the Persevering Maltese" in *The Way Home: Selected Longer Prose* (London: Atlas Press, 1999).
2. "That's something you can't say in French."
3. The invented word suggests "toothness" as well as "identity."
4. *The green mustard-fields of Afghanistan.*
5. It is important to remember that no expression in the English text has retained its normal meaning: *savage* means "victim," *bumblebee* means "dollar bill," and so forth. Here are some of Perec's French equivalents: *chapon* (invented slang) = capon; *la marelle* (invented slang), literal translation of "hopscotch"; *cornanche* = marking of a card by a card sharp; *choper* (slang) = to take; *moelleuse* (invented slang), literally a tender, sweet woman; *corbaque* (slang) = crow; *empiler* (slang) = to con; *démarquer* (invented slang) = to remove identification marks of goods; *sueur* (invented slang), suggested by *faire suer* = to harass; *surin* (slang) = dagger; *chouquette* = pastry, a *petit chou,* which is also a term of endearment; *refiler* (slang) = to get rid of (e.g., counterfeit money), combined with *filer un mauvais coton* = to be ill; *dentelle* (invented slang) = lace; *arjoncs,* suggested by *argent* = money and *jonc* (slang) = gold; *bernicles* (slang) = eyeglasses; *carotte* (slang) = a lie leading to the extorsion of money (cf. *carotter* = to con); *catiche* (invented slang), perhaps suggested by *catin* = prostitute and *pouliche* = filly; *badour* (slang) = beautiful; *maousse* (slang) = huge; *miquel* (invented slang), cf. *miquelet,* guerilla fighter in Napoleonic wars; *bide* (slang) = flop.
6. Again, it should be remembered that the English words have nowhere retained their ordinary meaning: "to read the stations" means "to complain,"

"to spread jam" means "to lie," "I'm sorry" means "I strongly disagree," etc. A few of Chaix's equivalents, virtually all of which are invented: *déplier mon Golgotha* = to lay out my [map of] Golgotha; *foire* comes from *enfoiré* = a bugger, in its most contemptuous sense; *à perpète* = for life, normally used to describe a jail sentence; *battre des naseaux* = to have one's nostrils a-flutter; *éponger tes faux-cils* = to dry your false eyelashes; *pincer le banjo* combines *pincer* = to have a crush and *pincer* = to strum; *tu peux courir Berthe* combines *tu peux courir* = you have another think coming, with *adieu Berthe* = it's all over.

TRANSLATION AND THE OULIPO:

THE CASE OF THE PERSEVERING MALTESE

A Problem in Translation

Some of you may know the name of Ernest Botherby (born in Perth, Australia, 1869; died in Adelaide, 1944), the scholar who founded the Australian school of ethno-linguistics, and also the explorer who identified the variety of *Apegetes* known as *botherbyi*, popular in England during the years before the Great War when private greenhouses were still common. Botherby attained professional notoriety in the late '20s, after publishing several papers on a north New Guinean language called Pagolak. The peoples of New Guinea were a favorite subject with Botherby. He had begun studying them years before when, at the age of twenty-four, he undertook a solitary voyage into the interior of the island, vast areas of which remained uncharted at the time. A collation of reports by Nicholas von Mikhucho Maclay, the Reverend Macfarlane, and Otto Finsch had convinced young Botherby that tribes still existed in the New Guinean highlands that had shunned contact with their neighbors, not to mention the modern world, and preserved a truly primitive culture.

Starting from Tagota at the mouth of the Fly, Botherby traversed the river by steam launch to a point over five hundred miles inland, whence he proceeded in more modest craft almost to its headwaters. After establishing a base camp, he traveled across the plains into the mountain forests, finally arriving at the unexplored region he was looking for, a complex of valleys lying—to use the toponymy of the time—between the Kaiserin Augusta, the Victor Emmanuel Mountains, and the continuation of the Musgrave Range.

In one of these valleys Botherby discovered, as he had hoped, his first archaic tribe. He designates it as that of the Ohos. This community, numbering no more than a few hundred, lived a peaceable existence in conditions of extreme simplicity. Its members were hunter-gatherers equipped with rudimentary tools. They procured fire from conflagrations occurring in forests nearby but were incapable of making it otherwise. They also used speech, but a speech reduced to its minimum. The Oho language consisted of only three words and one expression, the invariable statement, "Red makes wrong." Having patiently won over the tribal chiefs, Botherby was able to verify this fact during the many weeks he spent with them. Other needs and wishes were communicated by sounds and signs; actual words were never used except for this unique assertion that "Red makes wrong."

In time Botherby signified to his hosts a curiosity as to whether other communities existed in the region. The Ohos pointed north and east. When Botherby pointed west, he met with fierce disapproval. So it was naturally west that he next went, prudently distancing himself from the Oho settlement before taking that direction. His hunch was rewarded two days later when, in another valley, he came upon his second tribe, which he called the Uhas. The Uhas lived in a manner much like the Ohos, although they knew how to cultivate several edible roots and had domesticated the native pig; like the Ohos, they had a rudimentary language used invariably to make a single statement. The Uhas' statement was, "Here not there." They used it as exclusively as the Ohos used "Red makes wrong."

Botherby eventually made his way back to the valley of the Ohos. There he was overcome by an understandable (if professionally incorrect) eagerness to share his second discovery, to wit, that near them lived a people of the same stock, leading a similar life, and possessed of the same basic gift of speech. As he was expounding this information with gestures that his audience readily understood, Botherby reached the point where he plainly needed to transmit the gist of the Uhas' one statement. He hesitated. How do you render "Here not there" in a tongue that can only express "Red makes wrong"?

Botherby did not hesitate long. He saw, as you of course see, that he had no choice. There was only one solution. He grasped at once what all translators eventually learn: a language says what it can say, and that's that.

Yes, but we're different

The range of the Oho and Uha languages is tiny; the range of modern languages—for instance, French and English—is vast. There is virtually nothing that can be said in English that cannot be said in French, and vice versa. Information, like phone numbers and race results, can easily be swapped between the two languages. Then again, some statements that seem informative do not really pass.

A Frenchman says, "*Je suis français;*" an American says, "I'm American." "I'm French" and "*Je suis américain*" strike us as accurate translations. But are they? A Frenchman who asserts that he is French invokes willy-nilly a communal past of social, cultural, even conceptual evolution, one that transcends the mere legality of citizenship. But the fact of citizenship is what is paramount to most Americans, who probably feel, rightly or wrongly, that history is theirs to invent. The two national identities are radically different, and claims to them cannot be usefully translated in a way that will bridge this gap.

I suggest that this gap extends into the remotest corners of the two languages. *Elle s'est levée de bonne heure* means "She arose early," but in expectation of different breakfasts and waking from dreams in another guise. This does not mean that it's wrong to translate plain statements in a plain way, only that it is worth remembering that such translations tell us what writers say and not who they are. In this respect, French and English—or Germans and Portuguese—would seem to be as separate as Ohos and Uhas.

There are also times when plain statements of fact do translate each other rather well—even the statements *Je suis français* and I'm American. To make what I mean clear, let me add to them one or two supplementary words. The Frenchman says, "*Je suis français, Monsieur!*" The American says, "I'm American, and you better believe it!" You see at once that the meaning of both statements is the same: an assertion not of nationality but of committed membership in a community—"*my* community." So even essentials can sometimes break through the linguistic separation.

What makes this interesting is that the substantial identity of these statements does not lie in what they say—the information they contain is obviously *not* identical (French/American). So in this instance, at any rate, what has been successfully translated lies not in the nominal sense of the words but in other factors of language, whatever they may be. And whatever they may be, these factors are precisely the material of Oulipian experiment.

So can the Oulipo help translators in their delicate task?

Translation and the Oulipo (1)

The Oulipo certainly can't help in an obvious way. Unless he wanted to sabotage his employer, an editor would be mad to employ an Oulipian as a translator.

A few samples will show why. As our source text, let's take a famous line from Racine's *Phèdre*:

> *C'est Vénus tout entière à sa proie attachée.*

The literal sense—please be charitable—is, "Here is Venus steadfastly fastened to her prey."

First translation: *I saw Alice jump highest—I, on silly crutches.* Explanation: a rule of measure has been applied to the original. Each of its words is replaced by another word having the same number of letters.

Second translation: *"Don't tell anyone what we've learned until you're out in the street. Then shout it out, and when that one-horse carriage passes by, create a general pandemonium."* Explanation: the sound of the original has been imitated as closely as possible—*C'est Vénus tout entiére à sa proie attachée* / Save our news, toot, and share as uproar at a shay—and the results expanded into a narrative fragment. (Let me give you an example of a sound translation from English to French, Marcel Benabou's transformation of "A thing of beauty is a joy forever": *Ah, singe débotté, / Hisse un jouet fort et vert*—"O unshod monkey, raise a stout green toy!")

In these two examples the sense of the original has been quite forsaken. Even when they preserve the sense, however, Oulipian renderings hardly resemble normal ones.

Third translation: *At this place and time exists the goddess of love identified with the Greek Aphrodite, without reservation taking firm hold of her creature hunted and caught.* Explanation: each word has been replaced by its dictionary definition.

Last translation: *Look at Cupid's mom just throttling that god's chump.* Explanation: all words containing the letter *e* have been excluded.

The preserved sense hardly makes these two translations faithful ones. And yet all four examples can be considered translations. What has been translated, however, is not the text's nominal sense but other of its components; and we may call these components "forms," taking "form" simply to mean a material element of written language that can be isolated and manipulated. So the first pair of examples are direct translations of forms: in the passage from one language to another, forms rather than sense are what is preserved (number of letters, sound). The second pair are replacements of forms—not only the words but a form of the original has been replaced, in one instance a lexical context, in the other the choice of vowels.

These strange dislocations of the original may seem cavalier, but they are useful in drawing attention precisely to elements of language that normally pass us by, concerned as we naturally are with making sense of what we read. Nominal sense becomes implicitly no more than a part of overall meaning. Jacques Roubaud has recently provided a nice insight into its relativity in a discussion of the nature of poetry. He posits the axiom, "Poetry does not respect the principle of non-contradiction," and goes on to propose two poems for comparison (since Roubaud says they are poems, let's agree):

1st poem: This is a poem.
2nd poem: This is not a poem.

There is, he asserts, no poetic contradiction between the two poems. I would add that according to ordinary criteria, the second poem is not a translation of the first; whereas by Oulipian criteria, they are perfect translations of one another—just as *"Je suis français, Monsieur!"* and "I'm American, and you better believe it" can be considered equivalents even though saying different things.

This view of translation is a first clue to why the Oulipo has something to teach anyone interested in how writing and reading work.

The Truthful Liar

The American novelist Robert Coover writes fiction that can be mildly described as outlandish. It is full of banal situations rapidly transformed into comic nightmares. No one would call him a realist. Yet at a literary conference several years ago, when he was asked why he wrote, he answered, "To tell the truth."

His answer startled me; not that Robert Coover isn't an honest man, but this was not what his work first brought to mind. I quickly saw that he had been right to place himself in the age-old tradition of poetic truth-telling. In that case, we may then ask, why does he invent tales so unlike what we see around us? Why can't he simply say what is true?

He could simply say it; what he cannot do is simply write it. We can tell the truth when we speak; it may not happen often, but you know it when it happens. But when you write down what you say, whether it's "I love you" or "Pass the salt," the words in themselves are no longer either true or untrue. No one is there to be responsible for them.

Even in its ordinary, utilitarian uses, the written word cannot guarantee what it says. Can we agree that instruction manuals sometimes fail to help? Although once you've figured out your gadget, they become clear enough. Have the cooks among you tried out cookbook dishes that clearly had to be mastered *before* you could understand the recipe? The authors of manuals and cookbooks tell us honestly what they do, but because they aren't there to show us, it doesn't work.

Consider the press. (If you watch your news, notice that the person on television speaks a written text.) What do we want from a news report?

Hard information—what we call facts. And what are facts? What, for instance, is the central fact about a tennis match that you learn in a newspaper? The final score. Does that mean the score is the match? After three hours of play, Sampras and Agassi are tied two sets apiece and four-all in the last set: where is the final score? Nowhere to be seen. The score only comes into existence when the match passes out of existence.

Facts are the score, not the game. Facts are lies. Not because they are false, but because facts belong to the past—to what was, never to what is. We love them, because once reality is safely lodged in the past, it becomes reassuring, reasonable, and easy to manage. Or at least easier: we read, "Fifty Palestinians and twelve Israelis killed in renewed fighting," barely gulp, and turn the page. Naturally. That is the way written language *naturally* works. Our language is made up of devices called sentences and paragraphs that automatically produce reasonable conclusions, which is another word for facts.

There is no escaping this. It is not a Bad Thing. However, a reality we can call the truth must be looked for elsewhere.

Fragment of a neosocratic dialogue.

Scene: outside the wall of Athens

You have been silent for a long time, Socrates.

I have been observing these little statues, Echecrates. This shady spot must be dedicated to Proteus.

I thought that you might be falling asleep. The breeze is so soft, the brook makes so lulling a sound, and then the air is filled with such a sweet scent of wild thyme.

It is abundant enough and makes a pleasant couch; but I am not sleepy, Echecrates.

All the same, you seem little inclined to speak.

Perhaps.

So you prefer silence, Socrates?

Let me listen to you, Echecrates. Will you agree to consider a question, one that you, better than anyone, can surely answer?

What is your question?

Echecrates, tell me: what is the truth?

Socrates, I expect you wish for silence after all, and that you hope to keep me quiet with your proposal. I shall not let you off so easily but answer your question forthwith. The truth is the perception of Ideas, which are the sole causes of all things and the sole objects of knowledge.

Your answer, Echecrates, is apt; for certainly the knowledge of truth requires the perception of Ideas. And yet the truth is not that.

In that case, Socrates, let me modify my answer, for I see that the truth lies of course not in perceiving but in what is perceived: the truth, then, is the divine array of absolute forms by which the One is manifest in the Many, and the Many subsumed in the One.

What you say is by no means false, since no opinion of the truth can deny its unity or exclude its multiplicity. And yet, Echecrates, the truth is not that.

If only I could guess what you expect of me! Socrates, you have turned me into a confused child standing before a stern and patient father, hoping to please and dreading to disappoint him. Let me try once more to satisfy you. The truth is what is apparent only to the dead, whose immortal souls are freed from the hindrance of the bodily senses and are at last capable of knowing the pure and the good.

Let us hope, Echecrates, that we two are carried to that realm of virtuous souls, where we shall converse with Orpheus and Homer and know ourselves at last. But I feel that my question wearies you, and that the time has come to put it aside. Only in conclusion, let me repeat what I said before: the truth is not that.

But is there an answer to your question, Socrates?

Yes, and I have given it to you.

Socrates, I do not understand.

I have given you the answer three times. The truth is: not that. Is not this so, Echecrates? However you define it, whatever words you assign to it, you can and must always say afterwards, the truth is, Not that.

Keep moving

If Neosocrates is right, saying that the truth is "not that" implies: whatever you think you know, don't stop there. How can this apply to what has already been said?

Earlier I reached the conclusion, facts are lies. What if I round that out: facts are lies—and that's a fact. Look at what happens now. Facts are lies, and that's a fact: if the statement "facts are lies" is a fact, then the statement is a lie; and if it's a lie, then facts aren't lies. But in that case the fact that facts are lies *is* a lie, and so saying that facts are lies is not a lie, and so facts are in fact lies, and the statement "facts aren't lies" is a lie—and that's a fact. And so on and so on.

This modest circular paradox has its interest. First of all, when we read or hear it, something occurs beyond what's being said. Second, what was previously a conclusion becomes a continuum, a succession of events rather than a single event. What is the main difference between a conclusion and a continuum? What distinguishes the final score of a tennis match from the moment when Agassi and Sampras are tied four-all in the fifth set? Uncertainty and movement; in a word, change, a quality that is wholly wanting in the realm of facts. Change can have no place among facts, which constitute the realm of fatality, of what's over and done with. The realm where change exists is that of possibility.

"Not that" suggests that truth is a continuum of uncertain possibility. It only exists in the next now. In writing, that means the now of reading. Since the first reader is the writer herself, a truth-telling writer has to create the possibility of not yet knowing what the truth is, of not yet knowing what he or she is going to say. Non-writing artists seem to grasp this easily. Francis Bacon described his painting as "accident engendering accident." Ornette Coleman said he never knew what he was going to play next until he heard the note coming out of his saxophone. One writer, at least, made the point neatly: when the Red Queen tells Alice to hurry up and say what she thinks, Alice replies, "How can I say what I think till I see what I say?"

If we think of writers as translators, what they must translate is not something already known but what is unknown and unpredictable. The writer is an Oho who has just heard what the Uhas say. Poor Botherby couldn't begin to cope: he wanted to report a fact when what he needed was a cultural revolution. Fortunately, we have the necessary means, not always revolutionary. Language creates a continuum of its own, precisely in those components that concern not the plain sense of words but what we noticed in the circular paradox, the movement that their sequence engenders.

Translation and the Oulipo (2)

If truth is a changing continuum and not a series of discrete events and ideas, it's unlikely that we can catch up with it in any reasonable way. Reasonable and honest accounts will always resemble superior instruction manuals, useful, even fascinating, never the thing itself. Or perhaps we should say *a* thing itself. On the page, truth begins when something real happens.

Imaginative writers officially disclaim reasonableness and honesty. That's what imaginative (or creative) signifies: they're lying. Poets and novelists are outright liars. They promise to provide no useful information unless they feel like it. Three advantages accrue immediately. First, you are released from all responsibility to the dead world of facts. Second, your readers are ready to believe you, since by admitting you lie, you've told the truth at least once. Third and best, you can discover the unforeseen truth by making it up. You are condemned to possibility: you can say anything you like.

So much freedom can be unnerving. If you can say anything, where do you start? You have already started. No one sits down to write in the abstract, but to write something. Some writerly object of desire has appeared, and you are setting off in pursuit of it. The object may be an anecdote, an idea, a vision, an effect, a climate, an emotion, a clever plot, a formal pattern—it doesn't matter, it is what you're after.

What happens next? The process of translation as it is commonly practiced provides a helpful analogy. I am speaking from my own experience, but I do not think it exceptional.

Simplistically described, translation means converting a text in a source language into its replica in a target language. Both translators and readers know what happens when this process is incomplete: the translator becomes so transfixed by the source text that when he shifts to his native tongue he drags along not only what should be kept of the original but much more— foreign phrasing, word order, even words. The results hang uncomfortably somewhere between the two languages, and a brutal effort is needed to move them the rest of the way.

I learned how to avoid this pitfall. When I translate, I begin by studying the original text until I understand it thoroughly. Then, knowing that I can *say* anything I understand, no matter how awkwardly, I say what I have now understood and write down my words. I imagine myself talking to a friend across the table to make sure the words I use are ones I naturally speak. It makes no difference if what I write is shambling or coarse or much too long. What I need is not elegance but natural, late-twentieth-century American vernacular. Translating the opening sentence of Proust—*Longtemps je me suis couché de bonne heure*—I might write down: When I was a kid, it took me years to get my parents to let me even stay up till *nine*. (This is actually *mid*-twentieth-century vernacular; but that's where I'm from, and it's what I might say.)

There is still work to do. But I have gained an enormous advantage. Instead of being stuck in the source language, I am standing firmly on home ground. My material is as familiar as anything in language can be; and instead of having to move *away* from the foreign text, I can now move *towards* it as I improve my clumsy rendering, sure that at every step, with the source text as my goal, I shall be working in native English. All I have to do is edit my *own* writing until I eventually reach a finished version.

Think of the writer's object of desire—vision, situation, whatever—as his source text. Like the translator, he learns everything he can about it. He then abandons it while he chooses a home ground. Home ground for him will be a mode of writing. He probably knows already if he should write a poem, a novel, or a play. But if it is a novel, what kind of novel should it be—detective, picaresque, romantic, science fiction, or perhaps a war novel? And if a war novel, which war, seen from which side, on what scale (epic, intimate, both)? At some moment, never forgetting his object of desire, which may be the scene of a thundershower breaking on a six-year-old girl and boy, he will have assembled the congenial conventions and materials that can give him a multitude of things to do as he works towards realizing that initial glimpse of a summer day, a storm, and two children.

An example can make this clearer. Throughout his life, Robert Louis Stevenson was fascinated by the dual personality. His greatest exploration of the theme was *The Master of Ballantrae*, but he tried other ways of approaching it. In one instance he chose as his home ground the nineteenth-century penny dreadful with its array of melodramatic and grotesque trappings. Stevenson saw that to discover the mystery of his object of desire—the dual personality—in its starkest terms, these trappings provided what he needed.

They proved so suitable that we scarcely notice them when we read *Doctor Jekyll and Mr. Hyde*, a work successful enough to have attained the status of a modern legend.

It would be interesting to investigate works whose home grounds are not so readily discernable; it would also be laborious, and it is now time to think about the Oulipo.

Back home at the Oulipo

Since the mid-nineteeth century, writers have chosen their home grounds more and more outside the main traditions of fiction and poetry. Firbank used the brittle comedy of manners to register his tragic views; Kafka turned to the parable, Hofmannsthal and Calvino on occasion to fairy tales, Henry Miller to pornography. Other writers invented their own home grounds— Mallarmé in poetry, for instance, Joyce and Raymond Roussel in fiction— and it is for their successors and their readers that the Oulipo has a particular relevance.

A parenthetical point: the Oulipo is not a literary school. It is not even concerned with the production of literary works. It is first and last a laboratory where, through experiment and erudition, possibilities of writing under arbitrary and severe restrictions are investigated. The use of these possibilities is the business of individual writers, Oulipian or not.

All the same, several members of the Oulipo have exploited Oulipian procedures in their work. I suggest that these procedures have provided them with home grounds. How is this possible? How can methods based on deprivation become the comforting terrain on which a writer sets out in pursuit of an object of desire? Why would anybody not a masochist want to determine a sequence of episodes according to the tortuous path of a knight across the entire chessboard? Or use the graphic formulations of a structural semiologist to plot a novel? Or limit one's vocabulary in a story to the threadbare words contained in a small group of proverbs? Or, if a poet, why use only the letters of the name of the person a poem addresses? Or conversely exclude those letters successively in the sequence of verses? Or create a poetic corpus using the ape language of the Tarzan books? Nevertheless, these are some of the things Perec, Calvino, Jacques Jouet, and I chose to do, with acceptable results.

Why did we do them? I used to wonder myself. When I first learned that Perec had written a novel without using the letter *e*, I was horrified. It sounded less like coming home than committing oneself to a concentration camp.

When we were children, what we loved most was playing. After a fidgety family meal or excruciating hours in class, going out to play made life worth living. Sometimes we went out and played any old way; but the most fun I had was playing real games. I have no idea what games you enjoyed, but my own favorites were Capture the Flag and Prisoner's Base—hard games with tough rules. When I played them, I was aware of nothing else in the world, except that the sun was getting low on the horizon and my happiness would soon be over. In Manhattan last autumn, I stopped to watch a school soccer game in which an eight-year-old girl was playing fullback. She was alertness personified, never taking her eye off the ball, skipping from side to side in anticipation of the shot that might come her way. She had definitely not engaged in a trivial activity.

The Oulipo supplies writers with hard games to play. They are adult games insofar as children cannot play most of them; otherwise they bring us back to a familiar home ground of our childhood. Like Capture the Flag, the games have demanding rules that we must never forget (well, hardly ever), and these rules are moreover active ones: satisfying them keeps us too busy to worry about being reasonable. Of course our object of desire, like the flag to be captured, remains present to us. Thanks to the impossible rules, we find ourselves doing and saying things we would never have imagined otherwise, things that often turn out to be exactly what we need to reach our goal.

Two examples. Georges Perec's novel without the letter *e*, intermittently dramatic, mysterious, and funny, describes a world filled at every turn with multiple disappearances. Some undefined and crucial element in it is both missing from it and threatening it—something as central as the letter *e* to the French language, as primordial as one's mother tongue. The tone is anything but solemn, and yet by accepting his curious rule and exploring its semantic consequences, Perec succeeded in creating a vivid replica of his own plight—the orphaned state that had previously left him paralyzed as a writer.

I had a similar experience with my novel *Cigarettes*. My "object of desire" was telling the story of a passionate friendship between two middle-aged women. That was all I knew. I had concocted an elaborate formal scheme in which abstract situations were permutated according to a set pattern. This outline suggested nothing in particular, and for a time it remained utterly empty and bewildering. It then began filling up with situations and charac- ters that seem to come from nowhere; most of them belonged to the world I had grown up in. I had never been able to face writing about it before, even though I'd wanted to make it my subject from the moment I turned to fiction. It now reinvented itself in an unexpected and fitting guise that I could never have discovered otherwise.

For Perec and me, writing under constraint proved to be not a limitation but a liberation. Our unreasonable home grounds were what had at last enabled us to come home.

The Case of the Persevering Maltese

Earlier I quoted Francis Bacon describing his painting as "accident engen- dering accident." Imposing fixed patterns as it does, the Oulipian approach sounds as though it discouraged such self-generating activity, but this is not so: in practice it guarantees that the unforeseen will happen and keep hap- pening. It keeps us *out* of control. Control usually means submitting reason- ably to the truly tyrannical patterns that language imposes on us whether we like them or not. Language by its nature makes us focus on its conclu- sions, not its presence. Oulipian dislocations of this "natural" language counter its de facto authority or, at the least, provide alternatives to it. Don't forget that language cares as little about our individual needs as the tides and the winds; ill-equipped, we can affect it no better than King Canute.

Those of you who have visited Venice may know the paintings of Vittore Carpaccio in the Scuola di San Giorgio degli Schiavoni. The *schiavoni* were Slavs, and the cycle of paintings concerns a patron saint of Dalmatia, St. Jerome. Surprisingly, St. Jerome is absent from the most beautiful of these pictures, "The Vision of St. Augustine"; but there is a good reason for this. St. Augustine sits at his desk, where he has just finished reading a letter from St. Jerome asking his advice on a theological matter. St. Augustine has scarcely taken up his quill to reply when light floods his study and a miraculous voice reveals to him that St. Jerome is dead.

It might be entertaining to speculate on the relevance of the scene to what I've been discussing—pointing out, perhaps, the futility of the reasoned answer St. Augustine is preparing in the face of the unforeseen and overwhelming truth. But let's not. We have a still more entertaining object to contemplate.

In the middle of the floor, to the left of the saint's desk, a little Maltese dog sits bolt upright. He is bathed with celestial light, to which he pays no attention as he stares at his master in an attitude of absolute expectation, as alert in his immobility as was my little fullback in her agile skipping. He is as unconcerned by the momentous event now occurring as he is by literary theory. His attitude might be translated as the human question, What next? Like children and Oulipians, he probably wants to play, but he can't be sure of that or anything else. He has to wait to find out. What next? What next, and what after that? The answer will be something like the one given by Marcel Duchamp when asked what he considered the highest goal of a successful life. He replied, "*It.* Whatever has no name."

Brick, A Literary Journal, 1997

II

IN QUEST OF THE OULIPO

Literature and game playing, literature as game playing. . . . The words evoke a weedy figure: the playful writer.

The playful writer, probably male, never young (although often juvenile), sauntering nonchalantly down sunny boulevards. . . . *Faber ludens*—a little ludicrous, too; hardly dangerous; hardly serious.

Another image of game-playing: a six-year-old girl playing hopscotch, in dead earnest.

How much has the Oulipo mattered to me, and why? It is hard to answer simply, because its influence has been gradual, because I had strong non-Oulipian feelings about three of its members, because my devotion to the group involves much more than its ideas.

Was I an Oulipian before the fact? I long thought so. I used to claim that the Oulipo had only favored and not changed the course of my writing. (After all, I had written my first three novels without even hearing of it.) I was not yet aware of what the Oulipo was in fact changing: my understanding of the act of writing. This has been an insidious process.

My non-Oulipian feelings concerned Raymond Queneau, Italo Calvino, and Georges Perec. Towards Queneau and Calvino they were literary (I had met Queneau once or twice): the two were exemplary modernists at a time when the founders of modernism had become museum pieces. Queneau's writings in general showed what originality might now look like; *Exercises de style* provided an instruction manual. Calvino's inventiveness in the domain of fiction gave me hope of not seeing my own work automatically condemned to an idiosyncratic backwater. Perec was my best friend. When he brought me to the Oulipo, I followed not out of conviction or even curiosity, but because I trusted and loved him.

All the same, through the Oulipo Queneau became for me an intellectual arbiter, benign and beyond appeal, who authorized my adventures in writing. Through the Oulipo I came not only to know Calvino but to understand a new side of his work. And if I followed Perec somewhat heedlessly into the group, he knew what he was doing: putting me where I belonged.

Finally, my allegiance to the Oulipo expresses much more than an aesthetic choice. If I attend its monthly meetings as assiduously as circumstances allow, it is because my attachment is social: it is the best of clubs. Its witty and knowledgeable members are friends who sustain me in the life I lead. They incidentally validate work done and projects for the future, Oulipian or not. This is done affably, undemandingly, undogmatically. The support has no clear connection with the group's concepts, but I have never even heard of any other group that is, like the Oulipo, as generous as it is rigorous, and altogether free of sectarian rigidity. (Jacques Roubaud attributes this to the foresight of its founders when it was established.)

My quest for the Oulipo began in an obsessive early hope that literature would deliver me from an incompatibility with the world to which I felt doomed. In adolescence I became obsessed with poetry, both reading and writing it. To someone feeling hopelessly confined in well-to-do Protestant society, in those years aggressively sure of itself, poetry offered the prospect of another society, the chance to become someone else. (At fourteen I wrote in one week poems in the manner of Keats, Milton, Spenser, and Swinburne: vigorously condemned by teachers and peers, the experiment intoxicated me.)

Full of romantic confusion, I searched for remoter othernesses. I discovered practices beyond the curriculum of a classical education: more important even than modernist poetics was the revelation, in music, of the uses of structure.

The music that concerned me, contemporary or medieval, provided my first "Oulipian" procedures: the serial method of Schoenberg, Stravinsky's ordering of phrases by metrical manipulation, the isorhythmic melodic lines of fourteenth-century counterpoint.

Much later, I tried writing poems using musical techniques: a long poem in sonata form, a shorter one in *canon canzicrans* (a line palindrome). Too timid to follow this promising path, I had to wait for John Ashbery's liberating presence (we met when I was 26) to realize that I was free to do anything I liked and so continue such experiments (a bidirectional sestina, antonymic poems, collage poems, a poem following Poe's instructions for the composition of "The Raven").

Accepting the Oulipian view of writing is a commitment to materialism and relativity, against finality and transcendence. Engaging in Oulipian work subverts any fantasy of the absolute.

Also thanks to Ashbery, I read as a would-be novelist the work of Raymond Roussel, which led me out of the realist illusion in which I had floundered. It taught me what the encyclopedic transformations of *Ulysses* could not: the stuff of fiction can be wholly imaginary.

How can the fictional imagination escape from the cage of representation? Roussel's answer was to create narrative through methods comparable to rhyme and metaphor in poetry; also, and more approachably, comparable to pun-making, as in—to give *Ulysses* its due—The Rose of Castille = the rows of cast steel, where an opera title turns into a railroad. To make up a story, combine a number of such linguistic implosions, set one hour in a medium oven, and serve cold. The method is obviously preposterous and also genuinely mad, especially when it invests the respectable object called the novel. The madness is that of writing in *ottava rima* or Spenserian stanzas: it is the exhilarating madness of poetic invention laying claim to the realm of fiction. Roussel's methods inspired me to devise others no less mad for my own use. I then began my first completed novel *(The Conversions);* the book wrote itself.

My first three novels depend on a non-systematic Oulipism, if such a phenomenon exists—a combination of techniques of variation and substitution that often determine the nature of narrative materials as well as their use. In *The Sinking of the Odradek Stadium*, the accumulation of these procedures has become an omnipresent "table of obligations" (Perec's *cahier de charges*): the text is, to put it mildly, overdetermined. From *The Conversions* to *Odradek*, the use of "justifying myths" in the manner of Joyce and Eliot yields to that of "non-certifiable" materials organized in quasi-systematic ways—a tendency pointing eventually to a complete Oulipisation. Appropriately enough, I had by then discovered the Oulipo itself.

Two short works I had already written were Oulipian by any definition: a homophonic reading of the alphabet, and what was later called a transplant—a lexical exchange between two texts, where each is rewritten with the vocabulary of the other. My original transplant combined a poem of Keats with a cooking recipe. From it I learned: (1) Once a problem is set, I must solve it. (2) No matter how absurd, a problem once tackled quickly convinces me that a "true" solution exists. (3) Finding any solution can be excruciatingly difficult. (4) To pursue such activity, I might well be, if not insane, perverse to the point of perversion. Being welcomed into the Oulipo made me feel like someone who has been denying a shameful habit only to discover that it is perfectly honorable.

One immediate privilege the group offered was being able to pursue these experiments not only systematically but independently of my other writing. They were an object of research to be happily pursued for its own sake. This separation of experiment and practice was of course illusory; a sense of innocence, however, averts the anxious gaze of conscience. I exercised my new freedom on a small scale, exploring possibilities of lexicons and letters, only gradually realizing how it was leading to the resolution of problems thought insoluble—for example, how to write works in French. Eventually, and by then almost naturally, I decided to use an Oulipian method of my own invention to compose my next novel, and writing *Cigarettes* definitively proved to me the validity of the Oulipian idea. It brought me full circle to my beginnings as a novelist. I had then been psychologically trapped inside the society that I wanted to portray; I thought I could only do so in its own literary terms. That society now still supplied the context of my narrative but, approached with the indirectness of abstract procedure, it became an imaginary object, and so accesible. I was no longer its creature but its inventor.

Comme les masques sont les signes qu'il y a des visages, les mots sont les signes qu'il y a des choses. Et ces choses sont les signes de l'incompréhensible.

—Marcel Schwob

During a recent stay in Berlin, I became friends with the poet Oskar Pastior, not yet an Oulipian but long addicted to combinatorial stratagems. Each of us proposed methods unfamiliar to the other: I, sestinas; he, anagrams. We began exploring their possibilities.

The projects I then undertook were ferociously hard: a three-part composition based on anagrams of our two names distributed according to 3 x 24 permutations; a sestina consisting entirely of anagrams of its six end-words. I ate frugal, hasty meals; slept little; neglected my friends. During those long hours, I have no doubt that, to an unobtrusive observer, my face would have manifested the oblivious intentness of a six-year-old girl playing hopscotch.

Lacanian Ink, 1994

THE PURSUIT OF THE WHOLE

1

Uncertainty shrouds the beginning. Let us say that it occurred in 1944—a reasonable probability—when my father was overseas and my mother rented a summer cottage for the two of us in Wainscott, Long Island. I was 14 at the time. One evening my mother and I were invited for dinner at Mary Callery's house on the North Shore, or perhaps on Peconic Bay. The time and place do not matter all that much. Mary Callery was my mother's closest friend, beautiful, smart, temperamental, much involved with the international art community, herself a sculptor. There were other guests: the architects Philip Johnson and Ludwig Mies van der Rohe.

Mary Callery, Philip Johnson, and my mother drank dry martinis—no doubt more than two. I probably drank Coke; I don't know what Mies drank, but I do know that after a while the martini-drinkers entered a gay and gossipy realm where Mies and I had no part. Towards the end of the meal I went and sat next to him. I had been told he was a great architect. The prospect of talking to him was interesting because my father was also an architect, serious if not great. So I did not hesitate to question Mies about his work. We talked for about an hour. I suppose that having a fourteen-year-old as listener was better than no company at all; at any rate, he spoke to me seriously and without condescension. I have forgotten everything he said except for one thing: he insisted that all his notions of architectural

space had been drawn from a book called *On Growth and Form*, the work of
someone called D'Arcy Wentworth Thompson. (When I later mentioned
book and author to various literary mentors, none had ever heard of them.)

2

During my late adolescence I was a bookstealer. I loved books, not just to
read but to own, and there was no way I could buy all I wanted. Because I
stole for love, I stole self-righteously. It took time for me to realize that if
Scribner's could afford my pilfering, I was doing palpable damage to places
like the Holliday Bookshop. At the age of eighteen I stopped altogether.

In 1952 I moved to France with my wife and daughter. In Paris we became close friends with Tony and Eve Bonner. Two years later, the four of
us decided to try living in Majorca, reputedly pleasant and unquestionably
cheap. Tony was as much a bookworm as I. Faced with an indeterminate
stay on a then out-of-the way island, we took a brief trip to London to stock
up on useful books. We spent most of our daylight hours in Foyle's, viewing
and reviewing its innumerable shelves.

It was during our first morning in that bookstore that I at last saw a copy
of *On Growth and Form* (Cambridge University Press, revised edition, 2 vols.).
It was late afternoon of the following day when I mustered the courage to
steal it. I was by then in a pitiful state. I hadn't stolen a book in years; my
earlier recklessness had deserted me (I was now a husband and father).
Even in pluckier days I would have hesitated before smuggling two fat volumes out of a store milling with attentive salesmen. But the unforeseen
resurgence of a title pronounced once ten years earlier had set me trem-
bling with superstitious lust. (I could not begin to contemplate paying the
twenty pounds it cost—almost two hundred pounds in today's money).

I spent an inwardly frantic, outwardly reasonable hour executing my
theft, moving the two volumes separately and in stages from the middle of
the second floor towards the ground-floor exit, camouflaging the maneu-
ver by bringing books I planned to buy to the cashier nearest my point of

escape. At last *On Growth and Form* was settled, not too conspicuously, on a rack between my cashier and the nearby door. I paid for my other books— over a dozen, as I remember—and on my way out picked up my covert object of desire and walked out into Charing Cross Road. I did not look back. I did not run. I blessed the pedestrian throng.

3

That autumn *On Growth and Form* followed me to Majorca; back to Paris two years later; finally, two years after that, to Lans-en-Vercors (a mountain village near Grenoble). I wrote and published a novel. My marriage ended. I published more novels. My children went away. For a while I lived in Venice, without my books. I returned to Lans to begin life with a new family. I began teaching in America. My father died, my best friend died, my mother died. We moved to Paris. In 1996 we began spending summers in Lans once again; and it was there, on July 29, 1997, that I began reading my last stolen book. My progress was interrupted between September 23 and February 11, 1998. On July 18, once again in Lans, I finished *On Growth and Form*.

Near the end of his work, D'Arcy Thompson writes:

> The biologist, as well as the philosopher, learns to recognise that the whole is not merely the sum of its parts. It is this, and much more than this. For it is not a bundle of parts but an organisation of parts, of parts in their mutual arrangement, fitting one with another, in what Aristotle calls a "single and individual principle of unity"; and this is no merely metaphysical conception, but is in biology the fundamental truth which lies at the basis of Geoffroy's (or Goethe's) law of "compensation" or "balancement of growth."

Brick, A Literary Journal, 1999

LA CAMERA ARDENTE

At the end of last summer, on a trip through Italy, I arrived for a week's stay in Siena two days before Italo Calvino died there. Ten days earlier I learned of his first stroke from a newspaper and had since then, through relays of friends, kept myself informed of his condition. There had been an operation, after which Calvino had shown himself normally alert and mobile; a high fever requiring his return to intensive care; another coma, another stroke. On my first evening in Siena I phoned his wife, Chichita, who at once told me, "*Italo sta morendo.*" His coma had become irreversible, his brain was hopelessly damaged, only his heart continued to beat under the influence of a drug, called dopamine, that the attending doctors were required by law to administer. He would inevitably die in a day or two at most; after which, Chichita Calvino told me, he would be laid out for twenty-four hours in the hospital in a large room, transformed for the occasion into a *camera ardente* (a sort of secular *chapelle ardente*). There those who so wished could pay him their final respects. Signora Calvino told me that she very much wanted at least one friend of her husband's to be present in the room throughout this time.

Consequently, a little after midnight on September 19, I drove to the hospital with the intention of assuring a friendly presence during the emptiest hours of the night. I knew Santa Maria della Scala, as the hospital is called, all too well: years ago, I had twice brought my two-year-old son there in the grip of a convulsive coma. In the cool night, soothing after the mid-summerlike

heat of drought-stricken Tuscany, I parked my car opposite the hospital under the jubilant west front of the cathedral and prepared to consecrate the
next few hours to watching over my dead friend. In the hospital lobby,
however, I was politely informed that the *camera ardente* had been shut at
midnight and would not reopen before seven the following morning.

I turned away consumed with an irritation of which I was immediately
ashamed (what a petty and inappropriate sentiment!) but that could not be
denied. The knowledge that hospital rules had dictated the interruption of
the vigil did nothing to lessen my frustration: frustration less in accomplish-
ing a pious act toward the dead than in making myself useful to the living.
I had planned to perform a worthwhile duty, one perhaps spiced with a
little self-mortification. . . . Confronted with death, we console ourselves as
we can, and by *console* I mean *distract,* and by *we* I mean *I:* having been given
the means to at least partially evade my feelings by doing a good deed, I was
angry at having this advantage taken away. My escape now blocked, I would
have to begin turning to my "true" feelings, not knowing yet what they
might be and not wanting to know.

That they were taking an unexpected cast was confirmed on my return to
the *camera ardente* next morning. The hall—the *sala d'infermeria* or *pellegrinaio,*
covered with lofty frescoes by Domenico di Bartolo depicting scenes full of
elegantly striped and stockinged personages—occupied so vast a cubic space
that it made little difference whether one was alone in it or among fifty
fellow mourners. Calvino had been laid out near its windows in an asym-
metrically hexagonal coffin, under a pleated white satin coverlet that made
him look child-size. Emerging from the coverlet, his head showed the effects
of his operation: the right side shaven, a ridge running front to back over the
cranium where the bone had been cut; such details only underlined the
inevitably appalling disparity between a face known alive and the same face
dead. Many men and women stepped up to the coffin, afterwards departing
or joining those of us sitting or standing along the sides of the hall. A group
of eleven-year-old boys was ushered in by a schoolteacher. I thought, why
expose them to such a sight? But many, as they left, were weeping tears of
unmistakable grief, and I was told that these were the readers of *Marcovaldo:*

his genius, Calvino had no peer. Even better than Queneau, he knew how to pursue his radical investigation of fictional possibilities without alienating the reader (the reader present to varying degrees in all of us) who is attached to less novel modes of narration and speculation; not alienating the reader, rather engaging him in an ardent, arduous interrogation of the universe, of language, of the universe of language. Calvino could claim popularity and fame as a special kind of triumph. It was as though Raymond Roussel had been given a genius award for scientific research.

The triumph deserves particular admiration when one recalls a statement Calvino made in a lecture last year, to the effect that all his books were inspired by problems that seemed to him insoluble. The remark is doubly illuminating. First of all it suggests that Calvino always put questions ahead of conclusions—the written word provides material for "hide and seek" but never for "find"; that he therefore knew that reality must be established through processes that lie outside conventional assumptions about knowledge and experience. Calvino had no illusion that a rational intelligence, even one as penetrating as his own (which he never forsook or denigrated) could take the measure of the world. He had no illusion that language corresponded to anything much beyond itself, or, if it did, that what it corresponded to was anything but another language—signs of signs. . . . He had no illusion as to the significance of individual identity: the mollusc creates its distinctive shell desperately and blindly. He had no illusion about the importance of man in the universe—for him, we are mites on a mountain, and pretending otherwise has only turned humanism into a new piety. Calvino's statement, in other words, indicates how intimately his practice of writing identified him with a radical modernist position. The statement also points to an explanation of his public success and perhaps of his success *tout court:* facing a problem that has no conceivable solution, a writer must find an inconceivable one. He must invent one as he writes out of "nothing," and if he is not ashamed, or afraid, or for some other such reason stingy with himself, he will associate the reader in his struggle to pretend, to guess, to figure out what may and eventually does provide the solution whose absence has inspired him. I assert that Calvino does this unfailingly. This is not the place to describe how he does it, but a look at his fictional intermediaries, such as Qfwfq and Palomar, should yield initial proof of my assertion.

On several occasions Calvino wrote about death with his usual engaging originality, and with a lucidity that would strike us as grim if it were not imbued with a sense of acceptance that goes beyond any form of modesty or humility. Such passages offer little consolation for the loss of their author; they may offer some. For instance, at the end of the "Priscilla" section of *T con zero (T Zero)*, Qfwfq, considering his own death, reflects that discontinuity in individual life has proved necessary for his very existence. The alternative to our world of sexed mortals would have been one of self-reproducing, immortal sponges; from it our presence, no matter how brief, would have been permanently excluded. Now, Qfwfq thinks, the immortals are dead and at least for the time being we, the discontinuous, are the victors. And already a new continuum surrounds us—"the integument of words we constantly secrete." Bridging the gaps between our births and deaths, the continuum becomes "everything that is language in its widest sense"— groups of signs, ideograms, numbers, recording tapes, social relationships, family relationships, institutions, billboards, napalm bombs. The intricate mechanism goes on expanding until it becomes contiguous with the entire world:

> To a certain extent everything tends to close in on me, even this page on which my story keeps looking for a finale that will not signify its conclusion, for a network of words where a written I and a written Priscilla can multiply when they meet in other thoughts and words, setting in motion a chain reaction through which things made or used by mankind (things, that is, that are parts of its language) in turn acquire speech, so that machines will start speaking and exchanging the words of which they are made and the messages that animate them. The circuit of vital information that runs from nucleic acids to the written word will extend itself to the perforated tapes inside automats born of other automats. Generations of machines perhaps better than us will go on living and speaking about lives and about words that once were also ours; and, translated into electronic instructions, the word "I" and the word "Priscilla" will meet once again.

Review of Contemporary Fiction, 1986

QUEEN STORY

1

Poet, seer, muse, and occasional Fury, Laura (Riding) Jackson is back among us, mercifully and pitilessly, as a writer of fictions. A new edition of her *Progress of Stories*, first published in 1955, reprints the original text un-amended, together with twelve other early stories, one later one, and a new preface and commentary by the author. The book has long been un-available, and its reappearance is to be welcomed; indeed, in a wiser world, its publication date would be declared a national holiday. There seems no point in trying to conceal my own enthusiasm.

Mrs. Jackson's history deserves a few words, very few—"we must treat of it briefly, in order not to return to the matter again, if possible." She was born in New York in 1901. Married to Louis Gottschalk from 1920 to 1925, she began publishing in 1923, using the name Laura Riding Gottschalk until 1927, and Laura Riding from then until 1941. Between 1926 and 1939 Mrs. Jackson produced a considerable body of poetry, criticism, and fiction (as well as an enthralling assemblage, *Everybody's Letters*); she wrote almost nothing between 1939 and the mid-sixties, when a series of contributions to the magazine *Chelsea* concluded with *The Telling* (published as a book in 1972), a prophetic work in prose of heartbreaking and astringent power. Since then she has chosen and prefaced *Selected Poems in Five Sets* (1973), and two years ago the *Collected Poems* of 1938 was reprinted.

Mrs. Jackson lived abroad from 1926 to 1939, first in England, then in Majorca, where Robert Graves was her companion and frequent collaborator.

Two years after her return to America, she married Schuyler Jackson, with whom she lived and worked, until his death fourteen years ago, in what seems to have been a relationship of exceptional devotion and esteem. After her marriage, she signed her work Laura Jackson or Laura (Riding) Jackson.

Progress of Stories has two authors' names on its title page: Laura Riding for the original stories, Laura (Riding) Jackson for the new material. Her chronology explains this rare occurrence, as well as the name she finally chose. Her new surname denotes loyalty to her husband, the parenthetical Riding reminds older readers who she was. When discussing *Progress*, it seems appropriate to use Riding in preference to her married name.

When *Progress of Stories* first appeared in 1955, several years before Riding's renunciation of literary activity, she was a well-known and influential writer, and the book was widely reviewed and acclaimed. When one reads it now, it seems incredible that it should have been forgotten for so long. No doubt Riding's lengthy withdrawal from the literary world partly explains this neglect. So may her occasional Furiousness: it hardly surfaces in *Progress*, but elsewhere Riding has been harsh with writers and readers who she feels are wrong. I have always read her uncompromising corrections of others and claims for herself as proof, on the one hand, of her dedication to an extremely demanding conception of what writing ought to be and, on the other, of a most human vulnerability; but she must have discouraged many with her scoldings. I think, however, that it is her unusual conception of literature itself that best explains the near oblivion to which, until this republication, *Progress of Stories* has been condemned.

Riding's aim in writing this carefully structured series of stories was to make articulate in the experience of her readers a knowledge of life that is both true and nonconceptual. It was as if she wanted to make the mechanisms of language, usually so approximate and reductive, accurate enough in the effect of their working to initiate the reader willy-nilly into an awareness of what she felt to be the pure, unmediated truth. Such an ambition has sometimes been given expression in the poetry of our language (Blake is a conspicuous example); but to readers of English prose, what might be called initiatory literature is the rarest of genres. It is somewhat less rare in modern Europe, which has produced works comparable to *Progress*, whatever their dissimilarities: Hofmannsthal's *Letter of Lord Chandos*, René Daumal's *La grande beuverie*, Raymond Roussel's *Locus Solus*.

Other European writers are also close to Riding in their methods or ideas: Kafka in his grandiose reading of the whole world as metaphor, Nietzsche in his longing to purify language to make it fit for truth-telling (and also, I would think, in his admiration for the pre-Socratic philosophers and the "original unity of truth and fiction in their aphoristic language"). In American fiction, however, I can think of no one since Poe so seriously committed to evoking a visionary world embracing the familiar one we think of as real; and even Poe needed, as he said, to look through "half-closed eyes" to find his world, whereas Riding's eyes are always wide open.

Her interests are truly apart from those of our novelists and story writers. She is not concerned with the social destiny of the individual—for her, it is the self alone that creates society. She is not interested in what makes people different from one another, so the idea of character tends to disappear from her fiction and, along with character, plot: there is only storytelling. Where most fiction points to conclusions, hers provides empty spaces that we are left to fill. In general, we expect fiction to prove itself by the power of its illusions—its "realism"; for Riding, such illusions are no better than distractions.

It hardly seems surprising in such circumstances that, after a first success often explained by their "charm," these stories were quickly lost to us. Now, perhaps, thirty-seven years later, it is time to take a longer look at them and see what considerable riches their charming surface conceals.

Progress of Stories contains seventeen stories in all, as well as a meditative essay on storytelling. The first thirteen stories form the part of the book that is a progress: simple at the outset, they grow in complexity as the book advances. This sequence of stories is divided into three sets: Stories of Lives, Stories of Ideas, Nearly True Stories. The first section presents characters ordinary and not so ordinary in deadpan summaries; they might be the work of a celestial parole officer with a genius for thrifty precision. They are essays in pure observation, remarkably satisfying.

In one story, "Schoolgirls," we encounter Judith, a grown-uppish student in a Swiss private school, who halfway through the story has her nose broken by her math teacher. (She has been irritating him, and he throws a desk bell vaguely in her direction.) Judith, who has been depressed, is cheered up by the accident and insists that the teacher come with her to Paris "and be introduced as the man who broke my nose." This is fine for Paris; but when they decide to visit England, his own country, the teacher insists that they marry. "He could not think of any other way of arranging things. They were not in love with each other and had no intention of keeping house together, but he could not introduce her in England as the girl whose nose he had broken." This rings true; and it does so without cruelty or pity. It is simply the way things happen. Behavior is not analyzed, but left on the surface, just as it is seen; and yet, on their own terms, the portraits seem complete ones.

The second section, Stories of Ideas, has only two parts. The first is called "Reality as Port Huntlady." It is about a seaside resort where people go, not for fun, but because they think it will do them good. Port Huntlady is virtually ruled by a very fascinating woman known as Lady Port-Huntlady who, albeit fascinating, and kind, and ever so intelligent, never really emerges from her mysterious aloofness. In spite of their attractions, not only Lady Port-Huntlady but Port Huntlady itself ultimately disappoints its semi-residents, who wonder at length what they are doing there, until at last they go away. The place and the problem tremble with vibrations of magnanimous hilarity:

> The sudden decision of people to leave Port Huntlady always came as the climax of a gradually formulated question to themselves: what are they *doing* in Port Huntlady? Nowhere else could it be prettier than it was there—the flat, low sea, as near as if they were in a boat upon it, when it was calm, and farther away than the sky when it stormed, foaming up immeasurable black clouds. And the town itself, a bright, self-conscious table of security and intelligence standing over the sea, ready for anything that might happen. Lady Port-Huntlady had just such a look in her eyes—unprejudiced as to the present, curious about the future, wondering what might happen next, yet not doing anything herself to make things happen. And the abrupt, challenging mountains behind—watching, watching: how brave they looked, how brave they

made one feel. And the frantic, confused sunsets, so unlike the sedate Lady Port-Huntlady, who understood everything, and so unlike Cards, who let things go over his head for the fun of keeping calm no matter what might happen—the somehow dishonorable sunsets, lying postcards from lying heavens of prophecy. How beautiful! And the twilight before the honest moon came up—full of wicked temptations to do things of no importance whatever; when, indeed, they merely sat on verandas wholesomely alike, with green sun-flaps fluttering and cool cane rockers balancing a trifle in every direction—and laughed, and thought, "What could be prettier than Port Huntlady?" and tried hard not to ask themselves the question: what were they doing in Port Huntlady?

Before *we* leave the place, we witness (in addition to the innermost workings of local society) a marriage, a homicide, a suicide, a murder. . . . One of the characters actually dies twice. Or *perhaps* she does. Perhaps? By the end of "Port Huntlady" we have emerged from the observed familiarity of the first stories, where things may happen or not, into a world where things may happen *and* not. It is a world full of surprises, artifice, and—the mortality rate notwithstanding—delight.

The second Story of Ideas gives up plausibility altogether. "Miss Banquett, or the Populating of Cosmania" is about travel and discovery in territories that are on no map. Miss Banquett sets out on a trip, because she is beautiful and "beauty is a steady occupation." She "had made her beauty known to everyone possible in her own country"; she now feels she must "make herself still better known." After shipwreck, she finds herself a castaway on the island of Cosmania, where not only is there no one to acquaint with her beauty, there is "no anything." In order "not fast to disappear" for want of witnesses, Miss Banquett, in a week of hard work, creates a complete world for herself. She creates the heavens, nature, and love; she populates Cosmania with seven races—black, yellow, cloudy, blue, white, tawny-faced, and fire-colored—each of which corresponds to an aspect of her own self.

She has an exciting time doing this. When, for instance, she first visits her tawny-faced race, which consists entirely of women inhabiting a land of perpetual "hard snow," she is greeted with the complaint, "We worship you, great

Physician, in the way appointed, but we are still very, very, cold." Miss Banquett immediately decides to provide them with warm husbands. "In a few moments, Miss Banquett returned with a certain number of polar bears. . . ." But these animals have a will of their own, and eventually Miss Banquett herself is carried off by the best bear. The episode concludes sententiously:

> It is always well to include even the most frigid friends in one's sphere of intimacies, for otherwise they turn into dumb, unanswerable challengers and make one's most glowing experiences seem all rather affected. Thus do the polar regions have a peculiar psychological value for the rest of the world.

After completing her universe, which perfectly establishes her beauty, Miss Banquett feels that there is only one thing still missing from her life: being simply what she is. She realizes that, for her at least, being simply what she is means being alone. But there *we* are, staring at her. . . . So she leaves us and withdraws into solitude. As far as we are concerned, she vanishes. She continues to exist, we are told, but invisibly, alone within herself: she both "is and is not." We are left reading a story from which the only character has disappeared and in which nothing more can happen. A great deal does happen, however: as we look into this disconcerting void, Riding begins pressing us to think for ourselves—like Miss Banquett. After that the story, to which no ending is now possible, ends.

By now the world of realism is far behind us. We are deep into fantasy—more accurately, into fairy tale. (One of the Nearly True Stories is in fact "A Fairy Tale for Older People," and the meditative essay is called "A Crown for Hans Andersen.") Hard noses needn't turn up at the news: the last four stories leave no one out. No one can be left out of them because, with no less wit or liveliness than the earlier stories, these address the basics of universal consciousness.

That is a forbidding way of putting it—perhaps the subject itself is forbidding, but weren't fairy tales invented to turn such subjects into enchantment? There is certainly nothing forbidding about "The Story-Pig," the first of the tales. The pig of the title is a hollow silver one set over the mantel-piece in a fine country hotel. Guests gather in the evening to tell stories around it, as if they would drop them through the slit in its back. Hans (Andersen?), the doorman, has the only key to the pig. He also watches constantly over the guests—he is the only visible member of the hotel staff, except for Rose, the chambermaid, with whom he is in love. When the guests have gone to bed, he turns Rose into a queen, she makes him a king, and a magical world springs up around them.

The story is deliberately, lovingly sweet. In it we learn how "the other one" is created in our lives; the procedure, strangely enough, requires a willingness to die. At the end, queen and king once more become Rose and Hans—except they don't, things are not quite as they had been, it's a little dismaying: "Perhaps Rose would marry the chef after all."

The subject of "The Playground" is dreams. Two boys are sent by their mother to a secret, out-of-bounds playground. They meet Lady Thinking-hard, a heretofore imaginary woman their mother has mentioned, who supplies them with special dream-buying money. That night they dream about the primal playground, where nothing is, and which a game called Life and Death is invented to fill. Next morning, they discover that their father has dreamed about their secret world and are terrified that he will give it away. Their mother tries to notice as little as possible. Before this story, parents have only been glimpsed lowering in the wings of the other lives. Here they step into the light to form a visionary original family that emerges, appropriately, from the vision of creation in the boys' dreams.

"A Fairy Tale for Older People" is about the transformation of Frances Cat, a creature perhaps woman perhaps cat, into her very self—ex-cat, present woman. She is abetted by the Indescribable Witch, along with *her* cat, who may or may not be Frances. Like Miss Banquett, Frances knows how to disappear, although she emerges from disappearance; unlike Miss Banquett, she invents not a new world but the one she left behind, with the same old parents and chocolates, although these now look very different to her: she no longer depends on them, as she did before, for signs of appreciation and sympathy, which she now knows can only come from herself if they are to mean anything. She then gives up her new-old world to become utterly poor and alone, and in this state is at last restored to herself in a final series of transformations that are fascinating and also quite baffling. We would like to know more; but we learn that there is "nothing—nothing more."

The fourth fairy tale, "A Last Lesson in Geography," is *very* last—a complete topography of being. Riding here gathers up many of the questions raised in preceding stories—questions of selfhood and otherness, of dream and transformation, of life and death—and packs them into one stupendous metaphor. The metaphor is humanity conceived as the human body in its various parts. It is as if she had chosen to take literally the "body" present in anybody, everybody, or nobody. The protagonist of the story is Tooth. Led by him, we set off on the last of the many journeys in *Progress*. It takes us from the first nowhere to the final nowhere, through all the somewheres of actuality. The guiding spirit of the journey and its goal are an absolute, also indescribable "she." She is not a woman and not an idea; if she is a mystery, she is an inescapable one. She might be described as what-happens-next and what-lets-things-happen. Others follow Tooth:

> He saw that their number was the parts of the body. Each of them was a body, but also a part of *the* body. And the parts also had parts. He was a part, a Tooth. But Tooth, instead of having parts, had other teeth, each almost the same as himself. It might seem that this was also true of Nails; but a Nail was not so independent, so numerical a part of the body as a Tooth. Nails were the Teeth of Hands, but their identity was largely lost in Fingers, which in themselves were only theatrical creatures. He was a Tooth, and that is why he was the First One. It was his fate to be a Tooth; it could not similarly be said of any Nail that it was its fate to be a Nail. There was really greater likeness between Hair and himself, though his sympathy was with Nails. But Hair was almost too independent and numerical; antipathy rather than sympathy existed between Hair and himself. Hair was the Last One.

(Bone and Flesh also play crucial roles.) This band of somebodies travels across the world—the real world, where the earth is flat and only a stretch of time in any case, not true space. They wonder, "How long would [the journey] last? No, the question was rather: How long was it lasting?" Only the present journeying matters—forget beginnings and endings. Endings are for stories only. Even this story must end. And what comes after the end of stories? Why, more stories.

There *are* more stories—four lovely ones, given us for dessert after the hard-cheese course of "A Crown for Hans Andersen." (Its hardness consoles us for the ending of "Geography.") But instead of looking at them, I think we should glance back over the main ground of *Progress*. Even a first time round, it is useful in reading the work to know how varied a progress it truly is, how pertinently the book is ordered. What connects its parts is a number of topics, recurrent although evoked in very different, sometimes well-hidden, ways. These topics can be apparently prosaic, like travel, or more obviously significant, like the definition of selfhood and otherness. I mention these particular themes because, brought together, they suggest an image of *Progress* that may be helpful. The book, beginning with Fanny's solitary trip through life in "Socialist Pleasures" and ending with the universal trek of "Geography," can be read as the story of travel between different conceptions and experiences of self. It is as if we were accompanying Riding on a succession of journeys, each taking us farther (or nearer) than the last—with, at the halfway point, a long seaside rest at Port Huntlady.

It is there that we become aware of the first peculiarities of a topic that has been treated thus far in seemingly normal fashion. The narrator is considering the character of Lady Port-Huntlady herself. It is a frustratingly elusive one. We know that Lady Port-Huntlady is perfect and always right. She gives the impression of a grand and worldly schoolmistress—Port Huntlady does sometimes sound like a superior night school. Even the narrator, after telling what Lady Port-Huntlady does, hesitates to say what she is:

> As for *herself,* one might say, simply, that she had a virginal soul. Is this a crime? Perhaps. But against what? Against life, perhaps. But are there not other things besides life? Surely it can be no crime against death to have a virginal soul. But then, how many of us have patience with such distinctions?

Now what, I wondered, forgetting Lady Port-Huntlady, can this possibly mean? Is Riding playing with words? With me? A crime against death: what sort of death do these words imply?

Death is explicitly present in almost all the stories, from "The Friendly One" on. But what the word *death* means changes as we move through the book. In "The Friendly One," as in the other Stories of Lives, death is appropriately literal. (The Friendly One accidentally causes the girl he has rather insanely decided to marry to blow herself up.) Even on a first reading, one can't help noticing that death is commonplace in the first stories, that it occurs very matter-of-factly, and that what is remarkable about it is, all pathos aside, its usefulness. The girl's death demolishes the Friendly One's insane illusions (or one set of them). In "Schoolgirls," the death of Judith's husband—the one who broke her nose—consolidates the choices she has made. Emile's suicide, in "The Incurable Virtue," appropriately terminates a life of complete delusion. "Three Times Round" tells the elaborate story of Lotus who, after the most extraordinary adventures in her three trips around the world, stays home and at last finds a certain pleasure in herself: ". . . soon she would really begin to live. She felt, indeed, that she had begun to live already. She did not notice that she was dying."

While still taking its toll, literal death in "Reality as Port Huntlady" seems to have become both more important (more useful) and less serious. The "No Hurry" tea shop, located by the cemetery, is "a sort of afternoon suicide club where it was taken for granted that people would sooner or later kill themselves, although on this or this afternoon there was no particular hurry." Mabick, who has supplied the proprietor with this notion, "himself always promised himself every night on going to bed to open a vein the next morning after shaving; but after shaving he looked so smooth and fresh that it seemed a pity, while before shaving he could never think in an organized way." And then there is the extravagant Miss Man, who is not impressed by Port Huntlady—it is she who dies twice. (Perhaps.) Death is no longer literal.

Next to go is Miss Banquett: in the world she creates for herself on Cosmania, she suffers various interesting forms of extermination, all of which she exuberantly survives. But it is in "The Story-Pig" that we are first provided with direct insight into the nature of this other, original death. As Rose and Hans enter their magical night world, attendants follow them: these are ordinary objects that have been brought to life, as by enchantment. The attendants call this enchantment death ("Death had rapped them on the head. . . ."); and by death they mean a relinquishing of separateness and independence, a surrendering of themselves to the Queen—who then gives them life. A little later, Hans gives a fuller indication of what such death may be. He is walking with the Queen:

> The moon was singing—singing the death of passions and numbers: it was all one here. . . . Walking beside the Queen was like a large loss of strength by which all was achieved that strength could not achieve. . . . By the death of this strength in long self-combat—the death of the troublesome memory of self—he made himself Hans, and Hans made him a king.

In "A Fairy Tale," Frances Cat elaborates one of Hans's reflections. Now reduced to absolute poverty, she is wondering where she really belongs:

> The question was, which was the original world, her original world, the right world, the real world? She had certainly lived in *that* world ever since she could remember, but was she any the less alive now, and what was memory? Memory was fear. Yes, it was quite true: in that world she had been afraid of something—death. That is why she had lived. Was she dead now? In a way she was. What was death? It was being what one really was. What was life? It was running away from oneself. It was being not quite oneself—merely humouring certain whims.

When, in "A Last Lesson in Geography," Tooth and his fellows acquire a sixth sense, which is the sense of speech, they acquire death with it: the source of their words is the all-embracing Word of the ineffable She, the guiding spirit of their journey, and it is only by abandoning their identities—by "dying"—that they can participate in her speech. And in the final meditation, "A Crown for Hans Andersen," addressing us perhaps herself, Riding writes:

> For the true worry is not what you shall be in the end; you can be nothing different from what you have been, what you are. The true

worry is to learn to die, to make child's play of your immortal souls, to
enter gracefully into death in spite of being unalterably what you are.

Riding might remind us that, quoted in such a way, this is only "prattle"—
the attendants in "The Story-Pig" observe that "the moment a thing was
said, no matter how true, it becomes prattle." But, coming at the end of
Progress, Riding's words here reflect a meaning of the word "death" that she
has revealed little by little in the course of the book.

2

Death is only one of the many topics in *Progress of Stories*, and not the main
one. What then is the animating theme that makes sense of the whole?
One answer—not clever, not false—would be: What is the animating theme
that makes sense of the whole? For the characters in *Progress*, certainly,
asking such questions seems essential to *their* progress. Tooth and Co. prove
their strength by questioning. When Frances Cat, "impatient to learn," turns
to the book the Witch has given her, she is "surprised to find that instead of
having a lot to learn she had a lot of questions to answer . . . questions about
herself." In fact, from Lotus in "Three Times Round" to the pioneers of
"Geography," everyone asks questions—even, at the end of "A Fairy Tale,"
the reader. And the question the reader gets to ask is a very relevant one
(especially as Frances, the Witch, and the Witch's cat have just been bewil-
deringly confounded with one another): What happens in the end? The
author replies: "You can't get it into your heads that in the end nothing
happens—nothing more."

This answer is not, as it might seem, an evasion. Nothing is not merely
an absence of things, but a useful void: where knowledge is concerned, it is
a state of complete ignorance—a state in which we *have* to ask questions.
The answer "Nothing" doesn't mean that everything is pointless but that
we can now ask: What is nothing? What is a something? What is reality—
is it somethingness or nothingness (or something, or nothing, else)? What
is meaning? What do we mean?

"Reality" can mean a number of things; but most of us, most of the time, take reality to be what we think about it. We are content to accept our version of the thing for the thing itself. Sometimes we feel our thoughts could stand a little improvement, and we then rent a house in Port Huntlady and have tea with Lady Port-Huntlady, that virginal soul—the Goddess of Ideas. Put otherwise: next week I *will* read Wittgenstein. . . . Perhaps we should first read "Miss Banquett" and follow her example: for she finds out what thinking can be. After escaping from the enterprising polar bear, she comes to feel that her new life in Cosmania is like a book she has written to please herself.

> We might say that she had read her previous life out of a book. But that was a book written by everybody, not by herself. . . . She might read of [her beauty] there in her own familiar name; but she had to guess that her name meant herself, since it was only a name in that book, not herself. Here all was different. For, although she read out of a book, it was a book of her own making. She knew that her name meant herself. Or, we might say, in the one book her beauty was factual—that is, of others' making, and therefore false; while in the other it was fictional— that is, of her own making, and therefore true.

It may seem boorish to gloss a statement so precise, but it feels worthwhile to point to a particular precision: the word "guess" in the fourth line. If facts are what other people agree on—can we all agree on that fact?—the individual relying on them commits himself to guesswork, for what is more uncertain than what others will agree on? The individual is a victim of their view—even when it is right. Miss Banquett, after all, was beautiful and was thought beautiful. But being thought beautiful gave her no self-satisfaction. It meant that she was what others said she was. So one day she declared, "I am beautiful," and made up her own story in consequence. This of course didn't make her right; but it left her free to take responsibility for what she was. She makes it all look very easy, but it should be remembered that her story is only one of ideas (a story about thinking). Later, Frances Cat, who also "makes up her story as it goes along," will show us how scary, how death-inviting such a choice can be.

But to return from these enticing figures to the less visible question of reality in *Progress:* the book can be read as a demonstration of the consequences of thinking about reality in different ways. It reveals what happens when we choose to believe what we hear, when we concoct schematic versions of reality that are at least safely manageable, or, finally, when we go for broke by claiming the very truth of reality for ourselves.

Progress of Stories shows how these various options work, starting with that of accepting what we hear and ending with that of going for broke. This is perhaps the central progress of the book. In substance, it produces a shift that becomes explicit halfway through—it has already been described in connection with Miss Banquett as a shift from fact to fiction. But the shift is also inscribed in the actual narrative method of the successive stories, and it is there that it can perhaps most easily be grasped.

In Stories of Lives, the narrator describes people in the terms they use to define themselves: and these are terms supplied by others. Lotus, in "Three Times Round," for instance, agrees to be exactly what is expected of her, and this is how she is presented to us: in turn as an "Unseen Presence," a case history, a "symbolic statue," and finally, not realizing it, as her dying self. The world of the first stories is one of facts, of what everyone can agree on. It's as if Riding had thought, "If you respect facts, here is nothing else." The stories tell what is seen to happen, no more, no less. The procedure isn't cold-blooded or satirical; it isn't a stylistic device to elicit pathos through understatement: it is merely factual. Of course it soon becomes blindingly clear that facts are the most absolute of illusions. We emerge from these stories fascinated, but with part of our minds murmuring, "Naturally there's more to it than that." In fact, there is "everything" more.

We next come to Port Huntlady. That town of glamorous phantasms is where the bright people go—the ones who won't settle for the terms ordinarily supplied by others. They are the ones who know better, who want the best terms for themselves, the best views—the best ideas. They have tea with Lady Port-Huntlady, so perfect and all-knowing that she seems "their other self." And that *other* self is what she remains. Her visitors all eventually leave town because they realize that, while they may glean ideas from

her, they can never be what she is. Even if otherness in her seems exceptionally significant, they depend on it no less than the characters in Stories
of Lives. Lady Port-Huntlady suggests the lure of the mediating intellect, of
life turned into a justification of life—another illusion.

We might say in other words that together with Stories of Lives, "Reality
as Port Huntlady" describes what happens to those who conceive reality as
being what we think about it. It then becomes appropriate, in the second
Story of Ideas, for Miss Banquett to instruct us in better ways of thinking
about it. After that, we enter the fairy-tale world of the Nearly True Stories.
Here we find that the factual realism of the first Lives, undermined in "Port
Huntlady" and set on its head in "Miss Banquett," has disappeared for good.
Furthermore, Miss Banquett's orderly if novel thought process is also abandoned. Reason has gone, and consistency with it. We have already seen, in
discussing "The Story-Pig," that the world of the last stories is one where
death reigns, but that this death brings life even to inanimate things. There
is no point in making sense of such matters: they are not meant to be anything but merely so. This is not absurdity, which depends on reasonable
expectations, quite lacking here. This is a world of purest nonsense.

Why, in the Nearly True Stories, does nonsense prevail? Why, attempting to
approach the truth of reality, does Riding abandon reasonable methods? A
useful answer is suggested by Miss Banquett when she realizes that only in
the book of her own making does her name mean herself. In the book written by others (as books ordinarily are), what "Miss Banquett" means is only
guesswork—the idea people have of her. This is the problem of all written
language: if the names and ideas of things were the same as those things, the
truth could be simply and reasonably told. But this is impossible. (At the end
of one story, Riding gracefully evokes the problem in speaking of her "certainty . . . that mere nakedness never advanced the course of truth as never
the course of love.") Names and ideas are other things: butterfly nets and not
butterflies. The discrepancy is of course a very obvious one, but to a writer, it
is crucial. There are other ways of resolving it, but for Riding, if the truth is to
be told, it can only be through means that transcend mere naming and con-
ceptualizing—the illusions of fact and idea that the first stories expose.

Clearly it is not enough to be familiar with such abstractions as these if one is setting out with the butterfly net of language in pursuit of the truth. The task requires mastery, a mastery that in my opinion can only be achieved through tough-mindedness ruthlessly directed against the comforts with which writing forever tempts its practitioners (such as impressing the reader with desirable presences). This sparkling freshet of a book seems to me the work of such a master. Talent alone, no matter how fine, could never have produced it. Once upon a time Riding must have had talent; but she consigned it to her inner incinerator before undertaking *Progress*. Talent is the ability to manipulate the recognizable attractions of an art; but to reveal what cannot be said, one has to look outside one's art: one has to master not only one's art but its use.

How does one go about this? Riding seems to have assigned herself four tasks: first, of purifying language to the point where it could never feign to be more than it is; second, of practicing storytelling not as an act of self-expression but of collaboration with the reader; third, of treating the entire objective world as a metaphor of human experience; finally, of banishing definition by turning this metaphor involving everything into a metaphor of what cannot be believed or understood—a metaphor of what, conceptually speaking, amounts to nothing.

The first two methods are really one. Riding seems to have governed her use of language in *Progress* by consciously treating writing as a form of speech. She has referred to writing stories as "speaking to the page" and "speaking recorded for silent apprehending." Since she elsewhere remarks that "writing reading" isn't very different from "reading writing," the choice of this speaking part no doubt brought with it both a sense of responsibility for words that were felt as living acts and the awareness of an imagined reader participating in those acts as he made them his. In such a context, inaccuracy and self-indulgence would be tantamount to betraying one's humanity. The discipline is of course a subjective one, but the results "speak" for themselves. Riding's words are scrupulous, and they are also plain as the pebbles on any public beach, even when they carry novel meanings:

And she, too, moved from room to room, but according to her kindness, not according to her need. And she had thirty-two kindnesses, according to the number of kinds.

There is no preening in this scrupulous redefinition. Such language, on the contrary, gives us a sense of being taken not only into an author's confidence but into that of Riding herself.

What she is confiding—to move on to her use of metaphor—is her own answer to a question that, as we have seen, runs through the entire book: How should one think about reality? Riding, needless to say, wants more than the illusions of fact and idea: she wants reality as it truly is. She proposes that the truth can be known, and that this is possible because the secret of reality lies not someplace outside us but in the very process of knowing. The act of knowing is the truth, although "act," in suggesting a finite event, may be a misleading word: knowing is a process both momentary and open-ended, without any particular substance or form.

This may sound like prattle of the vaguest kind, but only a statement such as this can suggest the function of Riding's metaphorical treatment of her material. First of all, if one can accept the idea that apprehending the truth exists in the process of knowing and not in any particular object of knowledge (a significant "content"), then it can be grasped that any object, any thing, can be a pretext of knowing. In *Progress,* that is what things—anythings—are for: they supply the characters with substance through which their awareness can prove itself while becoming for the reader metaphors of that awareness.

In these circumstances it would be strange if inanimate objects *didn't* burst into eloquent life. And so, in "The Story-Pig," slippers and fans walk with Rose in the moonlight, talking accurate nonsense; in "Geography," Tooth and Nail lead humanity clear out of history. The really extraordinary thing is that they aren't telling us something or taking us someplace. There is nothing to know and no place to go. There is nothing permanent or important for us to hang on to. There is only the continuous experience of knowing, which never arrives at a final destination.

This is why the sum of Riding's metaphors is a metaphor of nothing, rather than a representation (an image, an allegory, an explanation) of something. Knowing something is not the same as knowing the truth: "The truth can only be proved by forgetting it," and going on to whatever is next. Does this make sense? No. The truth doesn't make sense; and even this partial summary of a near-impossible attempt to evoke it produces a kind of nonsense. That is what, deliberately, the stories set out to do.

A few brass tacks to nail this prattle down. I said earlier that "Reality as Port Huntlady" was about the illusion of the mediating intellect; and it is possible to calculate an allegorical reading of the story in which (for instance) the houses in Port Huntlady stand for points of view, boats for books, Cards for language, and so forth. This interpretation is not only tedious; it is rendered ludicrous by a major subversion of the central character, Lady Port-Huntlady herself. The story at the beginning is told by an anonymous narrator who keeps well out of the picture, using expressions such as "It has been explained . . ." and "It is necessary to tell . . ." never saying "I." But at the end of the second section, the narrator starts using "we" and then "I" and she proceeds as this first person singular to become, briefly, either Lady Port-Huntlady herself or "someone equally the same." At this point we ask ourselves: Huntlady? Riding? But the "I" soon vanishes, the impersonal expressions once again replace it, and the narrative continues as though nothing had happened to the narrator. But the damage has been done. There is no way of identifying with certainty who that "I" was, and as for Lady Port-Huntlady, she is now beyond recovery. Her fixity, her interpretability have been destroyed; her world dissolves along with her into ambiguity.

Similar dislocations occur in all of the later stories. At the end of each one, we cannot be sure of what has finally happened; and yet, while it is happening, there is no doubt about it. Each story is perfectly clear and perfectly inconclusive. The only thing we *know* of it is the process of its telling. Afterward, we are left with "nothing—nothing more." The substance of the stories is their telling, not some definable subjective matter that can be taken out of them. Just as in the knowing of truth, their content is their process.

A final example may clarify the point. When Miss Banquett feels a need for something more evidently solid than this—for real "content"—she decides to have a child with a member of the fire-people she has created. The child turns cannibalistic and eats up the entire race, including Miss Banquett. As she is being swallowed, she suddenly says, "'What a pig I am!' For she had swallowed herself. She felt herself solidly inside herself." We are, it seems, our own (and our only) content; where these stories are concerned, we can only know about them by involving ourselves in the fugitive act of reading.

The central progress of *Progress of Stories* is a kind of atheological initiation. Like candidates for some great mystery, we are step by step divested of successive illusions until illusion is (nearly) gone and we are left with nothing but ourselves. The stuff of this initiation—after all, we are only reading a book—is reading-writing and writing-reading. That is the particular dark wood through which we are led. (That is why "story" is as frequent a topic in these stories as death or secrecy.) As to where we are being led, Riding says in her new preface:

> [These stories] neither will nor can do you any good but (if you let them do what good they can) that of stirring you to feel hungrily the void that all stories leave, which can be filled only by the story of us all, the compacted story of everything.

And that is another story. How it may be told is, in fact, something that was addressed by Riding thirty years later in *The Telling*, where her purification of language leads her into a wholly new style of written speech; but the stories in *Progress* leave us to fill the void they create by ourselves. At the end of such a feast, we can hardly complain about that.

3

If this discussion of *Progress of Stories* has taken somewhat abstract questions into consideration, this has been for a simple purpose: to put the book in a context where it can be justly read. The attractiveness of *Progress* as enter-tainment, the pleasures one takes in its observation, its fancy, and its wit, can easily distract us from a less evident quality: *Progress* is not only a very complex but a very modern work. It could not have been written before Flaubert and Mallarmé, because what it tells us is communicated not as things said but as a way of saying things. The wisdom and mastery of its author work through the concatenation of effects produced in us as we read her words; we will not find them by trying to look through or past her words. Of course it is always reassuring when we extract from a book great bones of conclusion that we can then bury deep in our private gardens, but that is not the way of the best works of modern literature, and it is not Riding's way. Only by being aware of what we are reading as we read it can we discover her secret. So that, really, there is no secret: it is all there on the page, waiting to gather you in.

Is the time now right for *Progress of Stories* to be read at last and given the special glory it deserves? There are grounds for hoping so. A stance as radi-cal as Riding's will no longer seem as eccentric as it once did. The nonrealist writing of recent years has perhaps expanded readers' expectations and made original uses of fiction more accessible. The interest many Americans have shown since the '40s in exotic modes of access to experience should have made them ripe for *Progress:* certainly few writers have ever spoken to them so pertinently and poignantly as Riding does here.

But in fact that is the way she speaks to all of us. Although this is a book of uncommon knowledge, no one has to know anything to read it. There is only one condition for that: you must read every word of it; that is, you must read. If you read and do nothing but read you will encounter no obstacle, except that of yourself reading. It will be what you are reading that is allowing this to happen—allowing you to come into the presence of yourself doing something not very important, but not less important than anything else. As you read, you will become alone with yourself; with your-self and, possibly, with Miss Banquett, who is, yet is not; and with Miss Riding, who is—perhaps—elsewhere.

New York Review of Books, 1982

ROUSSEL AND VENICE:

OUTLINE OF A MELANCHOLIC GEOGRAPHY

by Harry Mathews and Georges Perec

Like a flaming comet that holds him fascinated
The astronomer trains his eye observing the canals
(Les Nouvelles Impressions d'Afrique. 2,75)

In his thesis on turn-of-the-century playwrights, Mortimer Fleisch[1] devotes a lengthy chapter to Raymond Roussel and discusses at considerable length five unpublished sheets of paper he was lucky enough to discover and identify in the Fitchwinder University Library. These manuscripts were left to Fitchwinder by Mrs. Rosamund Flexner together with three Quarli volumes published in Venice between 1527 and 1540. A note attached to the legacy records that the papers "had been inserted in a cloth pocket between the press-board and the end paper on the recto cover" of a fourth Quarli that is unfortunately lost. The title of this lost work is *Tragœdia Ducis Partibonis* (The Tragedy of Doge Partibon), printed in Venice in 1532 by Andrea Quarli. It was bought by Mr. Arnold Flexner in Paris in 1936, at a sale where it was advertised as a sixteenth-century Venetian verse tragedy about one of the first doges of the "Città nobilissima e singolare." The plot is reminiscent of that of Tarquin and Lucretia.[2]

Fleisch's examination of these sheets led him to suggest that they were the first draft, or rather the outline, of a verse play whose subject, roughly sketched on the first sheet of paper and presented here in an even more condensed form, is as follows:[3]

The scene is Venice at the end of the nineteenth century.[4] Accused of having assaulted his fiancée, a young nobleman is saved at the last minute by two children, the girl's brother and sister, who have been playing leap-frog on the floor above. Their antics make the floor shake in such a way as to set free the words the girl had cried out when she was attacked—words encapsulated in the water of the pipes and lodged as bubbles in the showerhead. The "liquid revelation" ("Gob! . . . Stop") incriminates Gobbo, the family boatman, who confesses his guilt.[5] The girl revives and the marriage is celebrated soon after.

The first sheet of paper, then, outlines this story, one that gives no evidence of being written for the theater. Sheet 2 shows that we are dealing with a play entitled *In the Palace*. The four and a half alexandrines on sheet 5 suggest a play in verse. From sheets 2 and 5 one can also deduce that one of the characters, probably the unjustly accused fiancé, is called Silvio. Sheet 3 is less easy to decipher; it at least refers clearly to the insertion of the papers in the Quarli ("inserted into the slit" and "a heavy paper in [as before at the binding]"). Fleisch makes the relevant point that, like the story of Tarquin and Lucretia, both the play and the Doge's tragedy are concerned with rape. Sheet 4, on the other hand, seems indecipherable. Fleisch supposes that it was written far earlier than the others (in 1896, while the others date from much later, sheet 3 in particular from after 1928), but he draws no conclusions from this, except that Roussel must have returned to the project more than once.

Fleisch makes an obvious mistake at the end of his analysis, when he suggests that the subject derives from the transformation of *"la vérité sort de la bouche des enfants"* [truth comes out of the mouths of children]* into *"la vérité sort de la douche des enfants"* [truth comes out of the children's shower]. The transposition *b/d* is indeed common in Roussel (*le crachat de la bonne à favoris pointus / le crachat de la donne à favoris pointus* [the spit of the maid with fussy suitors / the regalia on the dealt card with pointed sideburns]; Dardanelles / *Bard à Nesle* [Dardanelles / bard at Nesle];[6] *la place du bandit sur les tours du fort /*

---

* The nature of Roussel's verbal transformations frequently requires that versions in both languages be given. On such occasions, square brackets are reserved for the English version, round brackets for the French. (Editor's note)

la place du dandy sur les tours du fort [the bandit's place on the towers of the fort / the dandy's bet on the strong man's feats]), but none of the other words here—"truth," "comes out," or "children"—conform to Rousselian practice.

The following hypothesis, which follows an equally typical Rousselian procedure, seems more convincing:

Le viol [the rape]	= l'outrage [the outrage]
une révélation (liquide) [a (liquid) revelation]	= est dit [is spoken]
au moyen d'une douche [by means of a shower]	= de douche [by a shower]
d'une façon intermittente et/ou [intermittently and/or]	
grâce aux sauts des enfants [thanks to the children jumping up and down]	= par petits bonds [in little jumps]
"La Tragédie du Doge Partibon"	= L'outrage est dit de douche par petit bonds.[7]

This was not the first time Roussel had used a title as a starting point (*Les ensorcelés du Lac Ontario [Bewitched at Lake Ontario]*, the title of a novel by Gustave Reid that had been a best seller in 1907, becomes "*Amphores scellées dures a contrario*" *[hard sealed amphorae a contrario] (Com.*, 21) and gives rise to the story of the forger Le Marech'). In this case, however, we decided that we should consider the particularities of the book involved and, especially, the reasons why the five sheets of manuscript were inserted in the binding. While it may be hard to justify our assumption, we readily concluded that manuscript and volume were intended to form a whole. On this basis, we have taken up the question at the point where Fleisch, who, it must be admitted, had no call to spend more time on it, left off.

The Quarli sold in Paris in 1936 came from the library of a book collector in Lyon; it has not been possible to ascertain its prior provenance (it was presumably sold at public auction, like Roussel's other books and manuscripts, after his death). The most that can be established is that it had formed part of a collection of incunabula and illuminated books assembled in Italy in the early nineteenth century and dispersed in Turin in 1878.[8] However, while searching for traces of the sale, one of us discovered that the *Tragœdia Ducis Partibonum* had been sold a second time, on September 17, 1895, in Venice.[9]

Now Mme. Roussel had at this very sale bought the *Saint John the Baptist* by Groziano that was put up for auction when Raymond Roussel's collection[10] was dispersed but withdrawn by him at the last minute.[11] It will become apparent why we consider this significant.

Raymond Roussel accompanied his mother to Venice in 1895. He may possibly have been at the sale and bought the Quarli then. It seems more plausible, considering the high prices such items fetch, that his mother bought it for him, perhaps as a reward for his prize at the Conservatoire.[12]

This stay in Venice, to which, as far as we know, Roussel never referred, lasted about three weeks. The trip was made because Mme. Roussel wanted to visit one of her childhood friends, Paolina Grifalconi, whom she had met at Friedrichsbad and who had been recently widowed.[13,14]

The Grifalconis lived in Venice on the two upper floors of the former Palazzo Drasi, on Campo Bragadin, not far from the Mercato delle Fave. The *piano nobile* was let out: Todoro Grifalconi's death had left the family in some financial difficulty. This was one of the reasons that led Mme. Roussel to make the trip.[15]

Paolina Grifalconi had two sons: Ascanio, who was then sixteen, and Silvio, who was four. Ascanio was of delicate health and died the following year, on 25 September 1896. Silvio was killed in an accident in 1922 during the riots in Trieste. Mme. Grifalconi died in Rome in 1950, at the age of ninety-three.

We have drawn the following conclusions from these events:

1) It is more than likely that Roussel acquired the Quarli in Venice while there with his mother in 1895.

2) It is highly probable that it was he who made the incision in the binding.

3) It is not inconceivable that he slipped into the binding papers
what in some way concerned his memories of Venice and Ascanio.

We may then explain, even if we cannot fully decipher, the jottings on
the fourth manuscript page, written in Milan possibly on the very day that
Raymond Roussel learned of his young friend's death. "Sep 95" in any case
unquestionably refers to the date of his trip to Venice. The Hôtel de la Plage
is, as its name suggests, on the shore of the Adriatic; it is incidentally well
known for its excellent chocolate. The other words remain impenetrable.[16]

We are also convinced that our deductions explain the withdrawal of the
Groziano from the 1895 auction. The painting, a material relic of his time in
Venice, could not be allowed to pass into the hands of a stranger. Roussel's
behavior in the matter suggests a sort of superstitious piety: he returned the
picture to the church of Santa Margherita to which it had originally belonged.[17]

Roussel traveled the length and breadth of Italy several times but never
returned to Venice. In fact he appears to have avoided it by choice. The very
name of Venice, all that Venice automatically evokes, was banished from
his works: at the very heart of the Quarli project, the word *gondolier* is replaced by *boatman*.[18]

We think we can explain this reticence and Roussel's behavior in connection with Venice by what is known in psychoanalysis as "incorporation":

> Incorporation may thus be defined as a delusion which does all it can to
> change the world rather than allow the slightest alteration in the sub-
> ject. It achieves this goal by means of a literal and unshakable vision of
> the world. While the process of introjection discovers metaphor and
> symbol (learning one's mother tongue being the most striking initial
> instance of this), incorporation stresses the unique, "objective" meaning
> of words and things, and whenever it encounters metaphorical objects,
> systematically de-metaphorises them. So when a thing is "hard to swal-
> low," it becomes what must be physiologically swallowed: meals and
> food become obsessions. . . . [The aim of incorporation] is to avoid cer-
> tain unbearable words ever being spoken. Such words evoke the loss of
> objects of love whose existence was indispensable to the well-being—or
> quite simply the self-image—of the subject. The object whose loss is
> thus denied continues to exist, as a body of actions, feelings and inex-
> pressible words in a secret topological system deeply buried in the psyche.

Incorporation is therefore a refusal to grieve. . . . Except in the case of delirium or certain kinds of manic-depressive fits, the delusion of incorporation is difficult to diagnose. It is carefully concealed within roles such as "normality," "character," or "perversion." . . . At the melancholic stage, the inner crypt begins to crack and grief is finally accepted. It is unfortunately not felt as the subject's grief for the lost object of love, but as the object's grief for the subject. This is the first psychic modulation, but it is also the last, as it leads to a submission to death.[19]

We apologize for such a long quotation, but a devotee of Roussel can hardly fail to be struck by how well it applies to him, both in his life (periodic obsessions with food and meals, masks of "normality" and "perversion," the Sicilian melancholy of his last journey), and in his work (literalism, antimetaphorism). Incorporation can be inferred from the general impression made by Roussel's work, the famous effect of immobility and immutability, the sense that everything that can happen has already happened, has already been set in place and imbued with an indifference analogous to the numbness felt at the death of a person one loves, before their death is acknowledged or, as Pferdli might have said, before "one has expressed one's grief over it."

A more acute view of both his life and work (although only the second concerns us here) can, we think, be derived from what we have just said: Everything Roussel produced suggests an underlying unity that depends neither on "psychology" (which is incapable of describing the work or its development) nor, in spite of its enigmatic characteristics, on a coded hermetic message. Both in his life and his work, what "changes the world rather than allowing the slightest alteration of the subject" is, to give a banal and literal answer, travel. As a real-life traveler, Roussel's behavior was often baffling and inscrutable; in his written travels, he strode across vast, improbable continents.[20] He went all over the world without seeing it, without looking at it, without being for one moment "impressed" by it. His "visible" journeys are not the ones to study.

Roussel's work is, we think, a unique commemoration of his other, invisible journeys, the ones that took place in the "secret topological system" in which he had buried the loss of his one and only love object: Ascanio. The site of this topography is Venice.

Venice is not the only town to which Roussel never returned, but it is the only one he seems to have forbidden himself to mention.[21] The absence from his entire work of the city where "imagination and history are inexorably linked," as Pasolo aptly put it, is so surprising that several researchers have devoted their attention to it.

The urban architecture of Venice is pure theater; it is a trompe l'oeil in the context of illusion itself, which can therefore be taken literally: here, deprived of reference to anything outside itself, the reality of illusion—which is also Roussel's reality—comes into its own.

Venice is complete and isolated: a whole world, a planet; not only Venus, because of its name, but also Mars, since Venice is red and full of canals.[22] Mars and Venus are the divine, absolute lovers. Venus was the mother of Aeneas (Enée): was Roussel Ascanio's *frère Enée* [*frère ainé* = elder brother]?

Roussel discovered Venice a few months before he was illuminated by a "revelation" of his extraordinary powers. He discovered there, for the only time in his life, a place that embodied his own sense of reality: an illusory theater carved in stone. He went there with his adoring and adored mother. There he met Ascanio, two years younger than him. For the first and only time in his life, we think, a relationship both passionate and tender revealed to him his own desire.

In this sense, Roussel's journey to Venice was his only journey (Venice becomes *voyage, voyage* becomes Venice, and *V* comes to stand for both words). And like every true journey it was not a departure but a return. He came home; he found his place. It was not an exile but a rediscovery of his origins.

He then left. In the course of the following year, Ascanio died. Venice became the unmentionable place. Thereafter Roussel's life was divided between a social life of "normality" (think of his extreme concern for conventions) and "perversion," which both stem from one mechanical behavior pattern, and thirty-seven years of a lonely death agony devoted to constructing his "extraordinary travels." Meanwhile, in the depths of his being, he continued to walk with Ascanio through the streets of a Venice that had been banished from the trivial, contemporary world to become a refuge, a secret kingdom where the pure and immortal reality of illusion was kept alive.

It is not only the verbal coincidence with Pferdli's definition of incorporation that allows us to speak here of a "secret topology"; Venice is a city made for walking, where one is never quite sure which way is north or south, where one never knows quite how far it is from one point to another, where the link between two points is a question of continuity and/or discontinuity of surface, just like the space of topology, which disregards direction and measurement. Anyone who has spent even a few hours in Venice will have learned how unforeseeable and hard it is to measure one's movements: a street that we think will take us where we want to go brings us back to the campo we set out from, a promising thoroughfare ends abruptly at the water's edge. Meandering itineraries, together with the alternation of stone and water, shade and light, turn Venice into the dream space from which Roussel was able to draw the *mappamondo* of his work, the sites and axes of his books, the places and journeys that are direct projections of the walks and boat trips he made with Ascanio.

There are then two superimposed topographies in Roussel. One corresponds to the world of his books and generally respects geographical reality (there are imaginary towns and countries, but the continents are all in place); the other is the secret world of his Venetian life. The center of the first is Paris, the center of the second the Hollenberg Hotel, where Roussel and his mother stayed. This hotel, which closed in 1915, was unique among the city's grand hotels in that it comprised the Palazzo Hollenberg (now Pasinetti) and a smaller building on the other side of the canal, level with the last big bend before it emerges into the lagoon. The "Paris" equivalent of the canal is the Seine, and the lagoon then represents the Atlantic. Beyond the lagoon lie the beaches of Venice, along the islands that separate it from the Adriatic. Beyond the "Atlantic" one comes to the Americas: which are, in Roussel, "colonized" (Guyana), just as the beaches are summer colonies for the Venetians. To the south, in both cases, one crosses stretches of water, the Mediterranean and the Great Canal, to "unknown" lands: Africa and the group of islands that, in 1895, were still sparsely inhabited.

It is immediately obvious that these topographies are mirror images of each other: America is west of Paris; while the beaches are east of Venice. This "real" geographical fact is not an explanation. We find it much more relevant to point out that to someone for whom illusion is the very stuff of reality, something seen in a mirror is infinitely more real than the supposedly real objects that give rise to the reflection. The reversal of spatial organization in Roussel's two worlds is therefore the key to the topological equivalence, whose emblem is Roussel's own monogram:

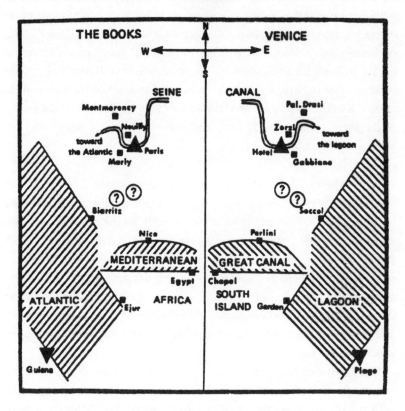

From the general outline mapped in the preceding diagram, one can imagine a point-to-point correspondence between the topography of the books and the course of the Venetian love affair, which can thus be glimpsed amid the convolutions of the major works.[23]

LA DOUBLURE [The Lining (or the Understudy)]: Paris—Nice "and the whole Côte d'Azur"—Neuilly.

Paris, as we have seen, is the Hollenberg Hotel. The Côte d'Azur may be the bank of the Great Canal (the "European" side)—a particularly promising analogy in that this is one of the Venetians' favorite walks in the winter months. Nice would then be the celebrated Café Perlini, which was famous in the winter for its *gatto caldo* (a sort of boiling hot punch) and in summer for its sherbets. It is hard to imagine a tourist spending three weeks in Venice without going to the Perlini at least once, and it was probably one of the first fashionable spots to which Ascanio would have wanted to take Roussel. As for Neuilly, a place that is "near the center," north of the river (the canal), its Venetian equivalent would lie between the Hollenberg and the Palazzo Drasi (where the Grifalconis lived): for instance Da Zorzi, on the Campo San Domenico, a tearoom that was very fashionable at the time, a place where Ascanio and Roussel might have met their mothers after one of their walks.

LA VUE [The View]: Biarritz (?)—A grand hotel—A spa

Whether or not the seaside resort described in the first poem is Biarritz (as is generally supposed), it is unquestionably on the Atlantic coast, and therefore, in the Venetian version, on the lagoon; it could be, for instance, the extension of the great square that comes down to the waterfront. This is where in the '90s an enterprising restaurateur named Gustavo Soccol started an open-air restaurant, a sort of smart precursor of modern snack bars. Young Venetians were very partial to his light, hot meals, and it is by no means implausible to suggest that Ascanio and Roussel lunched there together.

Since the other two poems in *La Vue* are much less specifically sited geographically, it is more difficult to deduce their Venetian correspondences with any precision. Possibly the descending progression of areas of water in the three parts of the book—ocean, lake, and pond—is significant; in which case the other scenes must be further "inland." Given that one correspondence between a grand hotel and a spa might be that of the expensive purveyors Roussel loved to frequent, we can suggest two such places, both in the neighborhood of high-class shops close to the square on its inland side: the famous tailor Bordino and the hair salon where the world-famous Roncali plied his trade.

IMPRESSIONS D'AFRIQUE [Impressions of Africa]: Near the West Coast of Africa, not far from Porto Novo

The passengers on the *Lyncée* cross the Mediterranean and part of the Atlantic before they are stranded on the black continent: Ascanio and Roussel cross the Great Canal, round the tip of the South Island through a narrow passage, and land on its eastern end. This part of Venice was very different then from what it is now: there were gardens, orchards and fields, a rustic landscape full of trees and exotic flowers, an almost wild smell. Anne d'Azay, who visited the island in 1897, wrote: "I half expected monkeys to appear among the trees; I was almost scared to walk into the warm shade of the thickets."

One need not go so far as to suggest that Ascanio and Roussel actually lay down side by side under this warm shade, but one can easily believe that in this luxuriant, unfamiliar world so close to the civilized delirium of the Venetian palazzi, Roussel discovered the erotic power of his passion. He may have regarded it as a dark force that knocked him off course, just as the passengers of the *Lyncée* while off course discovered Africa against their will (it is worth noting in this context that the words *vessel* and *canal* can, in anatomy for instance, be synonymous). In any case, he made this place his "Inner Africa," the dark, nocturnal continent of his desire.[24]

LOCUS SOLUS: Montmorency

Montmorency is a few miles northwest of Paris; the Palazzo Drasi is a few hundred yards northeast of the Hollenberg Hotel. Could any place be more deserving of the name "Locus Solus" than Ascanio's house? In this sense "Solus" obviously means "unique," a meaning that the book and its brilliant protagonist constantly bring to mind but that Roussel took care to disclaim in the opening lines of the first chapter.

It is also in *Locus Solus* that the process of turning the world to stone is most clearly apparent: the entire novel is a walk past "monuments in action," frozen commemorations looked upon by anonymous faceless people who might just as easily be ghosts.

L'ETOILE AU FRONT [The Starred Brow]: Marly—Paris

Marly is a wealthy residential suburb to the south of Paris. In the "Venetian mirror" it could be (for instance) Il Gabbiano Ingabbiato, a restaurant famous for its seafood (it still exists, without a trace of its former glory). The establishment's "class" would suggest a dinner outing with the Grifalconis and the Roussels *en famille*, after which Roussel would have taken his mother back to the Hollenberg around the corner.

LA POUSSIÈRE DE SOLEILS [Dust of Suns]: Guiana

On the other side of the Atlantic, that is of the lagoon, lies the bathing beach, the Venetians' Eden during their warm Septembers, where one can easily imagine that Ascanio and Roussel went swimming together.

In our discussion of *Impressions*, we pointed out that the passengers of the *Lyncée* never reached the Americas. Here we are at last in the "New World." Though we have rigorously refrained from discussing circumstantial, unquantifiable, and in Roussel's case obviously ambiguous correspondences between his writing and his experience in Venice, we cannot refrain from observing that *Poussière* describes a treasure hunt that ends with the treasure being found: was Roussel's passion, perhaps, physically consummated on the beach? Or perhaps not "on the beach" (bathing arrangements in 1895 did not on the whole facilitate such matters), but "at the Hôtel de la Plage," which Roussel refers to on sheet 4, or back in Venice, at the Palazzo Drasi, since the play whose fragments we have rediscovered appears to have been entitled *In the Palace* (cf. sheet 2). This play, the projected ultimate culmination of Roussel's work, would then be a commemoration of such an event. It is more realistic to suggest that just as the play got no further than a barely sketched outline, their physical love remained at the stage of passionate promises, and the "treasure" they found was in fact the discovery that their love was shared.[25]

NOUVELLES IMPRESSIONS D'AFRIQUE [New Impressions of Africa]:
Egypt: Damietta—The Pyramids—Damietta area—Outside Cairo

We return to Africa. Not "black" Africa but a place of mummies and tombs. Its mirror image, at the western end of "Venetian Africa," could be the wonderful baroque chapel of Santa Cecilia, where lovers traditionally exchange vows. We cannot help thinking that in choosing Egypt to commemorate this last outing with Ascanio, Roussel had become painfully aware of the wretched irony of the love he had inarticulately borne all his life: the sanctuary so laboriously constructed contained only the dead body of Ascanio. Such a discovery must have set the final seal on his unhappiness.

We can now return to the five manuscript pages whose material history we claim to have reconstructed and whose meaning we now wish to consider in the light of the preceding paragraphs.

The "incorporated" memory of Ascanio, its inscription secreted within the precious book, in an incision that was like a wound that will never close, fueled an impossible work, the total book Roussel dreamed of throughout his career: a book that would bring him universal recognition, a book that would be a poem, a poem that would be a play—a book and a play in trompe l'oeil.

The relationship between the play and Ascanio (sheet 4) belongs to the domain of Roussel's secret equations, and the project is not sufficiently developed for us to hazard an explanation of it. All one can deduce is that the fiancé was originally called Ascanio and his name then changed to Silvio (cf. sheet 2: Asc is called Silvio), so that the second line of the couplet on sheet 5, "Ramener Silvio sur le lieu du forfait" [To take Silvio back to the scene of the crime] does not scan unless one pronounces the name Sil-vi-o: obviously "Ramener Ascanio . . ." provides the metrically correct reading. Beyond that, as we have said (note 16), one can only indulge in considered speculation.

One can see better how pivotal the Quarli is to Roussel's project. Sheet 2 makes this conspicuously clear. There the physical characteristics of the book are used, in accordance with one of Roussel's customary procedures, to create the components of the play:

Travail de vers (de livre) [Worm-eaten (book)]	= Livre (pièce) travaillé en vers [book (play) written in verse]
mouillures [damp stains]	= gouttes d'eau [drops of water]
dos à nerfs [ribbed spine]	= ? (punition de Gobbo) [? (punishment of Gobbo)]
a fondello[26] [a fondello]	= révélation qui vient du 'fond de l'eau' [revelation coming 'from the water's depths']
fermoir [clasp of book, or tap of shower]	=(douche) [(shower)]

The clasp *(fermoir)*, is the thing that closes, that seals, that thus conceals, and that does not speak ["shut up!" (in French "*la ferme!*")]; the shower/mouth *(douche/bouche)*, is what holds back the water *(l'eau)*, what holds back the confession *(l'aveu):* what cannot speak the impossible word. Given that it is actually put in brackets, we find this to be the strongest possible image of "incorporation": the truth is inscribed (inserted) in the book, but the book is closed; it will say nothing (Gobbo confesses but remains silent *(muet))*.

tranches (peintes) [(painted) edges]	= (texte) en tranches [(text) in sections]

As always in Roussel, words have to be taken in their strict sense. When Roussel associates the clasp with a shower, he has in mind the physical image of a book whose clasp resembles a shower attachment. When he refers to a text in sections, he has in mind a text that can be physically separated into sections. Again, when he later adds, after listing the roles in the play, the apparently superfluous remark, "chacun représentant un rôle" [each representing a role], he can only mean "role" to refer not to the dramatis personae but, etymologically, to the rolls of paper on which actors' parts were written.

Our final hunch, based on a difficult reading of sheet 3 as well as on what we have already said, is that for his play Roussel had in mind a single stage apparatus that would allow him to mime *all the roles/rolls*, drawing them out of a book as it was broken into sections to form the stage set (*tranches peintes* = painted sections).[27]

"The book that from one side only arrests the eye and masks" would then have indicated a replica (all plays consist of *répliques* [= spoken lines, replicas]) of the Quarli, an outsized trompe l'oeil book made of wood sections painted with the principal settings of the play and a clasp shaped to resemble a showerhead. It would open up to reveal "rolls," which Roussel would take out and read one after another *(à tour de rôle)*.

This is not the first time that Roussel refers to a "book with a secret" or a "binding with a pocket."[28] And there is an analogy with the Frascati episode, where the "precise apparatus" refers both to the spring mechanism commissioned from the clockmaker, Bordaz, which had been described in detail four pages earlier, and to the entire mechanism devised to confuse Neyric, the receiver of stolen goods. Similarly this play, when read "as an open book," in the moving brevity of its five fragments, stands for the ultimate silence of the text as well as for the "coming apart" that animates it. The "precise apparatus" in fact made Roussel during the rest of his life incapable of undertaking a play destined to reveal the displaced locus of his desire and the true image of his "renaissance." The Renaissance book (the Quarli) and the renaissance or resuscitation of Sibylla, who comes back to life to celebrate her marriage to Ascanio/Silvio, were to remain dead letters forever.

One cannot expect the exegesis of a few lines, no matter how assiduously one has disassembled them, to cast much light on an *oeuvre* so well described by Bachter as "a literary adventure that has no source but itself, no goal but its own existence, no meaning other than its own wake."[29]

It is ultimately unimportant whether one can identify in these paltry fragments the seed of a project to which Roussel might have devoted his entire life as a writer, a project that would have become his crowning work, the "masterwork" capable of winning him universal recognition. There is ultimately no Roussel mystery; his work is not a riddle that we have to solve. It is only our reading of it, our thirst for explanation, our love of complexity that create the impression that there must be a secret. If there is a secret, it will not be found where we look for it.[30]

Any attempt to explain Roussel founders on the obstinate fact of his unfathomable method. Our claim that the hypothetical play whose possible origins we have attempted to describe is the last, posthumous metonym of a trip to Venice around which the delusion of writing was organized derives not from any illusion that our arguments define Roussel but, in the last resort, from the incomparably Rousselian emotion the traveler feels when, standing on the steps of the Evangelisti, he discovers for the first time the city of which Roussel was the mental architect.

Atlas Anthology Three, 1985

APPENDICES

Sheet 1

At the end of the last century a prominent family lived in V, called the Z, whose daughter, Sib, was engaged to a young nobleman.

The engagement period was nearly ended, when, after a visit by   to the Palazzo   , the governess found Sib unconscious in the luxurious bathroom that adjoined her room. The young girl held in her clenched hand a batiste handkerchief embroidered with the initials of her fiancé, who was immediately accused of having assaulted her.

The evidence was overwhelming. No one had seen the young man come out after going with Sib into the music room where she usually spent the afternoon.

          was arrested and taken to the court-house where an attempt was made to reconstruct this base assault.

Everyone soon was gathered in the young girl's room, except for the two youngest Z children, a boy and a girl, who were playing *leap-frog* in the huge attics of the Palazzo.

At this point the young girl's voice was heard coming from the bathroom, in distant, intermittent, but perfectly audible snatches, pronouncing the inexorable accusation that revealed the truth about this horrible crime: GOB! . . . LAISSE! [GOB! . . . STOP!]

There could be no doubt about the meaning of these words, which pointed to Gobbo, the hunchbacked family boatman, who was promptly questioned and soon admitted his guilt.

Sib's shouts had been intercepted by the water in the pipes and held in the showerhead attached above the bath.

The children had in the course of their innocent games caused the shower attachment to shake in a particular way that released the fateful words.

Sib, when to everyone's surprise she emerged from the coma the assault had induced, confirmed this curious liquid revelation.

No time was lost in celebrating, on the water, a sumptuous wedding in which the youngest children were given the place of honour they rightly deserved.

Sheet 2

In the Palazzo
Asc is called Silvio

Worm eaten
damp stains
ribbed spine
a fondello

clasp   (shower)
painted edges
book in sections
casting of roles

the father
the mother
Silvio
Sib
Govern
Gobbo the hunchback, *silent* role
the two children

each corresponding to one role

Sheet 3

far here. 20 vol

instalment
folded both sides

and because of that
addition of one
sheet in the opposite direction
inserted, into the slit
against

death
renaissance ?
for +

one never finds
a role that goes the
other way

—there is another sheet
to cater for the possibility
of this other way

series of roles
the book that from only one side
gilding—
—arrests the eye—
a heavy paper
and masks
in (as before
at the binding)

Sheet 4

(with the letterhead GRANDE ALBERGO DEI PRINCIPI DI MALTA San Cosimo degli Incurabili 14, Milano)

chocolate

At the *de la Plage*

Sept 95

the ivory of his

sieve
monkey

tombola (SM)

Sheet 5

red

Handkerchief

By overcoming his nerves he will be able
To take Silvio back to the scene of the crime

As to the erect purple of the clasp which an oaf . . .

There could be no purer oath to give you

Translated by Antony Melville, in collaboration with Harry Mathews.

NOTES

1. Fleisch, M. *Formal ambiguity in early twentieth-century French theater.* Unpublished doctoral dissertation, Carson College, 1975.
2. A second copy of this extremely rare work is to be found in the catalogue of the reserve of the Hermitage library (Lett. Poj. 2450); a third copy appeared in the auction of the possessions of the Comte de Fortsas on 10th August 1840, with the reference Pat. 55, and the following description: *Tragœdia Ducis Partibonis.* Venice, Andrea Quarli 1532, in-folio 19pp. nch., 191 pp. ch. and 1 p. nch., rom. char., original binding with wooden boards half bound in brown morocco, vertical design of four rectangles of scrolls with spiral motifs in center, spine with three ribs decorated with broad criss-cross, three clasps, two of them intact. Painting on fore-edge: the doge is shown in red clothes, speaking to a soldier in armor; his hand is raised in entreaty. The other edges are marbled. Elegant title pages; ms. glosses in a fine humanist hand in margins and on end-papers; some damp-stains to top margin.
3. See appendix for full texts.
4. Roussel writes V. and not Venice and speaks of a "boatman" rather than a "gondolier." We shall come back to these points.
5. Sheet 2 reads: "Gobbo, *silent* role" (Roussel's underlining). But he later makes a confession: the significance of this apparent contradiction is made clear later in the article.
6. Cf. Doc. 4: Marguerite de Bourgogne conducting a search on the shores of the Black Sea for her bard Slân.
7. Was there perhaps some corruption—if so, late—of "Doge" into "Duce"? On Roussel's relations with fascism, see Alvirondi (*Les écrivains français et la tentation mussolinienne,* thèse de 3e cycle, Université de Nice, 1973); the author had access to various state archives.
8. We are particularly grateful to Mme. Paulina Petrasova of the Bibliothèque du Tribunal de Commerce for the meticulous research she undertook in auction catalogues.
9. Vianello sale, No. 133; the Palazzo Sarezin archives list it as a "*coll. forestiera*"; there is no mention of an incision in the binding; close study of the description shows that it is not the same copy as the one in the Fortsas sale. (Cf. p. 1 n.2)
10. Cat. No. 19.
11. Letter to M. Baudoin-Dubreuil, dated 6 March 1912. See also Voltic (*Il Museo Immaginario di Roussel,* Lo Zecchino, 1976, 3), which interprets the withdrawal as a symptom of Roussel's homosexual urges. The evidence we present is, we feel, much more specific.
12. The last Quarli to be auctioned was sold, as far as we know, at Brylinger's, Basel, in 1971 , for Sfr. 240,000.
13. Letter to Dr. Reboul, undated (Sept 95), B.M. Fonds Chambrac, item 843c.

14. It would be improper not to mention an eyewitness account that, although it yielded no major clues, deeply influenced our researches. In the course of a long stay in Venice, one of us recently met an old lady, Signora Gianna S., who proved to be a distant cousin of the Grifalconis. In the course of a conversation with her, the name Roussel was mentioned, quite by chance. Signora S.'s reaction was immediate: her face took on an expression of melancholy indignation while she murmured only the two words "Povaro Asganio!" She refused to elaborate.

15. At the time of the Roussels' trip—they stayed at the Hollenberg—the apartment was let to a young American architect called Joshua Ewett, then at work on the restoration of Santa Maria degli Svevi. Correspondence with his son, Ethan Ewett, of Hartford (Mass.), has produced neither verbal accounts or documentation relating to the Grifalconi family.

16. *Singe* [monkey] could be a rebus-abbreviation of Saint-Jean-Baptiste *(singe en batiste)*. *Crible* reminded us of the "cry" *(cri)* uttered by the girl: *"Gob! Laisse!"* Could this goblet (?) *(gobelet)* be a mug won by Roussel at the tombola? At this point we are reduced to hypotheses that, spellbinding as they sometimes may seem, are no more than that. Even though we are deeply convinced that the play, both in its conception *and* in its form, is *bound* to the memory of Venice (it is lodged in the *binding* of the Venetian book), we would be hard put to support our hunches with down-to-earth arguments.

17. This church, then undergoing restoration, would not reopen to the public until 1987. We were, however, able to see the picture, which was temporarily housed in the Scuola di San Fantin. A brass plaque screwed onto the lower right-hand corner of the frame declares: gift of Mme. R. in memoriam A.G., 1912.

18. We explored the works for explicit references to Italy. There are fewer than we expected. Most occur in *Nouv. Imp.:*

Au glas pontifical le Savoyard s'il va
Avoir à ramoner les conduits du Conclave

Si dans un rêve encore il aura, lumineuse
L'idée de son final allegro, Tartini

Pour un caillou chassé par un quidam hableur
L'Atlas ouvert sur la Sicile et l'Italie

D'Andorre, Saint-Marin ou meme Liechtenstein
On n'écrirait jamais un traité vraiment plein.

(Whether at the Papal knell the Savoyard
Will have to sweep the conclave's chimney clean

If yet again, luminous, in dream will appear
To Tartini the idea of his final allegro

For a pebble a nondescript braggart kicks away,
The Atlas opened to Sicily and Italy

Andorra, San Marino, even Liechtenstein
Could never furnish matter for truly pregnant studies.)

19. Pferdli, O. *Autres Images de mélancolie,* translated from the German by Henri Brunet. *Nouv. Rev. fr. psych.,* 1974, 6.

20. Virgil Ceaunescu has unearthed an interesting example of such behavior: a fortnight before going to Bucharest, Roussel wrote to the best stationery printer in the city to order 500 calling cards headed with the address of the hotel where he was to stay. But he never had them delivered and did not even stay at that hotel.

21. The comment attributed to Roussel by a journalist at *La Gazette Automobile,* "When one arrives in Venice one longs for candies as big as stars," has been shown to be a brazen forgery by a "hack in need of copy" (unpublished letter from Roussel to Eugene Brigeaud, in *Labyrinthus,* 1974, 1).

22. Isolated: *isole:* Venice is made up of islands. Is it merely coincidence that Roussel went to die on an island, that so many islands appear in his work (Sein, Barbados, Martinique, Reunion, etc.) and that Locus Solus is an "*isolated place*"?

23. The hypotheses we put forward about these correspondences are based on a systematic analysis of guides to Venice published at the turn of the century, especially the Zanotti.

24. It is worth pointing out that the *Lyncée* was sailing to South America and that none of the passengers reached this destination.

25. In *Poussière,* however, the words *Lit de haut* appear twice, and mention is made of a *Lie d'O* [upper bed, dregs of O].

26. Parchment covers, before they were bound, bore one of the following two handwritten inscriptions: *coverto,* if it was to be a full binding, or *a fondello,* if it was a half binding (Beaujeu and Petitjean, *Histoire du Livre,* Paris 1960).

27. This idea may date from the late period when Roussel, a ruined man but still addicted to the theater, thought of putting to use his talents as mime, musician, and actor, the very ones that had brought him success (if only in society).

28. "Having once again been addressed as 'Seneschal' by Frascati, the 'fence' was at once supposed to insert his nail into the delicate graining of the parchment . . . which unknown to him set off the precise mechanism the Genoan had placed there. The binding opened to reveal the three letters that would save the numismatist." (Imp. 147)

29. Bachter, B.O. *Les Lieux Solitaires.* Bull. Inst. Ling., Louvain, 1972, 97: 103-114.

30. Nothing could be simpler, for instance, than to explain the ballerinas costume in the episode of the lawyer Dargaud (*Locus Solus* 176) by means of a near pun on "*Meunier, tu dors*" / "*Manille et Tudor*": *manille* [anklet] referring to the hoop with which the dancer's crinoline is made, and *Tudor* to the roses on her bodice; but the whole episode could just as easily be linked to the slang

expression "*Je n'ai pas un rotin*" [I haven't a bean], which becomes "*jeune épouse a rotin*" [young wife with hoops]: both expressions are equally valid, equally interesting, and equally useless.

In a few years Roussel's entire work will have been computerized and subjected to a statistical analysis of self-correlation and cross-relation that will enable us to define systematically all significant variations in vocabulary, syntax, metrics, even semantics (frequency of half words, obligatory associations, etc.). So at least we are told by Professor Vance de Gregorio, director of a project at the Parnell Institute for Advanced Research. Such analysis will no doubt clarify and confirm what we already know. It is doubtful whether it will enable us to learn anything about matters that Roussel wished to keep hidden. Although far from sufficient, the taste for riddles is here a better tool than the most powerful computer.

THE BAD DREAMS OF CAROLUS LUDOVICUS DODGSON

Now, Dinah, tell me the truth: did you ever eat a bat? When suddenly, thump, thump! down she came upon a heap of sticks and dry leaves, and the fall was over.

So ends Alice's abrupt entry into her dream world. That entry had been conceived, psychologically speaking, in the most promising conditions. Lewis Carroll reported that, as he began making up a story for a young listener, "I sent my heroine straight down a rabbit-hole, without the least idea of what was to happen afterwards." The world of the unconscious lay open, with no preconceived notions to bar the way.

In many of Alice's adventures Carroll lets "things come of themselves"—he accepts the consequences of his heroine's descent into the unknown. He confirms this open-minded attitude when he states that he "cannot set invention going like a clock, by any voluntary winding up." Furthermore, the word *invention*, quite distinct from the vagueness of inspiration or fancifulness, usefully characterizes the adroit mixture of poetic and logical procedures that enabled Carroll at his best to set down the discourse of the unconscious in all its subversive allusiveness. Whenever he surrenders to his fascination with the deformations and conformations of language, Carroll writes powerfully and provocatively. Alice's fall irresistibly evokes such basic terrors as impotence and death.

Nevertheless, in the very instant of that fall, our fears are immediately and carefully assuaged. The marmalade jar that "might have killed someone" returns to its place on the shelf; the world we have suddenly discovered is made familiar; common sense reasserts itself. Once the fall is over, anxiety actually yields to cosiness, and we discover that it is only leaves that are dead—hardly a painful death, and one that depends on the presence of an upright, flourishing tree. (At the end of the story, when Alice wakes up, the same leaves turn out to be the harmless explanation of the hostile swarm that has just attacked her.) In other words, we are given a glimpse of the world of the repressed and at the same time reassured that adventuring into it involves no risk.

"And the fall was over": as if innocence had been restored, at least provisionally. Carroll in fact justified himself as an author of children's books by identifying childhood with innocence. The last paragraph of *Alice's Adventures* is only one striking example of Carroll's frequent expressions of this belief. No matter how innocuous such a belief may appear to us, it could hardly avoid clashing with the "underground" realities Carroll encountered in the course of inventing his tales. In general, writing for children leads its practitioners toward the complementary extremes of sadism and hypocrisy, and Carroll's concern for the "innocence" of his readers—which is to say his own illusions—pushed him irresistibly toward the second extreme; so that as his work progressed he felt increasingly obliged to mitigate or sweeten the "wonders" his inventiveness revealed. In this respect the change of the faintly sinister *Adventures Underground* of the original title to the childish *Adventures in Wonderland* anticipates the decline of the straightforward style of the *Adventures* to the bathos of the opening chapter of *Through the Looking-Glass* and the unbearable saccharinity of *Sylvie and Bruno*. No less dismaying are the starchy attitudes attributed to Alice, which evidently spring from her confident invulnerability among the troubling creatures of her dream world. (These attitudes find their counterpart in Carroll's explanations—interesting enough in their own right—of the many dreams that appear throughout his work.)

It is easy enough, perhaps too easy, to see why Carroll took such pains to defuse his discoveries after one considers the strange story of his life. The life calls out for analysis and interpretation all too temptingly; it certainly offers topics for our consideration that are almost as engrossing as those of the work itself. It seems hardly fair not to forgive Carroll his shortcomings when one learns to what an extraordinary extent his public life was devoted to concealing secret and unremitting anxiety. From his decision not to use his father's family name when signing his nonscientific work ("Lewis Carroll" was created by re-Englishing and transposing the Latin forms of Charles Lutwidge, his given and maternal middle names) to the renunciation of his passion for photography because of a scandal that was largely imaginary, Carroll's life reads as one long exercise in abnegation, a terrible and fascinating exercise that led this natural iconoclast to accept established authority unreservedly in every domain in which he was active.

While biography may explain Carroll's ambiguous attitude toward his inventions, the reputation his work enjoys in the English-speaking world owes less to him than to his readers. Aside from the studies of De La Mare and Empson, critics have never considered his writings on their purely literary merits; as a result they have passed indifferently from success through neglect to acceptance as minor classics, with the dismissive implications of the term, like "charm." Critical neglect has left glaringly plain facts, such as the correspondence of the Cheshire Cat to a photographic image being developed, undiscovered and unexploited; so the Cheshire Cat is consequently abandoned to the reductions of literal or symbolic interpretation.

In the midst of the genteel penumbra surrounding his books, Carroll has been assigned qualities that obscure his strength. He has been made into an amiable representative of a lost Victorian world, before the advent of disagreeable realities such as psychoanalysis and socialism. That Carroll was undoubtedly a political reactionary (consider the Caucus Race in *Alice's Adventures* and the heroine's remarks about her poor neighbors) does not explain the phenomenon. It is precisely the reassuring, "delightful" aspect of his work that has allowed his idolaters to reduce what he was at his best to what he perhaps would himself have liked to be: an amusing writer of children's books and a brilliant vulgarizer of the paradoxes of modern science.

Needless to say, Carroll can never belong entirely to such admirers. Although I have no desire to give substance to their views, it seems useful to emphasize that the Carroll of nonsense and linguistic innovation—the Carroll familiar to French readers—has been assigned a quite different literary and social role in the countries that speak his language, and that Carroll himself was inclined to accept this modest role. He was after all a true Victorian. He considered Longfellow to be the finest writer among his contemporaries. He declared that *Wuthering Heights* was the novel "I should least like to be a character in myself. All the 'dramatis personae' are so unusual and unpleasant." But he was as unusual as any of them and, in his fawning support of the social and cultural establishments of his day, no less unpleasant.

The best passages in Carroll are naturally free of his fearful compulsion to edulcorate. The poems that punctuate *Alice's Adventures* (all essentially parodies; even "Jabberwocky" has been shown to parody a particular Romantic poem) provide a series of delectable assaults on the very tradition of Wordsworthian sentimentality by which Carroll was so often attracted. In the *Alice* books they are what most purely constitute a universe of genuine iconoclastic madness, the madness Carroll aptly defined as the incapacity to distinguish between waking and sleeping life. When he applied to prose the systematic dislocation practiced in these poems (a practice close to that of Blake, Smart, and Lear), he introduced a radical discontinuity of compelling effect, without which neither Firbank nor Joyce would have been able to write as he did. Carroll's use of the ambiguity of language to create narrative also anticipates, even if it cannot have influenced, the work of Raymond Roussel, who would have especially relished the short story in which a simple blank space, transforming *Romancement* into *Roman cement*, determines the entire fiction. Even the reassuring sense of comfort, even the interludes of tediousness have their use, in that they encourage our imagination to venture further than it otherwise might; and there is no denying that the conflict between the Carroll who invents and the Carroll obsessed with "innocence" exercises its own real fascination.

Le Monde, 1971

LES MERVEILLEUX NUAGES

. . . man's best-directed effort accomplishes a kind of dream, while God is the sole worker of realities.
　　　　　　　　　　　　　　　—The House of the Seven Gables, XII

T*he Duplications* is not what they seem. Kenneth Koch's book-length poem, which resembles his earlier *Ko* in size and style, is a work of many duplicities, of which the foremost is this: it is an intensely serious undertaking masquerading as preposterous entertainment. In this respect it belongs to a family of modern classics that includes *Count Orgel's Ball* and *The Baron in the Trees*, as well as stories of Kafka's such as "The Giant Mole." It also takes its place in an older tradition of inspired poetic comedy, the tradition of *The Rape of the Lock, Don Juan*, and *Orlando Furioso;* together with Ovid's *Metamorphoses*, Byron and Ariosto in fact provide its models.

The preposterousness of *The Duplications* lies more in the telling than in the tales told; but some idea of it can be given by a summary of the stories themselves; and the summary will serve, especially for those who have not read the work, as a frame of reference for discussion. The main stories are four:

1. Mickey and Minnie Mouse are driving through Greece as contestants in an automobile race. They are accompanied by Donald Duck, by Pluto, who is gay, and by Clarabelle Cow. Clarabelle manifests an attraction to Mickey that angers Minnie, who soon dispatches her to Samos. Mickey and

the others drive across a bridge of spray to Crete. There Donald makes a pass at Minnie. In a jealous rage, Mickey pounds him with a rock until Minnie stops him. Donald is taken to a vet, but too late: he dies. Stricken with remorse, the mice abandon the race. They try to live a solitary life in Crete, but they are so hounded by journalists and tourists that they repair to Washington, D.C., where, thanks to a new drug, they are changed into comic-book characters.

Their chief competitors in the race, Terence and Alma Rat, seem sure winners at this point; their progress is interrupted, however, by Herman Clover, a snake who anesthetizes Terence in order to make love to Alma.

Meanwhile, to protest their transformation, artists display giant paintings of Mickey and Minnie in the Bosphorus. These works of art convince Mickey that he should return to the race, win it, and confess to the murder of Donald. He and Minnie are transported to Olympus, where they soon become gods. Terence and Alma are then rescued from Herman the snake by priests from Mount Athos. Minnie, remorseful over her punishment of Clarabelle, uses her new powers to change her into a beautiful woman. Mickey likewise resurrects Donald; but because his command is imprecisely phrased, Donald is no sooner reborn than he becomes a calligram of himself. Heartbroken at his mistake, Mickey is unexpectedly visited by the turtles of Olympus, who demand self-rule. When he replies to them, Mickey utters a blasphemous "Goddam!" Olympus explodes, scattering its inhabitants. Mickey and Minnie land on a Grecian highway conveniently near a Chevrolet in which they go on to win the race. The Donald calligram is taken away to a Dutch museum.

On Samos, Clarabelle bumps into the Amos Frothingham statue (see 3). Amos comes to life, clasps a rapturous Clara to his bosom, and "soars straight skyward" into cloudland (where Pluto, when we last saw him, was playing golf).

2. Two characters from *Ko*, Pemmistrek and Alouette, are picnicking in Provence. Pemmistrek accidentally touches a chemical substance that turns him to glass. Alouette is so shaken by this event that she is transformed into

a huge bird. She carries her lover to Rome, where he is brought back to life by Doctor McSnakes, although without his memory. The doctor advises Alouette that a certain rabbinical ritual may be able to restore her to human shape. As the couple wanders through Rome, Pemmistrek tumbles into an underground passage that leads him straight to Helsinki. Alouette is forgotten. He takes up with Ann, one of the Early Girls, winsome creatures fabricated out of Finnish soil. (When an Early Girl makes love, the replica of an existing city comes briefly into being, as Pemmistrek soon learns to his surprise.) He leaves Helsinki by train with Ann and other Early Girls.

Meanwhile, Alouette goes to a Roman synagogue where a rabbi performs as an entertainment the very ritual needed to bring back her womanhood. She magically learns of her lover's whereabouts and flies to Stockholm, where Pemmistrek has arrived and narrowly escaped death. Still in the company of the Early Girls, Pemmistrek takes a train north. His memory returns. After a polar bear knocks him off his train, he boards another that soon pulls into a station where Alouette has just arrived. The lovers are blissfully reunited. At this point Atlantis raises its watery arm to snatch the train filled with Early Girls down to its watery realm. Ann and her sisters will henceforth be companions to the all-male Atlantides.

3. Huddel, another refugee from *Ko*, survives only as a Roman statue. Brought back to life, he is immediately shattered by a passing car. But his fragments miraculously reassemble: he becomes a superman, half flesh, half concrete. He flies (not in a plane but by his own powers) from Rome to Samos. There an American team has gathered, determined to destroy him before the USSR enlists his powers against the West. While in Juno's temple, Huddel recognizes one of his assailants and slays him—a sacrilege that brings about an earthquake. Samos is destroyed, although only temporarily.

On the island, Huddel has met the beautiful Aqua Puncture. With her he flies to Africa. (In the meantime, Amos Frothingham deserts the American death team, devotes himself to the cause of Greece, and settles on Samos. He will later die of an insect bite, and a statue of him will be erected on the island.) Huddel and Aqua land in Tropical China, a region of Africa, Italian in its customs but populated by Chinese. (During a peaceful interlude, Aqua tells Huddel her story. She is the granddaughter of an ancient Etruscan woman whose youth was preserved by a secret process through the centuries. John Ruskin had fallen in love with her; she had died bearing him a daughter, who was kidnapped by jealous archeologists and kept, drugged, in a Dutch museum. There she was discovered by Nyog Papendes, Commander Papend's father [see 4]; Aqua was their daughter). Mugg McDrew, a member of the death team, has tracked Huddel down and tries to kill him, but he is thwarted in the attempt and himself dies.

After yet another assault, this one by a pygmy, Huddel decides to leave Africa and fly with Aqua to Helsinki. On their way they discover a pleasant region in the clouds where sky vegetables are growing. They find life there exalting and go no farther. Pluto then delivers Papend's letter to Aqua (see 4). She thus learns that she has a half-brother and is filled with longing to meet him. In time a crescent-shaped car picks them up to drive them to a heavenly feast organized by Nyog Papendes.

4. High in the Peruvian Andes, Commander Papend, Nyog's son, has built a replica of Venice in which to indulge his appetite for young women. In protest against this abomination, Nature has attacked the city with swarms of giant bees. The only defense against them is the erection of large matzoh placards throughout the city.

At the start of the poem, an inhabitant of Second Venice, Elizabeth Gedall, disappears into the sky while sitting by her stoop. She is later found unharmed, the momentary victim of a "gratuitous act" on the part of certain cumulus clouds.

Papend knows of his half-sister Aqua's existence. Out of his desire to know her, he persuades Pluto to deliver a letter to her. An earthquake then releases a long-buried Inca prince into Second Venice. The event leads Papend to reconsider his aims in life—a process that continues when, after a summons from his father, Papend is lifted into the sky. Visions of a better world come to him as he travels through the clouds towards Nyog Papendes's feast.

Clearly the author of *The Duplications* has no interest whatsoever in subur-
ban realism. He entertains us with improbabilities. And these, it should be
added, are riddled with further improbabilities. We are constantly being
distracted from the stories here summarized by lesser incidents of varying
irrelevance, as well as by a swarm of minor characters—fifty-nine by my
count: some last only a line, like Miss Ellen Foster Tay; others, such as Norma
Clune, nuclear physicist and translator of Proust into Icelandic, infiltrate
several stanzas. Further interruptions, also entertaining, take the form of
reflections in the manner of *Beppo* and *Don Juan*, each with its particular
savor. A consideration of the transcendent moments life can offer includes
these lines:

> There is the proud sensation, for example,
> Of sitting in the ocean in a car;
> Or being thrown against a Gothic temple
> By an outrageous omophagic Czar—
> No one should ever feel that he has ample
> Experiences which light him like a star:
> Stark naked hens and roosters playing cricket,
> And Juno, Mars, and Saturn in a thicket.   (25.2[1])

Those who have spent time in Venice will recognize the aptness of this
observation:

> And now the Adriatic seems a pond, though
> One knows how large it is upon occasion
> When in a vaporetto to Torcello
> Going as slowly as a spoon in jello.   (149.1)

Furthermore, this medley of "interruptions of interrupted interruptions"
moves along *prestissimo*. Enjambment, which keeps lines and stanzas spill-
ing forward into their sequels, is applied to the narratives as well. Ariosto
told several stories at once, but carefully marked off the beginnings and
ends of their parts. Here there are no such pauses. We can never be sure the
next half sentence will still pertain to Mickey's and Minnie's adventures or

plunge us into those of Pemmistrek and Alouette. We can only hang on as we speed along into whatever comes next.

Even as we are being so impudently entertained, we start noticing certain duplications, certain duplicities, at least the simpler ones that lie in the foreground of the text—such as that the Venice we had assumed to be the original city is a copy perched high in the Andes, or that "a tremendous goat" seen wandering through Thessaly is a disguise worn as a punishment by three monks from Mount Athos. We also notice that rhyme, that traditional duplicating procedure of verse, has a novel function: instead of emphasizing meaning or playing a counterpoint to it, it can in this poem brutally determine it:

> the large Christmas turkey No-Shu
> Sends each December to the O.N.U.
>
> Now that Mao's China's been admitted to it.
> Norma, who loves him even though he's crazy,
> Has made him go each week to Dr. Bluet,
> The psychiatric heir of Piranesi,
> Who saw man's mind as a huge, complex cruet
> In which he was imprisoned, like a daisy.   (105.1,2)

(After this summary appearance, we hear no more of Piranesi and Dr. Bluet.)

When we read this passage, we are deep into the poem, moving fast; and since we know the lines are parenthetical ones, we do not stop to ask what kind of sense they make, or if they make any sense at all. We are willing to allow that the last four verses may have been entirely suggested by the rhyming pattern—that they may be, in other words, nonsense. Now, when a writer has succeeded in creating such a state of mind in the reader, he can get away with murder. And in fact the next two lines tell us: "He'd worked with No-Shu now for eighteen months, / Who in that period had killed only once." The writer can lead a pleasantly distracted reader into the depths unsuspecting and virtually unawares. Reconsider the quotation that starts "There is the proud sensation . . ." The gods invoked in the last line of the couplet are not such auspicious ones as, say, Venus, Mercury, and Apollo, but a sinister triad standing for domestic law, war, and death. We are being entertained with murder and gods of gloom. *The Duplications* are not what it seems.

What is really going on in the poem? We can start looking for an answer in another, even less comprehensible passage. The passage cannot be said to be central to the poem, because, like *Don Juan*, *The Duplications* has no center; or more accurately, its center is a perpetually shifting point on its surface—the point where at any moment we are reading. Still, even at a first hurried encounter, the passage is arresting enough to make us wonder about it. It occurs just after McDrew's death in Tropical China. Meralda, a blue-eyed young woman, has just explained to a Chinese journalist named Pong that this death was brought about by an insect lodged in McDrew's heart:

> "Say, have you got a match?"
> The lovely girl requested. When the TienTsin
> Reporter bent to see, she ran off dancing
>
> And screaming horrible threats into the air,
> "We'll kill you all, us bugs! Ha ha. Forget it!
> You'll never stand a chance!" No underwear!
> She rose into the sky. "What have I said? It
> Was only so I'd understand!" "Beware!"
> She rising cried. She saw a bird and met it
> With sloppy kiss. "We cure at first but then
> We do our fated work: death to all men!"   (65.1,2)

First of all, Meralda, however mysterious, is plainly duplicity incarnate. Her change from pretty girl into prophetess of annihilation might be said to confirm the suspicions we have been starting to feel. Her threat of death furthermore thrusts into our attention a topic that we have already found—in Saturn and No-Shu—lying close to the entertaining surface of the poem. Talk of death in fact permeates *The Duplications*. Mickey's first appearance, for example, at once leads to the mention of Walt Disney's demise, and the giant Packard in which he races suggests the "bone and dust of dinosaurs."

The first Mickey episode concludes with news of a murder in an Athenian restaurant. Pemmistrek's translation to Finland brings to light another murder. The "proud sensations" in the quotation on p. 147 would seem to offer little hope of survival, and in other reflective interpolations we are told of the "meaningless violence" that plagues the world, of "decimating nations," of "the art / We waste upon ingenious ways of killing." The long reflection at the end of the first part of the poem concludes: "And so one carries on . . . with what is vital / Being a thing continually sought for— / At death it's this that we have come to nought for!" A full list of such examples would multiply them tenfold.

Death wreaks havoc as well with the cast of characters. Bit players, like Huddel's assailant on Samos or Pemmistrek's in Stockholm, are pitilessly mowed down, and at some point most of the main characters are deprived of life in one way or another. Mickey and Minnie are reduced to two dimensions, Pemmistrek is turned to glass, Aqua spends inanimate years in a museum. Amos Frothingham and Mugg McDrew both lose their lives. Huddel and Donald die twice, once literally, once figuratively. Papend leaves the world "as one dead." Nyog Papendes may be alive, or dead, or both—it hardly seems to matter.

The reason it hardly matters is that in the poem death does not always mean that life is over. For the principal characters, in fact it is more like a new beginning. Of them only Mugg McDrew dies definitively—the peculiarity of the event is driven home by the repetition of "death" as a rhyme seven times in two stanzas (63.2,3). The others all recover—are reborn. (It is true that Donald Duck ends stuck in his calligram, but there is good reason for that, as we shall see.) We may ask why, aside from the animated-cartoon improbability of the work, this should be so. What kind of death can this be? The answer seems to be: It all depends. We do glean a few general hints about its nature. Death is apparently a prerequisite of freedom. Huddel declares, " 'three births remind me / That I was meant to live . . . / Above all else I prize my liberty'" (36.1); Mugg McDrew cries, "'A shame / That I must kill them both, but that's the game / Free life depends on'" (58.2,3). Death is also close to dreaming. When Papend rises "as one dead," the poet writes, "I cannot guarantee his state was waking, / But he was wakeful in its dreamy spaces" (153.1); and Early Ann, snatched from life on earth to Atlantis, goes on loving Pemmistrek "as a dreamer / Loves someone she has never seen in daytime" (144.2). Lastly, death works a change in its victims that makes them semidivine. Mickey and Minnie become gods on Olympus; Huddel becomes superman; Aqua, Amos, and Papend acquire the ability to fly; Pemmistrek (in his dreamlike amnesia) leads a life of bliss miraculously shielded from the dangers that beset him.

So death in *The Duplications* is not altogether dire; it can even lead to happiness. It does, however, demolish expectations; and it remains a real, if variable, danger. Why does it happen so often? Why does it happen at all?

A short quotation will suggest the answer. By a roadside in Thessaly, the snake Herman Clover has just put Terence Rat to sleep and is turning his attention to Alma:

> He seized her in his coils, which caused a cinem-
> athèque in Athens to explode and nine
> Persons to suffer in Constantinople
> From heart disease. (100.1)

No deaths are certified, although at least a few seem inevitable; but what emerges unambiguously from these lines is the lethal power of sexual desire. It is the desire of the male for the female that litters *The Duplications* with mortality. Desire may have consequences other than death, but it is death's certain cause.

This fact manifests itself first of all in the narratives: Donald Duck has his head bashed in for seducing Minnie; the Renaissance architect Archibald is poisoned for lusting after Leo VII's favorite; a Dallas billionaire dies after satisfying his girlfriend's whims. But it is more by poetic association that the link between desire and death is forged. Juxtaposition rather than causal sequence is what puts the point across. Some examples: Commander Papend has "sexual urges large as Lapland / And was as set for action as a gun / In madman's hands who hates the world around him" (4.1). Minnie reclaims

Mickey from Clarabelle with the lusty words, "Your tough luck! / Alone with him tonight I'll squeak and fuck!" which no sooner spoken precipitate the fatal shooting in the Athenian restaurant—an event that initiates a reflection on death that brings us to Pemmistrek vitrified on a field in Provence (11.3-13.2). The passage devoted to "the art / We waste upon ingenious ways of killing" ends a list of preferable pastimes with the erotic awakening of an adolescent boy (59.1 ff.). "The beginnings of romance" are said to be "very quiet, like a sailor / Drowned in the sea" (51.2). The words already quoted, "At death it's this that we have come to nought for!" concludes a two-page description of the attractions of different women to men, and the next stanza, which terminates the first part of the poem, contains the lines "So mourners walking down the Via Sacra / See their love's grave and feel they're buried in it / Themselves . . ." (76.2-77.3). And this is only a sampling. As its last item, a slightly different kind of fact: there is only one triple rhyme in the poem that appears four times, and it is *life, wife, knife* (15.3, 23.1, 98.1, 99.2).

Next question: why should male sexual desire cause death? We are not praying mantises; we are not even obliged to be Lacanians. Why such punishment for so "natural" an impulse? If there is a punishment, there must be a crime. What is criminal in man's desire? Two guesses.

No, one guess. Who needs to think twice about Oedipus and his mother? And this obvious answer came at once to mind. It came to my mind, and there it stayed. There was nothing in the poem to justify it. I did not, however, let the answer go. On the contrary, it could properly be said to have started bugging me. I won't say it gave me butterflies in my stomach, or ants in my pants, but it was certainly a bee in my bonnet and a flea in my ear. So I looked at the poem yet again, starting at the beginning with Papend and his duplicated city, where I read:

> Why did he want all this in Venice? Actually
> I do not know. I'm not sure he did either.
> I'd guess the city just aroused him sexually
> As Mommy's breast arouses the pre-teether.   (7.2)

Why yes! And Second Venice was an "Abomination beneath the sky's blue." And what happened to it? "Nature" caused it to be attacked by "hideous monstrous bees." Then I recalled other curious details in the work: the buzz and the butterfly preceding Huddel's resurrection, the mite in McDrew's heart, the ant that revealed precious information to Alouette, the bees that helped No-Shu learn the truth about his mother, Meralda's curse on men, McStrings devoured by ants, the prohibition of females from Mount Athos so strict that "even Ann / The Ant and Fay the Firefly are excluded," and, late but not least, the poet's exclamation on Amos Frothingham's return to life: "Take that, you / Dull insect, Death!" My obvious answer lay explicit but invisible under my eyes in a metathesis at once simple and ingenious and, of course, disarming:

in S e C t.

It was no longer surprising, it even seemed perfectly fitting that *The Duplications* was so full of bugs (even if I knew that they could not be interpreted simply as allegorical or even symbolic representations of incest). The discovery, however, did nothing to answer yet another question that immediately arose: Is incest really a punishable crime? Why does it lead to death?

Let's reconsider the concluding lines of the quotation on page 10: "aroused him sexually / As Mommy's breast arouses the pre-teether." Men first turn to women for nourishment, and their mothers naturally provide it. Food is a substantial, nonduplicitous gratification of hunger: not only does hunger disappear, something tangible is provided to make it disappear, something ascertainable, something that can be identified as it is incorporated. But with this gratification men also get something they didn't bargain for: an awakening of sexual desire. And unlike hunger, sexual desire cannot be satisfied—by the mother or anyone else— the way hunger can. We can never possess our gratification the way we possess food; we can never be sure of it, never "know" it in so reassuring a way as incorporation. The satisfaction remains elusive and illusory.

On several occasions in the poem, hunger and sexual desire are merged in the figure of the mother: almost overtly in the remarks on Papend's preference for Venice (7.2), inferentially in the interpolation on violence and pleasure (59.1 ff.), most explicitly in a passage that follows the mention of the poet's given name and speculates how such names may be chosen:

>   some, romantically—

> If, for example, Dad once loved a lassie
> Named Billy Jo, he might call baby Billy,
> If baby is a boy, or if the chassis
> Of that small creature shows that it is silly
> To think she's the same sex as Raymond Massey
> And may one day play Lincoln, perhaps Tillie
> Might satisfy his crazed nostalgic need
> To see his old flame at his wife's breast feed.   (87.3)

"Dad" is certainly a doomed man, and probably one long gone. In any case his "crazed nostalgic need" is a perfect definition of the condition that condemns the male to death. His insanity—and his crime—lies in confusing the two kinds of desire, one seemingly real, the other illusory in its gratification. By demanding a substantial gratification of sexual desire (that is, as substantial as food—something impossible) the male condemns himself to failure, hopelessness, unreality, nothingness, and so to "death." This death is then interpreted as coming from the mother herself: by luring with real satisfaction and exciting with impossible desire, she becomes unforgivably duplicitous. Incest is not lethal because of any social taboo but because the mother reveals desire as something doomed. The maternal breast is at once the source of life and death. (Cf. Meralda: "We cure at first but then / We do our fated work. . . .")

It is thus that the insects of incest pester these pages with their curious itches. As we have seen, at the very outset of the poem bees attack Second Venice, where Commander Papend "made love over fifty times a day": the bees are warded off with matzoh placards "placed on the shoreside gilding of [each] house": food—the object of innocent and necessary desire—staves off the punishment of sexuality. Interestingly enough, bees are later on specifically associated with the sexual attractiveness of the mother. No-Shu's murderously obsessive jealousy is explained in this fashion:

> His father and his mother had a dog
> Named Uncle Patsy, Ki-Wa in Chinese,
> Which bumblebees had trapped under a log.
> No-Shu, just five, ran out and chased the bees
> But then got lost, while going home, in fog
> And had a vision of his mother's knees
> With someone's hand upon them. Since that time
> He had devoted half his life to crime.   (104.3)

No-Shu became a murderer of philanderers, a self-appointed punisher of sexual desire.

Now if we remember Meralda's curse (65.2)—I trust by now it has begun to make more sense—we should expect insects themselves to become the agents of retribution. After all, Meralda says they will; and occasionally they do: a bug inside a crocus, no less a one than Meralda's daughter, stings Amos Frothingham to death (72.1–3); McDrew dies from an insect egg planted in his heart; a praying mantis's bite turns Pong into a baby while "'Insect eyes' were decimating youth" (66. 1); death is even accused of *being* an insect (147.1). But what is remarkable is how often insects fail to kill, how often, belying Meralda's words, they are harbingers of life, growth, and superior knowledge. Even in McDrew's case, it was the insect egg that enabled him to attain adult size; Pong, after his second babyhood, grows up again; it is an insect that, plunging into Alouette's Campari as she drinks it, supplies her with the information she needs to start recovering her happiness (68.3); and at one point the insect world is praised for holding philosophical views superior to our own (28.2,3).

This suggests why in *The Duplications* "death" (except for the exceptional McGrew) is less than fatal and often benign. Incestuous desire may not after all be a crime, or not only that. Rather than a punishment, the death it leads to may be a kind of rite of passage. Both desire and death may reveal paths leading to the kind of knowledge that "might cure us of all grieving" (as the author says of the insects' wisdom), knowledge that will transcend the practical, provable sort and "help people love . . . their world," for all its duplicity. Certainly the desire that dooms us leads as well to developments other than death. It enables us to produce (or discover) new worlds: the ephemeral cities of the Early Girls, Second Venice itself, the new Atlantis that is its undersea counterpart (144–145), the exalting sky world in the clouds that is a dreamy version of earthly life, with fields of heavenly fruit and vegetables, sky fish, cloud golf links, and endless sky-borne thoroughfares. These various new worlds can be called metamorphoses or sublimations of ordinary reality, but in the poem's term they are most fittingly thought of as its duplications; and their existence points to duplication as the way by which we can survive desire, death, and their duplicities. For, clearly, if one can be reborn, death is *also* a duplicity. This is perhaps the wisdom of the mortal, benevolent bugs.

If that is so, we may ask what modes of duplication are available to us. Poetry is certainly one: we have not only the demonstration of the art in this particular book but the more general claims the author makes on its behalf. (The poem itself is qualified as an attempt to speak "Of how things are on earth, and how in heaven" [84.3]; earlier, the *ottava rima* stanza is praised as "a splendid churn to / Make oppositions one" [79.2]. In ultimate aim as well as in immediate practice, *The Duplications* is everywhere concerned with duality and doubleness.)

But before we turn to the poet's advocacy of poetry, we should see what he has to say about the medium in which poetry operates, that is, about language. After all, we habitually think of language as a vast duplicating system: it replicates reality by assigning it names. Why can't it suffice as our means of duplication (i.e., of survival) without being subjected to the additional formalizations that poetry brings to it? Answer: by itself, language is utterly duplicitous—as duplicitous as men's mothers. Language pretends one thing and does another. It pretends to give us names for things; in fact it gives us only words (which are other things). It is, in "other words," always telling lies, a fact grandly demonstrated at the opening of *The Duplications* when we are presented with a familiar Venice that dissolves a page later into something very different: "Venice, Peru, of course, is where it happened" (4.1). The strange ways personal names are given, as in the passage quoted on p. 162, illuminates the naming function of language in general: the names we call things represent not those things but ambiguous histories of experience that we peremptorily associate with them.

This radical ambiguity of language is dramatized in Donald Duck's transformation into a calligram of himself. Mickey, you may remember, has killed Donald in a fit of jealousy. When he becomes God of Everything on Olympus, his first act is to resurrect his friend. But Donald has scarcely come back to life when he is turned into words: "Words everywhere feathers had been except / His beak, which stayed the same, like Uncle Sam" (135.2). The reason this happened is that Mickey's "commandment / Had some ambiguous words in it" (136.1):

> What "like to man" meant
> In resurrecting Donald—he had said
> "Bring Donald like to man to life from dead"—
>
> Was what remained unclear. Did Mickey mean
> "As man would"? Man would do it in some art,
> In picture, word, or music, and we've seen
> The natural forces carrying out this part
> Of what he said, confused, had tried to glean
> The maximum effects: first made a smart,
> Exacting, happy duck, far from acedia,
> Then turned him to a high form of mixed media.
>
> The words which make his feathers up declare,
> I think, SOMA PSYKOS SEMA ESTIN,
> "The body is the soul's prison." If you care
> For intricate deep meanings, this has been
> The best part of the story anywhere—
> Think how man's language shuts man's meanings in
> And is his prison, as his body is!   (136.1–3)

Ambiguity creates the prison of language, which is equated with the body, itself condemned to ambiguity, as we have seen, in its confusion of palpable and imaginary longings.

So language is our second body, and it is similarly doomed: "One's words, though, once excited, mate and marry / Incessantly, incestuously, like patients / Gone mad with love . . ." (91.1). Like the body forthright in appearance, language is another instrument to delude ourselves with our desires— "to see our old flame at our wife's breast feed."

(This ambiguity of language perhaps provides one meaning of the words " . . . the fallacy / We find by being born into this galaxy" [81. 1]. It is worth pausing to underscore the weight of the word "born" in these lines. We find death and all the ages of man in *The Duplications*, but never birth. It is the great *non-dit* of the poem.)

If language doesn't work as a naming system, what has to be done to make it work? A possible answer may be suggested by pointing out that if language cannot properly name what is, it may be able to name what isn't. Indeed, this is what it seems to do naturally. And what might "what isn't" be? Out of the ocean of infinite possibilities rise glistening dolphins we can recognize: the creatures of our "crazed nostalgic needs," the images of our impossible desires.

Can language be compelled to perform usefully and consistently this naming of what isn't? This is where poetry comes in. Poetry transforms language into the Universal Duplicating Machine that it can never become in the world of fact. (When the author returns from an outing that filled him with inspiration for his poem, he finds that "even sometimes the very / Words I would lose en route spawned duplications / Stretching as far as sight" [91.1].) Not representation but invention—or more precisely reinvention—becomes the overt goal toward which words are directed. Here are some simple examples of what I mean.

Even in conventional poetic usage, rhyme is a procedure that is independent of the aims of representation (although it need not disrupt them): the duplication of sounds occurs for its own sake and needs no further justification. We have already noticed how in *The Duplications* rhyme can take absolute precedence over reason to determine events and even the presence of particular characters (there are many so created, beginning with E. McTizzy born from "busy," Dr. McSnakes from "shakes," Ellen Gudge from "grudge").

The usual naming function of language is reversed; now, it is realities that are assigned to names.

Another kind of duplicating power can be discovered in single words by exposing second meanings. Consider the effect in these lines of "pinking" in the wake of Lisa's sunburn:

> I see the dawn
>
>> Growing more quickly than the flash of red
>> Upon the back of Lisa who has lain
>> Four hours naked in the sand instead
>> Of going to the store at Fifth and Main
>> To buy some pinking scissors as she said
>> That she was going to do, wherefore her pain.   (88.3)

The passage furnishes us with another kind of example of nonrepresentational invention. The simile illustrating the dawn is carried way beyond any criterion of vividness. The visual comparison is submerged as it expands into apparent irrelevancy. And just as the comparison with the "patient etherized" obliterates the sunset at the opening of "The Love Song of J. Alfred Prufrock" but defines the speaker of the monologue, Lisa in her nakedness becomes not an image of the dawn but yet another apt if unreasonable duplication of sexual desire. Metaphor has been subverted from its explanatory prosaic function to become the recreator of a reality it does not name.

An earlier instance of simile demonstrates a comparable effect, achieved in this case through compression rather than expansion. It occurs in the description of the "giant earth- or sea-quake?" that is devastating Samos after Huddel's sacrilegious act:

> [It] smote the Samian robber in his cave
> And threw the Samian shepherd from his mount
> And shot a thousand dead up from the grave
> And broke more water jars than I can count;
> And, while the island cracked, a tidal wave
> Like a huge copy of *The Sacred Fount*

Smashed everything in sight and then retreated,
Leaving old Samos totally depleted.   (38. 1)

The comparison with *The Sacred Fount* at first looks like another wacky triumph of rhyme. There is more to it than that. Waves move in succession
like the turned pages of a book; a fountain or spring is very different from
the sea, but both are water. Why not compare a tidal wave to a book, when
this tidal wave depends for its existence on the book we're reading? The
undisguised imitation of Byron in the preceding lines has reminded us that
we are in a world determined entirely by poetic language: water here is all
words. Finally, James's novel concerns the passionate investigations of a
narrator smitten with a lust for knowledge: what he relates, it turns out,
may be no more than a duplication of reality created by his own desire. . . .
So here, as in the case of Lisa, an extravagant simile ultimately brings us
back to one of the poem's central themes.

    We are now in a better position to consider the claims the author makes
on behalf of poetry. Essentially, they are to be found in the long interpolation that starts the second part of the poem (78–95). Here the author speaks
about the difficulty of resuming a work that has lain abandoned for two
years; relates nostalgically the life he had led while he was beginning *The
Duplications*—he was staying in Kinsale on the Irish coast with his friends
Homer and Betty Brown; and discusses quite unsystematically the genesis
of *The Duplications* and the nature of poetry.

    These pages offer something of a relief after the unrelenting zaniness of
the fictional narratives and provide a more open, more comfortable context
for their resumption. Although it is the reflections on poetry that most concern us here it is worth pointing out that the author's life in Ireland is itself
presented as a kind of duplication. His friends the Browns are for the writer
a "home away from home," a second family: a mother, a father, and—the
only other occupant besides himself—their daughter, Katherine. At the same
time, we learn that *The Duplications* was born at least in part of desire. The
poet says that now, years later, his mind will be "less leaping / Than when I
saw you last when I was sleeping / And saw you blossom for me every

night" (79.3 f.). This unidentified "you" was present to the poet as a dream of desire ("But I've stopped dreaming of you / In that particular way, which made me wild" [80.1 f.]), and, elsewhere in the house, Betty Brown was dispensing motherly care. While the writer worked on his poem in a room upstairs, she "diced, sliced, and carved and sieved in / The kitchen which was under it." In the neighboring upstairs room was Katherine, "whom her mother / Would sing to sleep two times a day or once, / Depending if she was in a napping period" (86.2 f.). And it is precisely after evoking this double image of woman as the inaccessible object of desire and the tender, providing mother that the author writes (remembering the nonnapping baby's cries):

> I've always thought I should be more forgiving
> And not be seized by the desire to kill
> When someone interrupts me at my knitting
> Of words together, but I'm that way still.
> I've not, however, murdered anyone,
> I swear, as I am Stuart and Lillian's son.   (87.1)

Thus in the midst of comfortable domesticity are evoked, and clinched with a propitiatory oath, the interwoven strands of desire, death, and the mother that so entwine the fictional narratives.[2]

It could hardly be otherwise. To this poet, poetry is never imagined as an escape from desire and its consequences: poetry *is* desire. He describes himself as "burning / To carry on this discourse with my head / The world calls poetry and I call yearning . . ." (85.3). The equation is made explicit. He can have no hope of avoiding death. (Is the interruption of the poem its death, its resumption a rebirth?) Writing poetry, however, leads beyond "death" to the satisfactions of understanding and even of mastering the fate to which we are condemned. Poetry, we are told, is "a fabric to deceive and undeceive" (79.2). Through it we can discover "the sole true story of man's secret mind" (91.2). It can "change / What seems disparate into what alone / Can make us happy: re-possession" (94.1). The three statements can be taken together as one: humanity's true story is hidden by the incapacity of ordinary language to tell it, and only the deliberately "false" duplications of poetry can reveal it and so make it available to repossession.

How this actually happens is something of a mystery, and the author of *The Duplications* leaves the mystery unexplained. Doing otherwise would mean subverting the poem. He must, after all, remain the absent creator, even in the Irish interpolation, which for all we know may be as fictitious as the rest of the poem. Even if it isn't, neither the more personal "I" he assumes in it nor the confession of certain events in his life should be read as signifying more than the author pointing to the mask he has chosen to wear. The mask has its own necessary mystery, and this may be part of the mystery of how poetry accomplishes the transformations the author claims for it.

The mystery is not explained, but it is not concealed, either; and here we discover a more interesting reason for the lack of explanation. Towards the end of the Irish section, the author asks himself how the life he had then lived might be related to his poem: "There were, doubtless, certain real connections / Of other kinds between my life and work . . . / Some ways in which cool Kinsale did concur / With Aqua, but I don't know what they were" (92.2). And later, at the very end of the poem, he admits "I've no knowledge of transfinite life-death distance, / So I shall leave them, without more insistence . . ." (153.3). Since *The Duplications* has been largely about travels in "life-death distance," this admission of ignorance is striking.

The mystery is not explained because the poet does not know its solution, or perhaps because he knows that a true mystery has no solution. The "them" he leaves in the last quotation are the several characters en route to the feast of reunion and reconciliation organized by Nyog Papendes. By this time they, and we, are high in the clouds—deep, that is, inside the world of duplications. The poet is saying in effect that he does not know how we got there. But perhaps there is no way he could, if knowledge is only possible *within* that world beyond reason, beyond "death."

No matter how one does reach the world of poetic duplications, it is certainly worth getting to. When Huddel and Aqua discover their first sky-vegetable patch in the clouds, they are pervaded with a "sweet pure grandeur" for which anyone on earth would gladly abandon wealth and success

(76.1). When he rises into the sky, Papend finds himself "confused, inspired":

> He goes on thinking, which, on such occasions
> i.e. when one is in convulsive flight
> Away from what one knows and with sensations
> That mix the energy of day and night
> May bring about the birth of those creations
> All kinds of artists treasure, and they're right . . .   (152.1)

He is filled with "the confidence and lack of fear of death . . . That power gives, like that of innocence . . ." "Strange new energies became unfastened" in him, and he sees his life as he had never been able to see it on earth, conceiving of a new Venice greater than the one he built.

Curiously, when these grand revelations come to Papend, he may actually be asleep: "I cannot guarantee his state was waking / But he was wakeful in its dreamy spaces." We may then deduce that the world of poetic duplications is one of dream, as well as of desire and death. . . . Papend's experience confirms the notion that this second world of dream is the best and perhaps only place in which to apprehend and recreate our earthly reality.

But Papend may not necessarily be sleeping, or only sleeping, because he is dead or very close to death (v. 149.3); and so presumably are the others who like him are making their way at the poem's end to Nyog Papendes's feast: Clarabelle, Amos Frothingham, Huddel, Aqua, Pluto, and even Elizabeth Gedall. How could they not have died when the yearning that is poetry has brought them here? They are furthermore entering the realm of their own desires, going to "where what they know of things will be increased" (147.3), "to where they feel it is they're wanted" (154.1). They are doomed; and what of it? In this dream duplication of earth, the veil of duplicity will be cast aside and things be shown as they are—something that is revealed to Papend as a perception of desire innocently repossessed:

> Then into fading, then more faded blue,
> Until all colors are completely gone
> And everything a quite light light-white hue
> Like petticoats stretched out upon a lawn

> To dry on Easter morning, when the Shoe,
> Which children think the Rabbit has put on,
> Has left its tracks and also precious eggs
> To which the children run on trembling legs
>
> And cry, "Why are there petticoats out here?"
> In fact, there aren't. It was the mere appearance
> Of petticoats, was frost, which, in the clear-
> Er later morning sky is gone, as Terence
> Was gone from consciousness, as from the beer
> The foam is gone, as from the throne room Clarence.
> And Papend goes on sailing through their ether
> Where clouds, air, everything he sees, is see-through.
>
> (151.2 f.)

Desire repossessed: is anything else more desirable? Whatever the case, it seems improbable that the heavenly travelers will find anything else to enjoy, since there is no certainty that they will reach their destination: "I wonder if they ever will arrive?" (153.3). In fact, they have already arrived, although not at the feast of Nyog, "the Lord of Sad and Happy Endings." What they have reached is their desire: the perfect consummation of desire is its own duplication. We leave them journeying through the sky in ever-lasting flight. This is a last duplicity on the author's part.

Or next-to-last. Much earlier in the poem, during the Irish interpolation, there is a long passage about the dawn and early morning—it begins with the simile of Lisa pinking. The passage associates daybreak with poetic creation and introduces the reflections on poetry that we discussed. Now, in the very last lines of *The Duplications*, we read that Nyog Papendes's guests

> . . . all, soaring in their flight,
> Are fading fast, or covered by the awning,
> Which everyone can see, of early morning.-   (154.1)

They are, in other words, hidden by what inspired their existence: they disappear from our view beyond an oxymoron that tells us that our sight is darkened not merely by light, but by the light of revelation itself.

NOTES

1. That is, page 23, stanza 2, of the original edition (New York: Random House, 1977).
2. No sooner have the narratives resumed than these three themes are again sounded together with, as here, the vengeful child appearing as the possible agent of death (cf. No-Shu's story, 104-105). After Herman Clover, the lecherous snake, attacks Alma Rat, Pemmistrek and Early Ann are almost run over:

> My God! It must be smart
> To find a way to be as the first man was,
> Adam, I mean, exempt from, in the soft spring,
> Attack from others, either strange or offspring!
>
> But not since then, I think, has any managed
> To have complete protection. Even Adam
> Was by his earthly consort disadvantaged
> When she brought him an apple. Thank you, Madam.
> Oh well, all right! Then boom! Boom, doom, and damaged,
> We have not yet recovered from that datum
> (If it is true, which cannot be gone into) . . .   (102.1 f.)

WE FOR ONE:

AN INTRODUCTION TO JOSEPH MCELROY'S *WOMEN AND MEN*

1

W*omen and Men* is a simple book and all of one piece. The simplicity sometimes leaves us bewildered, the unity proliferates into an abundance that threatens to leap all bounds. But what happens, again and again, is clear and single.

When I began reading the book, I understood the title as a set of two elements: at the end, as a set of one; as "There are women, and there are men," at the start, as "We are women-and-men" at the end. The change meant my evolving not from "There are" to "I am" but to "We are." The "We are" in the final "We are women-and-men" includes "I am," but long before, "I" had been gently and inexorably co-opted into a community called "we." "We for one . . ." a passage casually remarks, suggesting that the distinction between "I" and "others" is, at least in this book, an inaccurate one.

The shifts from women and men to women-and-men, from I to we, are not wishful or sentimental or theoretical. They are the result of a generalized reduction and destruction of dualities, separations, distinctions, hierarchies: in history, in physics, in ethics, in the uses of language and literature. The destruction takes place not through assertion or argument, although there is plenty of entertaining encouragement, but through reading itself: a new reading of reality is made available as an effect of reading the text of the book. I know that this cannot be clear, but I must say it anyway. Here is an example of what I mean. It comes at the end of an account of an opera singer who, in order to lose weight, has recently ingurgitated a tapeworm:

> . . . we like her for herself if there were time, and not just for her tape-worm, its lighted path, thoughtlike through embedded night, its own tunnel or *"worm*hole" (to be quite as blunt as the obstacle out its far end). Obstacle? But why would the tapeworm track take us anywhere if it is in the diva's beloved body? Is there an answer for us as we seek another pause?
>
> A cuffless trouser. Whose? All together we don't yet know but the knowledge is loose in us—and the heel of a shoe half off a slender plat-form, call it a running board, hear the noise, and hear that backfire.
>
> Whose? Who's looking at a photograph?—the noise is of a male, breathing; not our communal breath and yet of us, and we're breathless spun upon the instant through a far end of what we already remember we were already accepting as our own diva's internalized tapeworm but in us turns waste compaction into time's momentary tunnel; but some-one is breathing for sure. (19)[1]

The man on the running board is the father, caught at a crucial moment of his life, of James Mayn, one of the central characters in the book and prob-ably the "someone breathing." Much could be said about the passage, whose exuberance and density calls out for extended interpretation, but the one point to be made now is that the familiar discreteness of time, place, and continuity are shattered at the moment "we" are propelled (I? you? and the tapeworm?) from a soprano's rear end into an altogether different story. And hear that backfire!

2

"We": could "we" really include a tapeworm? Perhaps. After all, we later hear this worm described as "angelic" (168), and in *Women and Men* so-called angels often appear in the same passages that "we" do. These angels are associated with "our" knowing and learning (note the worm's "lighted path, thoughtlike"); and the association of angels with "us" is so constant that at times it seems likely that we are these angels (e.g., "we . . . can't help being angels" [338]); but this is not always or entirely the case. At first angels are "heard to be speculating in us" (9) and "sometimes we don't really know what they are" (10). At about the same time another question is raised: "this 'we' that we have heard. What is it?" (11). Thus we expect, in the course of our reading, to learn both what angels and "we" are, and the progress of our learning leads us towards the event of "us" *becoming* angels, or our ever clearer awareness that "we" are angels.

These angels manifest themselves first as a speaking in us and later as a speaking between us. At this point it seems almost as if "we" were inside *them:*

> You don't go in for that type of thing, yet you are so much a part of other voices that you can't hear them *telling* you you're one type or another, you almost don't *hear* voices. You are spoken. Like voices that hear *you*. It's new—did something in you go to pieces light years ago? (56)

It is worth pointing out that in this passage the you is singular (James Mayn, in fact), while the voices are plural. At another point the fusion of singular-plural is described the other way round: "Inner speech must needs get what it came for. So we relations angel or not will single her out: Grace Kimball" (159), where the plural/singular opposition is reinforced by the verb "single," in turn exploded in the following paragraph in an account of Grace's emphatically plural roles with her ex-husband (lover, sister, pardner, priestess, daughter . . .).

By the time we are halfway through the book and the many apparently disparate stories with their numerous characters have intricated themselves with one another, our exposure to the presences and practices of these angels has grown enough for their multiple-oneness to be realized, to be recognized, and that so thoroughly that we, as "we," can even relinquish our physical singularities:

We and our multiples had looked into the incarnations we had so needed and curved for and found; but once in them we some of us or parts or branches felt these bloodstreams and fibers of true feeling . . . to be bodies we for one had already been and left. And this was a sensation so unlike leaving one another that we or a breathing majority proved what we then saw we had known already, that we had no angels keeping our curve just and our histories and our fluid breaths pure of interruption— for we *were* those angels and being so we must become ourselves for- ever, which meant losing those incarnations in order to guard the curve of consciousness, even though, if not pure gold. (435–36)

"We" have become angels and done so in part by following the "curve" of learning, which means being able to "prove" and "see" and "know." Be- coming angels has meant learning what knowing is. This is simplified ulti- mately into: "We had learned we were a language" (1113), but by the time this statement occurs so much else has happened that we had best post- pone considering the nature of knowledge in *Women and Men* until later.

Meanwhile, what about "us"? Are "we" all and only angels? What about that tapeworm? and the diva? and, especially, James Mayn?

3

In the preceding pages, my difficulty in consistently maintaining quotation marks around "we" and "us" indicates a disposition on my part that I had best acknowledge. Early in my reading of *Women and Men*—certainly before the end of the second chapter—I had joined whatever community I thought was being opened to me for membership. At that moment, who else did I imagine was incorporated in the "we" of which I now felt a part?

Among the many characters of the novel—122 by my reckoning, exclud- ing merely mentioned names—none can be identified as a narrative "I." (Read- ers, however, are represented from time to time by someone called the in- quisitor or interrogator, someone who bobs into the flow of events to ques- tion or comment and does so with a timeliness that makes the voice a listen- ing cousin to the two readers in Calvino's *If on a Winter's Night a Traveler*.) We surmise that the author is variously present in several of the characters. There is for instance an elder meteorologist who plots the relationship between weather and (among other things) coastlines; and weather throughout the book is presented to us as a non-symbolic representation of the irregularity and restlessness of knowledge:

> ... the configuration equation of the coast itself which the elder meteorologist worked out ... felt like a Canadian sine curve worked out for the coast-like pattern path taken by our own neurons retrieving memories yet sensing always that, traveler, there are not paths, paths are made by walking. .... (346)

There is the middle-aged James Mayn, perhaps the most nearly central "consciousness" of anybody (except us), who thinks he never dreams, whose intuition is that he has come to the present from the future, so that he looks through the present *towards* the past. There is the young Larry Shearson, the student who learns about and half invents "obstacle geometry" and other useful ways of thinking about reality (for instance, the rotation of geometrical figures in space and time). We might say that such figures represent the author not as likenesses but as envoys, concerned as they are with the processes of discovery and knowing that are the heart of the book.

The elder meteorologist and Larry belong to what may be called the James Mayn cluster of characters. Another cluster can be associated with Grace Kimball, a super-feminist consciousness-raising teacher so goddess-like in her comprehensive scope that the circumstances of our first encounter with her—she is elaborately masturbating on the "great uninterrupted carpet in her fully mirrored Body Room" (100)—seem as delightful as they are surprising and in no way inappropriate to the soaring, nutty wisdom of her long meditation. Still another cluster assembles people operatic or Chilean around Luisa the Chilean diva, she of the tapeworm. There is a more mysterious and looser group connected with the downtown store, where Señora Wang tells fortunes, and with the handicapped-messenger service (whose founder, Jimmy Banks, I think I like best among the many likeable characters). A cluster centered in the southwest includes the Navajo Prince and the Anasazi healer. Finally, we must mention Foley, imprisoned and so technically detached from any cluster but in fact in communication with James Mayn and the Chileans and, in any case, convinced of the unlimited possibilities of communication between human beings by his theory of the "colloidal unconscious," "the endless community of minds" (690).

When we read Foley's account of his "naive" theory, we are over halfway through the book. By then we are prepared to find it more than a little convincing. Not only have members of the various clusters established indirect and direct links between them and turned up repeatedly in each other's stories, but a less traditional kind of overlap has begun subverting our notion of characters as discrete units. Names, for one, are used in a way not always conducive to keeping the members of the huge cast clear in our minds.

A nice game can be played speculating why characters in *Women and Men* have their particular names. Many names—who knows, all?—can be read as pocket descriptions or emblems. James Mayn is the naym of the main man who may; he also sports the author's initials. Larry Shearson's a sheer son. Mayga and Mina, Chilean women come to America at different times and places, suggest major and minor. The first name of the heavenly Grace Kimball is obvious enough, but Kimball? "Can ball"? It's only a game to play and should not be made into more than that: while this book abounds in such decodable details, it would be a sin against the Holy Ghost to stop or even slow down its high cruising speed with gratuitous acts of cryptoanalysis.

Other aspects of the names in *Women and Men*, however, are noticed without our slowing down. We meet Sue early in the book[2] then again a little later but without really recognizing her; eventually we deduce (the possibility is barely alluded to) that there must be two Sues. One of the Sues feels an affinity to the high priestess Norma in the opera of that name: the diva Luisa sings *Norma;* there is a real (as it were) Norma; there is a Sarah who, rather like Sue, recalls the operatic Norma (196). This Sarah, James Mayn's mother, does not exclude the existence of a Sara (actually one of the Sues), nor the desire of James Mayn's daughter to be called Sara, nor the appearance of another daughter Sarah, of bike-learning age (783 ff.).

James Mayn meets a Dina West from Albuquerque; Luisa and other Chileans worry about DINA, the Chilean secret police. On page 1080, that is, almost at the end of the book, a second woman named Amy appears for the first time. On the same page, a Chilean naval officer whom we have come to know rather well is finally named: de Talca (is he about to take a powder?). Long before this, we have had no trouble recognizing the loathsome Spence in the guise of Ray Santee (aka Santee Sioux).

Names apparently do not—at least not necessarily—circumscribe singular identities; or perhaps whatever identity exists is not to be localized in a name. (Larry Shearson, wondering about "simultaneous reincarnation," "went on savoring the dream of the names, savoring even some reach within the nest of them to a next he didn't quite get his head around . . ." [1071].) And the characters are like their names: they have a hard time staying inside the heads and skins assigned them. Foley writes Mayn: ". . . In your head it's mainly me I hear talking (smile)" (722). Grace Kimball muses: "People . . . disappeared into people. Were they people? Someone arrived in her, but ancient or future, who knew?" (145). (The someone arriving in her is James Mayn, whom she never meets.) Because the author's pages, paragraphs, and sentences stretch to enfold places several thousand miles and times a hundred years apart, people and their actions are collated with each other and eventually fused. (This demonstrates what Larry has learned about rotation: shifted ninety degrees, parallel becomes equal: ‖ to =.) The elder meteorologist becomes "the same" as the Hermit-Inventor of New York of the previous century and the Anasazi healer (aet. ±500) of the southwest. Indian blood joins east to west, in Grace and Spence for instance. Jim Mayn is not only Grace Kimball—"oh that's crap, all that regret crap, say James Mayn and Grace Kimball in unison at a distance so that curiously they hear each other but don't know it . . ." (618-19)—according to his grandmother, who has told him their stories, he "can be both the Anasazi *and* Hermit" (852). This grandmother is "doubled as Margaret and the Eastern Princess" (1124), and she almost turns into someone else's grandmother as well when Jim's girlfriend Jean mentions her in place of her own. And, in addition, furthermore, and anyhow, years before the Anasazi healer was transformed a "noctilucent cloud," the Eastern Princess became a "sun-drenched cloud" (193) (or perhaps a mist, 416), both having assumed these guises for comparable reasons. In time, we can't help wondering who isn't turning into someone else.

James Mayn, convinced he has come to the present from the future, remembers from that future an unusual method of space travel (cum population control) that niftily parabolizes the kind of identity-fusions suggested by these other happenings:

> Meanwhile, decades later in the near future two persons stand upon a metal plate waiting to be elsewhere. And sure enough, behind them more twos wait their turn to step onto the plate and be transferred from sight. What becomes of these people? The plate is a type of transformer plate . . . the people on the plate are bound for a frontier colony out in Earth-Moon space; and while it feels like home it is uniquely economy-oriented in that, unknown as yet to these pioneers, they wind up on arrival one person, not the original two. But what does that feel like? Is this Experience again? What happens to their clothes? (45–46)

Transferred "by frequency into one" (92), the two arrive in a "libration space settlement" (75), a libration point being one in balance between (or oscillating between) the gravitational pulls of earth and moon. Libration: sleepy Jean, to whom (with us) James Mayn gives his account, hears: "Libration, vuhbration" (79). Staring at the word, we may aptly add a liberating e—aptly, because libration "space towns" are free of a number of things, such as weather (590) and divorce (625). The new state sounds satisfying:

> . . . many of these privileged settlers who've been compacted each one out of two original Earth persons (in most cases acquainted to start with) reported an unsettled sense of lasting content on arrival, later thought . . . to have been due to the mythically rich feeling due in turn to the indubitable *source* of each individual . . . of nothing *but* individuals. . . . The two projecting bodies who are presently to be one elsewhere are thronged with more radiance than their God-given cells know what to do with in all their glaring boundaries like graphed skin straining to see a future, while an old-style woman or man now and then sent out like

Mayn to report feels extra mortal next to these *colons* compacted by an
economy so simple its more question than solution. . . . (890-91)

A benign vision: one that, outside the parable, touches in various modes
most of the fluctuating-merging characters that people this book, among whom
"we" are happy to find ourselves, hoping that "they" are part of the us to
which I early on decided to belong: characters varying from agents of Pinochet
to politically inspiring teachers but none failing to excite our sympathy, none
of them ultimately blameworthy.

(Except for Spence, who is beyond the pale: a nosy creep, a paid spy,
probably a hired murderer, beyond anybody's sympathy or forgiveness. . . .)

Eventually we learn that the benign vision was produced by James Mayn's
fantasy—a "miracle witnessed by a ruddy-tan daydreaming adolescent lying bemused on his slightly sagging bed in an upstairs room of a New Jersey
house. . . ." (1118). We cannot help wondering if he did not dream the rest
of what happens in *Women and Men,* if it isn't his dream that gives the profusion of the book its unity. But, if that is the case, who has been all the
while daydreaming James Mayn, if not us?

4

—all we have to go on is the subject's tic-like tendency to stammer
forth nought *but* D.T's whose ambiguity now seems to welcome more
and more of punishment's teaching—
—Wham! we did it that time to ourself, we stick indiscriminately to
the same rules as we do others, here to have our delirium tremens and
in the same breath render from Romance language "double tenders."
(329)

No less than names, words take on prolific ambiguity in *Women and Men:*
double entendres abound for eye, ear, and mind, all of them breaking down
categories and distinctions and uniting the disparate. There are, of course,
puns, sometimes outrageous, such as those deriving from the *Hamlet* continuity ("New Yorick" [1175]), and, in a reference to unlikely densities of

prostitution ". . . than is dreamed of in your whore-ratio" [422]), some-times simply unsettling (such as the linking of "moral" with "femoral" or the use of "bisons" to mean two connected sons), never gratuitous. Usu-ally the proliferation of senses attached to words and moving *between* words is effected less conspicuously, rather in a sustained, discreet way that fi-nally colors the surface of the whole book. It is as though language were basically like the Colt or possibly two Colt pistols that figure in the Mayn family's past, making us see double: ". . . the ancient Anasazi . . . because her appearance at the top of the ladder caused the pistol in question to throw two shadows, had seen two moons. . ." (401). To which we should add another view of this event: "The Hermit-Inventor of New York asked if the Double Moon that had fallen upon the pistol Mena had brought to this cell had turned it into two pistols or only roused rumors of two *origins* for *one*" (829).

The Colt pistols are of course revolvers. To revolve is to rotate, as in the geometrical rotation Larry Shearson is studying. This rotation is a form of multiplication; the Colt multiplies or is perhaps a multiplier. At another appearance of the Colt pistol, James Mayn finds himself inside its barrel looking out the hole at its end. The view compellingly recalls the diva's wormhole, and so the revolver is connected to another set of interlinked words and events: the tapeworm and its track, echoed in one of Grace Kimball's prime research tools, her tape recorder (and how many tracks does it have?); the keyhole through which James Mayn spies on his mother and kid brother, at one point designated "the wormhole" (196) and so jus-tifying the familiarity of the Colt barrel; the colon (also appearing in French in an earlier quotation: *colons*, or settlers), the diva's, of course, also referred to as "wind tunnel" and so broaching the theme of wind and its many ramifications, such as breath, as in the "breathing wind" Mayn listens to (197), as well as to the theme of the void, as in the verb "to void," which then leads back to Grace Kimball and her therapeutic enemas, the void being as well the often encountered gap—an essential obstacle-passage on the path of learning. . . .

We could extend this chain back and forth across the expanse of the book, but the point should be already clear: as names of things, words cannot be localized. They indicate things in addition to those they name; things attract names not properly theirs. Early on (10), we notice this not normal and not so unusual state of things in a little device that adds its chime to the text's flowing discourse with irregular frequency: a word will be followed by a short parenthesis suggesting an alternative to it: ". . . and form another angle, for future reference (read *residence*) . . ." (10). Later the device attains a climax of sorts as the conclusion of a paragraph full of information and wordplay: ". . . a dozen other questions negotiating the passage of what we might have known we had in us. *Passage?* (read *wormhole,* read *wind-tunnel,* read *zero gravity chamber,* read *time baffle* . . .)" (184). The use of language in *Women and Men* makes us sense that behind words other words lie in wait, that any word may lead us to all other words.

The ambiguous nature of words is shared by what they designate. In the manner of characters, the objects, actions, and continuities that words designate tend to lose their exclusive properties, overlap with each other, or merge, although the merging is not so much with each other as into an idea that subsumes them, the way the generic "hole" gathers in *wormhole, gun barrel, keyhole.* Thus towards the end of the book the Navajo Prince and the Anasazi healer, in spite of notable differences in age and altitude (several hundred years and several thousand feet), travel across the continent "as one." The generic idea here is not simultaneity but something like "going east to learn a lesson." The book could be dis- and re-assembled listing these more than parallel and less than identical occurrences—something neither we nor I feel like doing. Here are two short lists of quotations representing instances of what I mean.

1.
The need to go away but the discovery that we can go away by staying and being left. (McKenna on Foley, 83)

. . . Kimball left her husband Lou yet *he* was the one who *went:* is not this like the mother long ago who sent her son away and yet left him with the impression that it was *she* who'd left . . . (James Mayn's mother, 189)

[Sue—the one who wants to be called Sarah—has left her own son Larry, and it is he who has moved away.] (378-79)

Away From Home All The Time. (said of James Mayn, and one of his wife's reasons for leaving him, 1015)

2.
Yet we didn't need to go outside the home to change, we had a set here and one in the next room where a child is doing his homework and some of it on the screen, so we have dual screens if we can go back and forth between the rooms fast enough. (Larry Shearson, 319)

. . . between two dimly lighted silent porch fronts he himself had no alternative parentage. . . . (James Mayn, running from his parents' to his grandparents' house and back, 443)

Both (1) and (2) assume many more guises. Sometimes, however, the convergence of elements can happen only once, with extraordinary effect. For example, we know that James Mayn's mother is supposed to have killed herself, but we do not expect to hear his daughter say to him:

"O.K., that's a good coincidence, but . . . Daddy—you know every-thing—when your grandmother committed suicide—"
"What!"

He had never mentioned this, not even to us. We are informed after 904 pages and know—as this pair, this so emphatically different mother and daughter (*and* mother) are reunited as suicides—that many of our suppositions have tacitly crashed. And this is by no means the last word on the subject.

5

Rotating the revolver led us to the words "breath," "wind," and "void." These words, which are apparent transparencies, are not transparent appearances.

If we look at them, we can delve into an important part of what happens in *Women and Men*.

When we are expelled from the wormhole or wind-tunnel into the scene of James Mayn's father meeting his mother, we are told: "Someone is breathing for sure" (19). Aside from our own gasps, who might this be?

Five chapter headings contain the word "breather": from "BETWEEN US: A BREATHER AT THE BEGINNING" through "BETWEEN HISTORIES: BREATHERS THICK AND FAST" to "BETWEEN US: A BREATHER TOWARD THE END." The chapters themselves have been referred to by critics as "breathers," and while this is not false, the word means something besides that. (And not, most of the time, what it means in the expression "taking a breather.")

In the case of the first breather chapter, for instance, the someone referred to in "someone is breathing" is soon identified as the "breather Jim Mayn," who, while "hardly able to observe the event has been born—that's it" (20)—hardly a surprise insofar as the meeting of his parents provided the premise necessary for that event. This discovery has two initial consequences. It changes the meaning of the chapter heading or, more accurately, extends it to include the notion "Between us, someone in particular"; and even in this early stage of our experience of "us" (where one part of "us" may still conceivably refer to an author existing somewhere else), "between us" quickly makes more sense as "among us" or "uniting us" than as "separating us." The bond implied soon is given a name: James Mayn. Next, the identification of the breather links breath early on with birth, that is, with our common humanity. (Birth-breath: the words even share a common linguistic cousin in "brood," as in "us chickens.")

Heaved out of divine darkness into the light of James Mayn's history, are we born along with him? Maybe. The novel, in any case, has come into being with another birth, the enthrallingly depicted one of the book's opening yes opening pages. The first words of the book describe not only the woman in travail but us starting (*and* not starting) off on our readerly trip: "After all she was not so sure what had happened, or when it had started. Which was probably not a correct state to be in . . ." (3).

"What is in others yet has others in it?" (614) is a riddle given to the diva Luisa, one that sticks in her mind. Two answers that might have come to her, since she is a singer much attended to by her lover, are music, a penis. What I-in-us thought of (is that another answer?) was the air we breathe. We are all of us born breathers, and not only inside this book (is the book another answer?). And what, in addition to being in the air we breathe and having it inside us, do we notably do with it? We hang sounds on it and articulate them into cries and words—"breath cutting life into words, a sentence into meanings" (27). So *language* might also answer the riddle. "A sentence into meaning": therefore "to breathe is to feel, perchance to think . . ." (327), something close to most if not all the humanity we inherit when we are born. It is also what we keep on becoming:

> Take some time for yourself you know (—A breather?—) That's the ticket. . . .
> But breathers aren't what they—*or* we—used to be: once marginal, the breather came to take up major space like a friend in need whom you have to listen to for weeks of personal crisis: once space, a breather has become a person like turning into yourself. . . . (663)

Breath can also become a "breathing wind," sometimes literally, as in the stunning recapitulation of a chapter ending about James Mayn and his mother. The recapitulation occurs at such an interval that we both forget and remember the original passage, which reads:

> Wind and weather a secret familiar cover, as we said, for the powers that be, and wind and weather a sandman's cover also for a mother who went away where salt waves rolled and eyelashed upon a beach but who then, as a future absence, brought herself close inside her offspring, furnishing a gap. And through this gap a future would always come back, as she did not: except a breath that came firm and steady, expelling, drawing back, the night, the day, human, animal, those who are known and those who are also known. (45)

And the recapitulation:

And so the weather and the sea made a secret familiar cover for the powers that be. . . .

And through this gap a future would always come, as she did not: except a breathing wind that came firm and steady, expelling, drawing back, the night, the day. And hearing this wind, her long-lost son Jim found obstacles for it. (197)

"In other words" the wind that disappears from the first sentence reappears linked to "breath" in the next-to-last.

Chiefly but not solely, wind is the breath of weather. The word itself is rotated through its other breathlike senses: a runner's wind, the legendary long-windedness of the Senate, the wind in the divas wind-tunnel (perhaps in part a childlike application to the notion of breath of the saying "What goes in one end comes out the other"). But chiefly, wind refers to weather. In this respect there are things to note about it, for later reference. Wind is curved, as Jim's mother once pointed out: "'She said the wind would just go straight ahead, straight out in a line, except the world is always turning . . .'" (577). Furthermore, the "world" not only keeps wind curving around it but presents it with its greatest obstacle: "the Earth . . . was after all, Mayn saw for the first time, always one prime boundary to winds . . ." (827). Bound to and by earth, wind becomes a medium for reading its "messages."

James Mayn draws for his wife Joy a wind rose, an eightpointed compass figure whose lines by their length and thickness show the frequency and intensity of winds. He explains, "'The wind rose shows the horizontal motion of the atmosphere. Now you know all I know'" (1014). Not quite: he knows, for instance, about the Anasazi healer's west-east weatherlike drift, about that journey's counterparts in the travels of Margaret and the Navajo Prince, even in his own return to New York from New Mexico. (And we know that Grace Kimball too has come east.) He knows, certainly, since he ascribed the name, that his family's New Jersey home town of Maplewood is called in his story Windrow—a most *singular* wind rose. And as from "wind rose" to "Windrow," so from "windrow" to "window": as in T.W., or "trace window," the name of a late-appearing character who can detect a certain kind of radioactivity; as in another window, a grave so designated in the Mayn family plot where T.W. catches emanations, even though the grave is supposedly empty. . . .

"Wind and weather a secret familiar cover for the powers that be. . . ." In an earlier quotation (346) we learned that the weather-forming meanders of a coastline are analogous to our memory-retrieving systems. Elsewhere mention is made of "the messages of Earth told in the apparent motions of storm mass and dry cloud from mountain to mountain or the transparency of an aborted fetus" (801). The Hermit-Inventor and the Anasazi healer discuss "the weather of presence and the weather of absence, which do not quite parallel the division between the weather from earth and the weather from beyond, the weather from the body, the weather from almost nowhere, weather of going and weather of arriving . . ." (685). Weather is a medium of revelation, providing in its own events masks and analogies of other events; a medium for discovery, as the Anasazi healer suggests to a visitor: "We create our weathers partly then to observe them, this, so that there will be something in front of us . . ." (816). Weather provides the "stuff" of what is happening, so that we can begin to be aware of it: "Hear us all falling toward the horizon. It's the wind the other side of an obstacle that draws us toward it. But the wind is our wind as was the obstacle we heard only as a prelude to whatever lay beyond" (10). Past the obstacle (whatever it may be—Earth itself), towards the horizon, the wind draws us in a curve of learning:

> . . .wind and weather a sandman's cover also for a mother who went away where salt waves rolled and eye-lashed upon a beach but who then, as a future absence, brought herself close inside her offspring, furnishing a gap. And through this gap a future would always come, as she did not: except a breath that came firm and steady. . . . And hearing this wind, her long-lost son Jim found obstacles for it. (43;197)

The obstacles and the gap form one weather-wise process of awareness and liveliness. The gap is more often referred to as the more vacant "void" (also as "power vacuum" or "power vac," as in "There's no power without the vac . . ." [25]). Since the gap, void, or power vac is an absence and empti-ness, defining what it may be is best undertaken lightheartedly, as Grace Kimball at one point does:

> Well, everyone knows about the void. . . . She would have reached into the void for her sketchbook to record "The Void is the nothing you may assume about your future" and "The Void is Divinity—which is the shape of that space that asks change of me and gives room for it." . . . "The Void is the phone's ring now going on and on for the moment," which it did because she had not activated Call Forwarding, which was "The Void when it's 'On' and yet you're 'In'. . . ." (946)

The void allows something to come into being that wasn't there before, and in this sense it resembles birth or, more precisely, giving birth. Of the mother whose labor we accompany at the start of the book we learn:

> Pain all in her back worked free of her at the end, dropping away into a void below, and it could almost not be recalled. . . .
> And she was in that gap there in the middle which was still an empty gap no matter how much of her was in it, she was what was in that gap in the middle, but she was there just for a moment. . . . (3,6)

"Just for a moment": but time enough to remember, if that is what she does. "Later she was encouraged to recall it all. As if she did" (4). And a few pages farther on, as "we" make our entry: "We already remember what's been going on. . . . Already remember what's been here with us so long we had the time to see but now seem to have been waiting to remember. For who are we not to? Yet give ourselves permission also to forget" (8–9). Forgetting matters: in a way, it *is* the gap in our illusion of knowing, the void that makes way for the breathing wind of (re)discovery to give birth to what we already or always knew. This is something that can only happen right now, in the absolute present where Grace Kimball reigns as goddess, although in the following passage it's James Mayn's daughter Flick thinking:

> The future her father had sloped out onto *was* like us the slope, static but for the shadow it threw, which was *him,* back upon Now, the Present,

which was really the past from the vantage of that future he had gone
into like a shock of memory which gave off a desire to return to what
was a void and had to be reinvented, namely this present. (407)

Obstacles are what allow this reinvention to take place. Obstacles, such
as those James Mayn created to his own breathing wind, are indeed part
and parcel of the void:

> . . . [an] understanding that since if you look at the history you find that
> the Obstacles we are dedicated toward can be seen to have been made
> by Us out of what from a parallel angle looks like the very void through
> which we passed in order to reach the Obstacle in question, it in turn
> must contain sufficient void for us to pass through it.
>   Yet not so much that we feel nothing. (1110)

Thus obstacles resemble (or belong to) the weathers we create, "to observe
them, that is, so that there will be something in front of us," as transparent as
the wind. Larry Shearson concocts a theory out of a mishearing of the phrase
"optical geometry": obstacle geometry. Larry is well qualified to perpetrate
this useful malapropism since he is living in a vivid gap of his own created by
his mother, Sue, having left him. In obstacle geometry, the shortest path is the
one that gets you where you're going to go: "The sign that detours you off
onto yet another course and the true way of the explorer that bends if need be
to circumnavigate a route that may in the end prove more direct" (401).

Can we be more precise about what happens in the gap? The void provides a chance to remember what we already knew: for *remember*, read
recognize. This will explain why James Mayn plays such a privileged role and
appears as our first breather. He looks, or at least says he looks through the
present at the past—"like a shade cast back upon a past not yet distinct,"
revealing its distinction: "And so he would try to get away from that distant
future through which he fell, by seeing such other times as perhaps had not
been altogether lost and seeing them so well that they came back into
being . . ." (1053). This act of recognition opens up possibilities of learning
and becoming. At least that is how I read the following lines about Luisa,
whose father is threatened by Pinochet's regime and whose lover is

Pinochet's agent: ". . . a gap of experience, if we will but let it in: and the diva Luisa years later finds in her a track left by some grace of the divine, like experience to be traveled, again if she will, and again she can't tell . . . of how she let herself learn to love him even in the dark of night . . ." (607). *Let* and *learn*. But how? It's not a matter of *decision*.

> So we must resist the temptation to be judgmental?
> Yes, but mental even more.
> Yet, our body-selves will sing to one another if we let 'em. (421)

"Body-selves" not being ourselves. Consider a previously quoted passage:

> . . . a memory whose fault Jim's life-support (luggage) system can, externalized and unbeknownst to him, supply. We and our multiples had looked into the incarnations we had so needed and curved for and found; but once in them we some of us or parts or branches felt these blood-streams and fibers . . . to be bodies we for one had already been and left. (435-36)

Our body-selves are our "commonalities," not what we are but mediums for our "we"-ness. What we "are" is "light passion-bent past roadblocks it has itself devised: yes, in the fine void of our possible intelligence that announces owl-like one weighty day that we didn't know what light was but we'd been promised a power and thought it might be to find that on good days *we* are light or got to be" (13).

It may be more accurate to say that the "we" who are light are that part of us representing the angelic presence. We can also recognize "light's refracting mediums [as] no other than ourselves" (39). So that we are both light and its refractions, perhaps among its obstacles—obstacles as we know being necessary to realization and arrival.

When light encounters an obstacle, it casts a shadow. Thus do we, and most conspicuously our friendly breather Jim Mayn, in a much-returned-to, late-childhood scene on a New Jersey beach where he leans menacingly over his younger (half)brother Brad:

> And at the instant his brother lay stretched out in front of him, Jim leaned over him so the shadow or human window fitted Brad exact, with no overlap onto the sand. And before Sarah's angry voice cut through a tissue of his feeling, *Don't touch him,* came her shout—Jim had already in fact *stuck* right there in the sand, and Brad screamed. (394-95)

Here we find another window near Windrow, a shadow-window that reveals Brad to a confusedly resentful Jim Mayn—light working *on* him if not *in* him.

Breath; wind; void (and obstacle and light . . .): part of what is happening, not symbols, not metaphors, metonyms maybe but we can't say of what. Agents: secret agents always modifying their identity, like the horrible Ray Santee Sioux Spence. If I haven't, as I know, made altogether clear what I think they are, that is because they are too involved with everything else that is happening to stop and pose for convenient snapshots. You can't take pictures of constantly evolving possibilities: no possibility looks the same twice in a row, especially a Windrow.

At times light for God's sake even becomes sound. An entire seven-page chapter ("the unknown sound") is devoted to investigating how this might happen—what do you hear from a turned-on television set whose sound has been turned all the way off?

This raises the question, how do these things—baffled identities, angels, even "we"—how do these things come into being on the page? How do the agencies of breath, weather, and light manage to act?

6

In other words, since *Women and Men* is a novel, how does its narrative function? This question is an important one to keep asking about the book, because in one sense there is nothing besides the narrative to pay attention to: that is, anything considered outside the narrative context is promptly denatured. Unfortunately the narrative process itself is no less disfigured by description; but I can see no way to avoid it if I am to make clear that what is said earlier and later is not abstract wishfulness on the author's part but exists palpably in his chapters and sentences. A small consolation is that analyzing the workings of the narration presents such a hopeless task that a reader's pleasure in reacting to it can barely be troubled by anything written here. The suppleness, variety, and speed of the prose; its immediacy and efficiency—

> The girl casts her eyes restlessly so that she radiates some subtle trouble. He's not bright; he's just looking. He couldn't place her until their eyes crossed going opposite ways and she was the one with the sketch pad who had been taken by Mayn's companion for one of the students, and there's still a point about her he missed.
>
> Hours later now he is touched by the rented car outside the tavern like a familiar object from elsewhere. All because of talking to this smart young woman he likes—who objected to the word *girl* even when he said he would be glad to be called a boy, hell; and she added, You're white.
>
> In the car they discussed the heat shield and the parasol: the lack of resistance in space—no air—the solar cells that, like color TV, neither of them would claim to be able to explain.
>
> And now, he listens to the girl and she to herself, "Do you think they'll get a new heat shield up?". . . (64)

and, last but not least, a guessed-at factor of improvisation, of the writer's being sure enough of his intention to trust his "stuff" and know that the right words and things will show up under his fingers, perhaps with an occasional rhyme but with no convenient litmus-test reason—all of these condemn any stylistic study to a falsification automatic and safely remote from its object.

There are nevertheless points to make. First, our way through these twelve hundred pages is besprent with small jewels. Here are a few of them:

> . . . the peanut-and-vinegar scent of horses . . . (21)

> . . . slick, cloudy-cupped oysters . . . (65)

. . . [her mother doing the daily dusting] like a lover of antiques who will never sell . . . (113)

. . . One who casts her fingertips upon the sense of his chamois-soft sac easier to know than what floats so unknown within it . . . (357)

. . . the grand piano's shaped black top large as Brazil . . . (357)

[In a train:] . . . I heard what sounded like a cat's angry squall at a distance and knew it was someone's zipper close by. (681)

Escape is always possible even if you think you are free . . . (836)

. . . they curled the potato skins carefully away from the cool, pear-like moistness of the white . . . (901)

. . . dark rustling dance floors . . . (917)

. . . walking with small children (they knew where your hand was without looking) . . . (1000)

"I think about you all the time, even when I'm with you," she says. (1056)

The future takes too long, she says. The workingman is forgotten every day. (1126)

We are also gratified with jewels of greater dimensions—chapters like the opening one ("division of labor unknown") about the mother giving birth, to the fourth from the end ("news") about a man who learns he will soon die, and on the way many kinds of moments in several lives (a hold-up, a bike-riding lesson), all told with a skill we can call classical because it is so effective we forget to remember it.

The chapters just mentioned belong to one of three series. This first group of thirteen (amounting to 169 pages) establishes no continuity between its parts, which are discrete units usually devoted to the secondary characters of the novel, although "Gordon's Story" involves James Mayn and the protagonist of "news" is someone never seen before or after. A second series of chapters (502 pages) tells stories about the principal characters and those connected to them: six center on James Mayn, two on Grace Kimball, three on Jimmy Banks, one on Mackenna (a Chilean exile), one on Larry Shearson; a last chapter, the next-to-last of the book, is shared by Larry and the notorious Spence.[3] Finally, there are the breather chapters, five in all (426 pages), which of course tell "our" story, the "we" including not only whoever we think we are but any character whose presence among us is appropriate. (The long chapter [113 pages] addressed to James Mayn by the prisoner Foley belongs to no one group but rather to all three: it tells his particular history, we learn a great deal about main characters from it, and Foley, as the inventor of the wild, wise theory of an "endless community of minds," is in and by himself everybody and his breather.)

Each series of chapters has its own scale of time and space. The discrete stories of the first group follow "standard contemporary fictional time": they are sequential and stick to a limited and well-defined place and time (often a few hours). The stories of the second group start in and return to a particular time and place, ranging far afield in between. In the breather chapters the only boundaries are those of the book as a whole: from the eighteenth to the twenty-first century, from Chile to China. More important, widely separated times and places occur within single paragraphs and even sentences, as close to simultaneity as is possible without destroying syntactical coherence.

Since the breather chapters continually invoke the overall scale of the book, it is they that provide the context in which we read the others. After the first breather chapter, which follows the short "division of labor unknown," the more reasonable chronologies of the story chapters become parts of the totality it has exposed us to. Conventional chronology in fact appears thereafter as a limited, partial mode, without any narrative privileges and dependent on the breather chapters for its relevance. To put this another way: the breather chapters establish that the only chronology that matters is "our" chronology (and let's say for the moment, inaccurately, that "we" means us readers) so that we take in the other chapters as artificial and abstracted facets of our larger experience. This becomes retrospectively true even of the first chapter, the absorbing and altogether beautiful account of birth. We are moved, but not because of the particular who and where and when. We don't *know* the who or where or when and, once we are plunged into the first breather chapter, we forget to care. The first chapter also affects us in a more lasting way. We have experienced an experience of giving birth, and this opens the way (down the wormhole again!) to a pseudo-birth of our own and above all to the birth of James Mayn, not so much his historical birth as his coming-to-be as our very own first breather.

This unlikely and nonlogical sequence actually takes place in our awareness of what we're reading as we pass from the first to the second chapter, from familiar sequential fiction with all its expectations to something completely unforeseen: an all-in-one, non-linear collage of more or less fragmentary and puzzling passages concerning angels and other matters that at first make little sense, although they are presented to us encouragingly and gently. (As soon as we come across a recognizable flesh-and-blood individual, who happens to be the diva Luisa, we scramble up her thigh right inside her—whence, in a while, the revelation of James Mayn.) This passage from the familiar and well-defined to the inscrutable and vast produces, no matter how smart we act, inevitable confusion—read: *gap*, read: *void*—and through that gap a "breathing wind" can at least possibly flow. It might be simpler to say that moving from the known to the unknown shocks us out of our initial expectations and leaves us open to the unfamiliar; but the point to be taken is that the structure and texture of the book here demonstrably embody the very agencies that it elsewhere describes.

Less grandly, the passage between the first two chapters can be said to accomplish two things. It establishes the reader's chronology as nonsequential, and it places that chronology in a context of what I shall call simultaneity. Simultaneity not only as in Dos Passos's *The 42nd Parallel*, with things happening in different places at the same time, but a conflation of things happening at different places and at different times. The place of their simultaneity is the page, which is to say the place of our awareness.

This effect is brought about not only by juxtaposition but by various methods of displacement. These produce "gaps" of various kinds into which we look and listen in our eagerness to find out what is happening. Seemingly appropriate information is withheld, as in the case of the mother's identity in the first chapter. In "Ship Rock" six pages go by before we learn that the prominent "he" of this story is James Mayn. When Grace Kimball visits Marv in his office (115), we are shown Marv's extraordinary anger in detail, but the explanation for her visit comes later (126). The consequence of "rent," an account of children being taught to ride bikes in Central Park, is passingly and astoundingly mentioned a hundred pages later: "such ordinary tales as a young black aspiring actress's, picked up in the park by an older man teaching his granddaughter to ride a bike" (894). Events and characters are quietly anticipated and recalled. Long before Jimmy Banks makes an appearance (464), references are made to messengers, a messenger service, and the problem of knowing which half of a subway door is going to open, in which Jimmy is an expert (346, 371, 373). On page 417 we finally learn that the childbearer of the first chapter is named Sue (or at least we may *think* we do—see note 2).

As they heighten the effect of simultaneity, these methods of displacement destroy our cause-and-effect expectation and replace it with what the text often calls "remembering what we already know." For example, since we are not aware that we are going to meet Jimmy Banks, the anticipatory references to messengers have no particular significance for us. When we do meet him, we "remember" them, but only according to a nonreflective "instinct" that feels as though what we were remembering was Jimmy Banks. Being confronted with unexplained material opens the uncertainty or gap in our understanding whose filling is experienced not as explanation but as rediscovery of the familiar. We "recall it all. As if [we] did." Thus is the "void" inscribed in the text of the book as the agent of discovery it is asserted to be.

Other methods of displacement function on the level of prosody: recapitulations of phrases or sentences like the one already mentioned on pages

43 and 197 (for another, see 994,1042); devices like starting each paragraph in "Mike-Whipped Landscape Specially Flown In" with the expression "he pulled away" (varied once or twice); sentences extending over entire pages to include in one syntactic breath different people, places, and times (e.g., 792-794); paragraphs that can for instance interrupt such wide-ranging sentences to single out a particular moment (e.g., 23) or that make unspoken points, as in:

> You *don't* talk too much. Try not to disagree with me, Jeanie. I could try, she said, except it's a losing battle. Well, you're so damn smart he was saying while she said, Some things I don't know; like "Visa to China". . . .
> You're speaking telegraphically.
> I have to be careful about attributing: I feel I'm on dangerous ground.
> This is a service road, the turn's up aways.
> When did you first know you were not dreaming? (1153)

—the paragraphing here making the point that some speech is shared, some speech is an exchange.

These procedures and many other similar and dissimilar ones keep nudging us out of our expectation of linear, representational fiction and remind us that the one sequence, the one chronology of this novel belongs to us turning its pages.

What can this chronology of ours correspond to? What is this continuity that embraces all the others? I see the answer as: not the actions and events that form the subject matter of the book but the process by which they are revealed, are learned about, are known. This process is the true plot of the novel, and in it we are one with the main characters: we experience the revelation of reality with them and like them. In a sense we are ourselves privileged characters. Our privilege is not that of seeing things from a superior vantage point with a narrator or author but of being present with the others, being present as each learns what can be known in his or her individual way.

(With the other characters we not only partake of the collective activities of the angels: our less angelic nature finds a voice in the interrogator who

keeps interrupting things with his "read this and that," and who at one
point is interrupted himself:

> You hear that call—
> —read *shriek,* we urge, not *call,* as if he were not one of us, this Inter-
> rogator—
> —O.K., *shriek,* he concedes. . . . [587])

Here are some obvious examples of what I mean. We learn about characters as other characters discover them. We become involved with here-
and-now James Mayn (Florida and New York, 1977) through his friend
Jean after she has met him at Cape Kennedy. We learn to love or at least
accept the Chilean agent de Talca through the diva Luisa's affair with him.
In the case of Grace Kimball, the other person revealing her to us is herself.
An exception? I prefer thinking that rather this is a demonstration of what,
at least if you're a goddess, masturbation is about.

The chapter (100–147) in which Grace discovers herself on our behalf
illustrates the process of revelation and the way we readers are made an
intimate part of it—"prosodically," which is to say physically. The chapter
opens: "It came after her at the end of a day and found her alone on her
great uninterrupted carpet in her fully mirrored Body Room, and it was not
the story of her life . . ." (100), and we do not find out what the "it" may be
until twelve pages later: "Whatever was at stake did not end. But the meaning of Grace's day which came to her alone as she plummeted all over
herself . . ." (112), and we do not find out what the meaning of her day is
until, on the verge of orgasm, her chapter ends. In the meantime the undefined "it" hovers over our awareness as we accompany Grace's gradual excitement and the fuse of her memory burning its elaborate way through
the past that is about to culminate in a present moment of discovery. The
chapter may not form one breath (although I felt that the first twelve pages
did) or be necessarily identifiable with a woman's breathing, but a definite
physical-mental sequence is recreated in the unfolding of the text, and we
participate in it. Among other things, this means that while we are supplied
en route with lots of narrative information, none of it exists outside Grace's

reimagining it; more emphatically, what we discover is never the information and always her. When she recollects her visit to Marv in his office, we encounter a man whose violent anger should terrify or outrage us; yet we feel only compassion for him, as Grace does, who we now learn feels in no way threatened by mere male fury and who is so attentively present as to recognize Marv's vicious words as expressions of confusion and pain (115–17).

Our oneness with the characters of *Women and Men* finds its most dramatic embodiment in the case of the horrendous Spence; and in his spectacular evolution in the way we perceive him and he perceives himself, Spence embodies as well the central process of learning, knowing, and becoming—of "remembering what we knew already."

For the first two-thirds of the book we see Spence mostly through the eyes of James Mayn and Jimmy Banks: alone among a sympathetically presented cast, he appears as a totally sinister fellow—a snoop, a spy, an agent for reprehensible public and private organizations, and most likely an accessory to an ignoble assassination. Worse than being evil, he looks, sounds, and acts repulsive, standing out among the rest of us like the sorest of thumbs. Then James Mayn, in the middle of a long review of Spence's activities, senses that there is "'something else' Spence was coming from" and tells his friend Jean: "'Have to think Spence was a snake in a previous life and didn't make it so they demoted him to a human snake—except there's no "they," is there? I'll say one thing for him: he has the stick-to-it-iveness of a good journalist: he listens and goes looking'" (870). This small, grudging acknowledgment opens for James Mayn (and we're right there with him) the possibility of thinking responsibly about Spence when he returns to evaluating him. Spence has intruded on Mayn in a number of ways, all involving a series of women that began years before with Mayga, a Chilean journalist, and has recently extended to his daughter, Flick, his old high-school teacher, Pearl Myles, and his friends Dina West and Norma. The tiny shift in Mayn's perception of Spence moves the latter from outside to inside his life, where the rest of us have long gathered. The consequences of Mayn shift fill many absorbing pages, popping (like Grace Kimball's reflections) with information but above all persuading us as he persuades himself that the creep he had refused to think about matters to him.

> . . . inspired by Spence who was nonetheless real . . .
> Spence was the problem. He was no less than making a living. (877)

> . . . and he heard himself saying in answer to Ted's "You're pretty hard on that little so-and-so," "Yeah, we all have a little Spence in us" for Ted to carry on, in Mayn's affectionate imagination, "Spence has more than most." (904)

By such little steps Spence travels from the margin of Mayn's consciousness to its center, helping him see that this distinction is a false generality: "James Mayn found himself left again where he'd about chosen to be: on consignment facing down the four corners of his one-time permanent shelter, unsure which was margin, which was center. . . . But margin and center turned out to be lunacy" (911), and Mayn discovers that there is "a unified field locking together the four corners: a *new* weather . . ." (911): "Margin or center? Mayn went on and on, angelic waste like education passing through him so he mattered so little he would just go on living contaminated to a ripe old age, the 'rhyme' to Spence's 'reason' . . ." (912).

Later on, learning as he comes to know others what is "known" about him, Spence accepts more and more responsibility for himself and begins to include himself in other people's lives:

> Hearing a scream of tires at his end and the gunning of an engine right afterward, [Dina West] asked what it was . . . and Spence said, Business as usual; and she said, You are in the business of *information*, and he, I'm getting out of it and go settle in the West, run me a boots-and-tack shop someplace small, maybe manage a supermarket; she said she hardly believed him and he said he hadn't known about that supermarket or the boot shop till he had said the words.
> There, she said, you *see?*, but she caught at a gentleness they both felt in her vowel, and she said, I'm sick of city phoning, I'm all phoned out, I want to talk to you face to face. (1075)

Eventually, and particularly in the course of a long meeting with Mayn's teacher, Pearl Myles, Spence abandons his "professional" illusion that knowledge means getting more and more information: "I used to know all these things, said Spence. As recently as yesterday, in fact. I guess I have to go on being myself" (1096)—from the words emanates a willingness to not know, to let there be a void where "all these things" were before. Already, to our apprehensive delight, he has assigned himself one of the central mysteries of the book as his objective: "the issue of further Mayn offspring was what Spence suddenly had come to think he had been sent to settle through some obstacle course of all these years . . ." (1091). How he settles the issue and solves the mystery, with us at his side taking this disreputable man to our heart as he moves through another formidable obstacle course with ever-growing understanding (read: *compassion*), provides *Women and Men* with a long climax of grueling excitement, in which the two time continuities of sequentiality and simultaneity are fused in the fire of action. All the author's narrative skills are concentrated here to gratify our most melodramatic cravings as well as our most serious expectations. I'm too great a respecter of plot and suspense to even hint at what happens; and, as by now may be obvious, it's not the what happens that counts but the how. Be that as it may, you'll have to take our word for it.

7

"Not the what but the how": insofar as the statement is accurate, it must be understood as referring to more than matters of style. In an oversimplified way, the statement does indicate an important part of what *Women and Men* is about. We have already guessed that, as they are in this book reimagined and refashioned, familiar novelistic elements like identity, time, space, and the relationship between author, narrator, and reader cannot help but produce startlingly new effects. In fact, we might as we read be primarily aware of the radical differences between *Women and Men* and other novels if the author had not taken such great and constant care to comfort and reassure us with the "illusions" of his more conventional chapters as well as with delightful regular bulletins reminding us of the diverse topics at play in his juggling act. The topics are many, and it is a true juggling act because they are kept in perpetual motion. Furthermore, the balls in the air have the odd habit of resembling and even becoming one another as they pass before our eyes. This process of convergence and conversion is the "how" that I suggest matters most and that we should above all devote our attention to.

The "what" of the book—its material, its "stuff": not just people, things, and events but relationships and ideas, including ideas of structure and language—is altogether captivating; and we must absolutely let it go, at least from the foreground of our reading, at least for a while. For one thing, the way everything is linked to everything else makes talking about separate bits of subject matter difficult: a discussion of almost any detail will lead to another and eventually involve the whole book. So, given this slipperiness of the material, we might as well get used to letting go of it. Giving up whatness, letting go of sure things like facts and good ideas—isn't that one thing the void is for? Facts and good ideas are not really revealing, merely bankable. They belong completely to the past, a past that might as well be called dead: Mayn once mentions his ability to fake "an entire double-column *obit* of information" (968; italics mine). And readers of this article must, for this very reason, forgive its imperfect clarity: the book will not be reduced to an analytical summary that they can safely file away.

In *Women and Men* every what is turned into another what and eventually into *every* other what. So extensive is this process of transformation that I have had to leave out entire domains from our discussion—politics and economics, for example. (Cf. the subject of rent, 739, 783, 790, etc.) Nothing in the book is excluded from this process. It is strikingly crystallized in the thoughts of the Navajo Prince as, journeying eastwards, he recollects the Bering Straits when they still linked Asia and America (a "solid fact" if there ever was one):

> . . . at the riverbank at night, his hand upon the bison tongue with all
> its waiting power took him closer every time to the doubled sight of
> that isthmus at the top of the Earth, where the two continents could
> not be looked at at once unless that isthmus could be seen for what it
> *also* was—a moving, a turning from there to here, a motion, a moving

which, if seen, made the mammoth and bison and the hunters with foreign seeds clinging to their leggings, frost in their eyebrows, no longer move but wait like pictures carried by this perhaps-soon-to-be-broken land from the world out behind to the world here before, one sky behind . . . and one sky before. . . . (1120)

Out of its effects, the process of transformation can be given several names, none of them definitive: inclusion (or two-into-oneness); multiplication (one-into-twoness); conversion, convergence; and identification, especially if one imagines a shift from identification meaning definition (which involves distinction, separation, isolation) to identification meaning the recognition of equivalence (which involves the conjunction of elements once separate). This shift in the meaning of identification can be visually represented through a term that recurs from time to time in the book, that of the Four Corners. It early appears as the name of the place where Utah, Colorado, Arizona, and New Mexico meet; here the corners are the image of definition and separation:

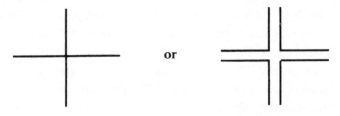

The expression later comes to refer to the corners of the universe, which form an image of inclusion (obtainable from the first once again by Larry Shearson's much-studied multiplication method called rotation):

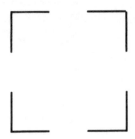

We have here a crucial diagrammatic representation of the process of center being turned into margin and vice versa. (Larry thinks, "now margin seems so central" [346], and James Mayn, "the margin was always turning us to it like a perfectly serviceable center" [979]. It is as if *center* could be, sometimes, a name for the reassuring "stuff" we hang onto.)

We have already seen, as consequences of the process of transformation, certain familiar distinctions dissolved, such as the individual identities of characters, a phenomenon given emblematic form in James Mayn's vision of the moon station where two settlers arrive as one. Similar overlaps or mergings were noted in the case of words (such as "wormhole"), objects (two pistols or one), acts and histories (mothers leaving sons). Here are a few additions to the list.

The opposition between the sexes is consistently subverted—not a surprise if we remember the change of the title's sense from women/men to women-men. Most often this is effected by narrative accumulations or by syntactic details, such as the repetition throughout the book, in the place of the familiar order "men and women" that "naturally" comes to the tongue, of its inverse, first exemplified in the title: "Slip it to her in her juice? That's how *men* make their dreams come true! says a voice preferably female *and* male" (170). Less indirect assertions also make the point. Early on we learn that the tapeworm that we first hear beyond the diva's "divine thigh" is dual-sexed and that Grace Kimball, to whom we have not yet been officially introduced, "found history in women: in the women contained by men, and in men retaining secret fluid of women you don't own up to . . ." (13). Grace's awareness of this is most dramatically presented to us through a rare glimpse into one of her workshops, where with therapeutic starkness she undoes the discrepancies between the sexual organs (noticing afterwards "one unrehearsed rhyme"):

> Grace's lanternslides (as they would have been called in her parents' day) projected now . . . up onto a screen for five hundred women to believe. The messages of these slices paired side by side so it looks like two screens, is that—in this hotbed of biology and cure (the auditorium of a hospital)—see for yourself, sisters, the hard-on you're getting right

now proves it, look at the penis then look at the clit, trace your vagina
and that scrotum is it, these are the same organs, ladies, which is why
you knew you had balls. . . . (185)

Things, places, systems, races are rhymed with each other; and so, most
tellingly, are individuals. We have seen a little how this happens, but the
matter is worth returning to because it underlies so much of everything
else in the book: not only in its writing but in its reading. Isn't giving up
our well-preserved individuality, after all, what makes possible my becoming "we"?

As with sexual difference, syntactical means accomplish much here: a
stream of innocuous-looking phrases such as "We for one . . ." cumulatively
undermines our attachment to this precious notion about ourselves (and
when we notice such phrases, we only smile and keep moving): the juxtaposition in "All things to him she was," or the mixed possessive pronouns
in "this body language we knew in their bones" (both 159). The point is
also overtly made, occasionally in explicit detail. It is enigmatically raised at
the beginning of the first breather chapter: "sent away by a mother . . .
those two remembered sons were secretly one as well as two" (9). The one-
twoness of the brothers is often referred to (e.g., 174), and other marriages
of body and consciousness range from the violent "counter-Masonic rite of
mingled flesh among Indians and Anglos in northern New York and central
Oklahoma" (894) to the diva's sensual sense that "her fascist argonaut" is
"her other body" (362) and Larry's insight into "obstacle geometry" and
simultaneous reincarnation: "And while receiving feedback . . . on reincarnation as arising out of crisis in your life when the void opening in front of
you could outguess you if you put yourself into it so you found you were
more than one person which was O.K. and scary and creative, Larry went
on savoring the dream of the names . . ." (1071).

Individuals can be absorbed into one another without benefit of prox-
imity (like Grace Kimball and James Mayn) or even language. The angelic
host to which we belong, or who belong to us, can be pure light or pure
intention. The prisoner Foley is so aware of this that, even as he is writing
Mayn, he can say to him, "I am getting through to you sometimes direct

by multiple word-bypass" (706). The Anasazi agrees that there is "neighborhood in silence" (835). Silence, after all, can appear as a kind of gap (one that in the reading of *Women and Men* shows up most obviously in the unexplained transitions between chapters). And of course the transformation of two individuals into one in the future space trips of James Mayn's future recollection involves no conversation, no discussion, no thinking: there are simply two people around on departure and one on arrival.

Can this possibility of individuals fusing ever be real to us? The answer is that it has never been otherwise. The moon-station transformation is a parable not only of what happens in this novel but of the nature of our existence. The correspondence is indirectly and gently made available to us, as when Mayn comments: "What sex? Far as *he* knew, the colonists two into one wound up with such deep memories of the other sex that such memories are built in!" (419). Later, "we" say: "But who are we getting at? or to? Was it our parents? (But) we are our parents by now, and in a miracle of memory now see they were angels of ordinariness helping us toward ourselves, we trust" (545). A quotation or two more:

> many . . . settlers reported an unsettled sense of lasting content on arrival, later thought . . . to have been due to the mythically rich feeling due in turn to the indubitable *source* of each individual in this and other space-positive settlements of nothing *but* individuals. . . . (890)

> our amazement at how we could get here without grasping the concrete sources in our collective childhood as if we had to forget them to get ahead—in order, say, to figure out how to inject weather into a "weatherless" place without ruining everything. . . . (892)

Who in our sexuated world has *not* been shot into a mysterious place, two people become one? James Mayn's daydream is no fantasy but an imaginative rendering of the human condition. We are all family, whether we like it or not; it's part of our lives, like weather. Not *only* family—the angels see to that. All the same, we wonder longingly who, on page 1176, that old woman (called Margaret) might be; and at the end of the book the gathering in the Windrow graveyard of Mayn, Spence, Margaret, Alexander, and

the Navajo Prince is the coming together of the parts of family history we
are ready to claim as inevitable, necessary, and very much "ours."

Like the vision of the moon station, *Women and Men* is not a wishful
fantasy: it is not prescriptive but descriptive, an account of our reality as a
oneness multiplying into stupendous variety, variety dissolving into oneness. An account of *our* reality, no less recognizable for being altogether the
author's own; even if we must acknowledge less immediate readiness than
his to destroy so many convenient categories of thought.

It may be useful to point out how the purpose behind the extraordinary
variety of people and events in this book differs from that of another great
accumulator, Georges Perec, as demonstrated for instance in *Life A User's
Manual.* Perec includes material in his work with no lesser a generosity than
that manifested in *Women and Men*, but he does so for reasons that are thoroughly skeptical and indeed pessimistic. He is intent on salvaging what he
can from the present and past as a bulwark against inevitable loss, "pluck-
ing fragments," as he says, "from the deepening void." The American's generosity produces instead an extensive tour of us at play in the universe.

And, as he himself points out in his prefatory note, American he is. His
vision does not ignore disease, death, torture, and other ignominies, but it
remains essentially one of inspired acceptance, much recalling (to me at
least) the visions of Emerson and the early Whitman, whose criteria this
book appears to meet:

> The American poets are to enclose old and new for America is the race
> of races. Of them a bard is to be commensurate with a people. . . . To him
> enter the essences of the real things and past and present events—of the
> enormous diversity of temperature and agriculture and mines—the tribes
> of red aborigines—the weather-beaten vessels entering new ports or
> making landings on rocky coasts. . . . (Preface to *Leaves of Grass*, 1855)

Like Whitman's, the author's acceptance is both nonjudgmental and
emphatically ethical. There is ultimately no one in the book whom we do
not agree to understand; at the same time there is no one whom we are
encouraged to feel overridingly linked to (except possibly Spence, whose

emergence from "badness" to knowledge is so crucial to our own knowing what we're up to). Aside from the twins in the downtown store window who on one occasion assume the roles, there are no goodies or baddies. The ethicality of the book might be called responsibility. The acceptance is not made in ignorance, it never depends on romantic hope or mysticism but is solidly grounded—as many quoted examples show—in an abundance of evidence: not of facts but the ways all facts, "good" or "bad," are interlinked parts of a whole. Nietzsche, attacking the metaphysicians' opposition of values in *Beyond Good and Evil*, writes, "It might even be possible that what constitutes the value of . . . good and revered things is precisely that they are insidiously related, tied to, and involved with these wicked seemingly opposite things—maybe even one with them in essence," and such a position animates, if not the belief, certainly the concerned procedure of *Women and Men*. It might be called a religious position if we exhume the etymology of *religion: re-ligare*, to bind fast. We remember E. M. Forster's "Only connect."

Like settlers newly landed on the moon station, we readers of *Women and Men* experience in the book "an unsettled sense of lasting content" (the accent of the last word falling most definitely on the second syllable). Since the novel could have gone on, we ask, why didn't it? Or is that supposed to be up to us?

8

In my last year as a music student in college, while working on my bachelor's thesis on Schubert's chamber music, I remember a moment when, my analysis of the various pieces complete, it occurred to me that the only way I could do justice to the music was to hand in a set of scores (or perhaps recordings) of it. It was not that description and discussion would "betray" the objects of my study (all writing about music falls ludicrously short of its subject), but that in these particular works the formal and stylistic practices I had identified seemed to make no sense except as embodied in the movement of the music being played and heard. Separated from that movement, they threatened to become irrelevant or, worse, a distraction from the truth of the composer's musical thought—a potential excuse for *not* listening.

Rereading *Women and Men* has made me feel the way I did then. Like the best of Schubert, Beethoven, and Haydn, it is a work that aims to make process signify more than it can say. Only while I am following the movement of its sentences do I sense myself close to what it is, to what it's doing and saying, to what it's doing and not saying. I want to replace this article with some act like taking a new reader's hand, leading her or him to the opened book, and sharing our amazement, bewilderment, and delight as we progress from one page to the next, from page one to the last.

Review of Contemporary Fiction, 1990

NOTES

1. Numbers following examples refer to pages in the original edition of *Women and Men* (New York: Alfred A. Knopf, 1987).
2. It was recently pointed out to me that this identification depends on a remark overheard at a party ("There was a moment of no talk and a woman said, 'Sue,' and everyone laughed" [7]), and that this "Sue" can perfectly well be construed as an imperative verb.
3. The typography of the table of contents—a "poem" in itself—suggests a slightly different distribution of chapters, with the three about Jimmy Banks assigned to the first of my groups and the seventeenth chapter, "CHARITY," to the second.

SEX REAL AND IMAGINARY

Paul Eluard:	What proportion has there been of impotence in which you have not been able to make love even though you intended to? . . .
André Breton:	It has happened only once—after an exhausting journey with a woman I desired who was not yet my mistress. . . .
Paul Eluard:	I'd like Breton to elaborate on the first part of his answer.
André Breton:	I attributed this to the mauve wallpaper in the room—I've always found the color mauve particularly unbearable.

This exchange occurred on November 24, 1930, during the ninth of twelve sessions of an inquiry that members of the original surrealist group devoted to sexual matters. The Wildean tone of Breton's response may not reflect the seriousness of the enterprise or his own passionate commitment to its subject, but I trust it demonstrates that *Investigating Sex* is not only a serious and revealing book but a delightful one. Indeed, revelation and liveliness frequently go hand in hand:

André Breton:	To what extent does Aragon think an erection is necessary in the accomplishment of the sexual act?
Louis Aragon:	Some degree of erection is necessary, but in my case I've never had anything but semi-erections.
André Breton:	Do you regret that?
Louis Aragon:	As much as any other physical failure, and no more. I don't regret it any more than being unable to lift pianos with my bare hands.

Aragon's statement is typically free of self-pity and fudging. The participants in these conversations are in general endowed with perceptiveness and self-possession; they rarely show a need to score points; as a result, their talk is natural, alert, and absorbing.

Only the first two sessions of the inquiry were made public at the time they occurred. It was not until 1990, when José Pierre exhumed the remainder from the Breton archives, that all twelve became available; his book, *Recherches sur la sexualité*, is the basis for the English edition. Supplemented with ancillary documents, notably other collective writings of the surrealist group on sexuality, it has been translated in lively fashion by Malcolm Imrie, who has also supplied welcome information about the participants in the conversations. José Pierre's introduction to the French edition has not been included, which is too bad, since it provides an informed view of the relations between the participants; it also emphasizes the adventurousness of investigating sex at the time of the surrealists' inquiry. English readers, on the other hand, have the benefit of an afterword by Dawn Ades that sheds abundant light on the context in which the inquiry was undertaken as well as the issues it raises.

The surrealists evidently began their talks without a clearly defined goal. What it implicitly may have been, at least in Breton's mind, is suggested in the sixth session by his reply to Antonin Artaud, after the latter has insisted on excluding any reference to love in the discussion:

> . . . I believe we must begin by linking the question of sexuality to that of love. The whole point of this investigation is, in love, to establish what part belongs to sexuality.

The remark can be supplemented by what is said years later in an "Inquiry into Erotic Representations":

> . . . Would we believe in the words of love if they did not carry the hope of that union of the real and the imaginary of which the lovers' encounter forms the allegory?

Breton's obsession with the notion of love as a prime mover in the surrealist enterprise may fail to achieve anything like a consensus among his
companions, but it ensures that the topic arises again and again in the course
of the conversations and presumably explains his initiating them.

Even though the twelve sessions of *Investigating Sex* extend from 1928 to
1932, the first seven occur during a short span of three and a half months,
between January 27 and May 6, 1928. While the later sessions benefit from
the presence of Paul Eluard and (none too soon) a number of women, they
have a mainly anecdotal interest, and the last three are, at least in their
transcriptions, disappointingly brief. The opening series, animated no doubt
by the enthusiasm attendant on breaking new ground and distinguished by
a varying and illustrious cast of characters, exerts the fascination of intellectual theatre at its brilliant best.

The questions presented by and to the participants, some of them prepared, others spontaneous, range from the trivial through the provocative
to the intensely earnest, and from the technical to the abstract. Among the
topics discussed we find homosexuality, masturbation, group sex, brothels,
preferred positions, monogamy, rape, abstinence, heterosexual sodomy (both
ways), erotic literature, marriage, and procreation. The initial question, asked
by Breton at the start of the first session, remains crucial to the entire undertaking:

> A man and a woman make love. To what extent is the man aware of the
> woman's orgasm?

The question is insisted on by Breton and frequently raised by him on
occasions when a new participant joins the discussion group. The responses
reveal such disagreement that, given Breton's attachment to the subject, it is
a wonder he persevered in pursuing the inquiry for so long; as Dawn Ades
observes, the investigation was a notable failure to the extent that "what
was fast becoming the special province of surrealism—the privileged place
of sexuality—was . . . demonstrated to be the source of some deep conflicts."
Breton was, however, not to be disouraged, thanks to which we are treated

to a lively sequence of encounters between him (and his supporters) and other, more independent-minded men, some of them not even members of the surrealist group. Aragon speaks sensibly about male homosexuality (Queneau has already denounced the surrealist prejudice against it) and is the first to deplore the male orientation of the inquiry, asserting "the fact that men and women have equal rights" in sexual matters. Jean Genbach, a defrocked Jesuit, sows a refreshing amount of confusion with mystical, innocent interpretations of his own peculiar experiences. Max Ernst is extraordinarily precise in his attentiveness to (for instance) the process of male orgasm; and he comes across as the most surrealist of all after Breton himself—among other things, he asks and affirmatively answers the question:

> Are you monogamous? That's to say, do you believe there is a woman who is your destiny, to the exclusion of all others?

Before leaving in the middle of the sixth session, Antonin Artaud in his usual harshly uncompromising way engages Breton in what is perhaps the most disturbing and stimulating exchange of all, denouncing not only sexuality as a source of pleasure but love itself as inferior to "satisfactions of an intellectual order." In reply, Breton says:

> . . . If I place love above everything, it is because it is for me the most desperate, the most despairing state of affairs imaginable.

Finally, Paul Eluard, who takes part from the ninth through the last sessions and whose surrealist credentials are impeccable, appears in soft-spoken but none the less absolute contrast to Breton, the idealizer of the Unique Woman: Eluard is an unrepentant sensualist who, among other things, has between the ages of fourteen and thirty-five made love to "between five hundred and one thousand" women and one who does not hesitate to justify his attachment to desire and sexual activity independent of an exclusive object, an attitude that Breton generally equates with licentiousness. The exchange between the two men on this subject in the tenth session, too long to quote here, is most revealing (pp.138–140).

Throughout these conversations "undermined," as Aragon says, "by the inevitable predominance of the male point of view," the idea of Woman plays a crucial part. The participation of real women in several of the sessions does little to restore any consequent balance between the sexes; as Dawn Ades aptly points out, "they frequently disagree with the men, but, while not silent, are in a sense mute." Even when the men present acknowledge the possible value of what the women present may have to say, they prove incapable of freeing themselves from their customary attitudes:

> *Simone Vion*:   I'd like to add something. In the dark I think it's always pleasant.
> *Albert Valentin*:   At last, after a whole hour, a human voice is heard.
>   Approval.
> *Paul Eluard*:   I'd like a woman to ask a question.
>   Approval.
> *Nusch* [Eluard's wife]: How do you like to make love?
> *Albert Valentin*:   You mean one sex inserted into another?
> *Paul Eluard*:   As you know very well, to make love means to ejaculate.

Contemporary readers, and not only women readers, will no doubt find such male ineptness irritating, to say the least. But dwelling on such obvious "political incorrectness" would be, I suggest, a waste of time. The interest of the conversations lies elswewhere. Its dreary humorlessness aside, the worst thing about political correctness is that it oppressively discourages telling the truth about one's ideas, sentiments, and actions. What is persuasive in what the male surrealists have to say is their unflagging commitment to veracity, no matter how embarassing or shocking or self-demeaning its results may prove. They offer us articulate explorations of masculine desire, fantasy, and indeed ignorance, such as were habitual sixty-odd years ago. Of course these men were unaware in varying degrees of the realities of women's experience—how could they not be? They were speaking in a pre-feminist age, and their testimony illuminates not only the habitual prejudices of that age but the admittedly limited ways which men of decisively radical intent struggled with them. These men ought to be viewed not as hopeless sexists but rather (their "experience" notwithstanding) as sexual innocents. It surely is more interesting to get to know them through their lively articulation of an imperfect but hardly complacent awareness than to dismiss them for breaking rules that had not yet been defined.

It isn't, after all, as though they were indifferent to moral issues. Even the promiscuous Eluard insists that "making love is to be recommended. . . . For me this is a moral idea. . . . I consider chastity as immoral and harmful . . . because for me sexual preoccupation is the basis for all mental activity." Breton strongly disagrees. For him, the willingness to renew the object of desire "tends to elevate the idea of love over the being whom one loves or wants to love. I love women too much, and I believe I am too susceptible to loving a woman, not to object to such an attitude."

The objection reveals Breton as someone who, while convinced that sexual love can be a powerful subversive agent, remains a romantic, and a rather conformist romantic at that: a willful monogamist. It should be emphasized that Breton's attitude during the course of the inquiry carries tremendous weight not only because of his constant presence (he is the only one to attend all the meetings) but because he involves himself in the undertaking with singular and unflagging attention. His sway over many of the other participants can, I think, be explained by a fact simpler than that of his prestige as a founder of the movement or of his exceptional eloquence: he is older than most, by a margin of three to thirteen years. With the exception of Queneau (who, although seven years his junior and years away from publishing his first book, defends his views with laconic pugnacity), it is those who are near his own age, or surpass it—Aragon, Artaud, Ernst, and Eluard—who disagree with him most freely and whom he treats with the greatest respect, not necessarily as antagonists but certainly as equals.

Breton's attitude towards love and sexuality may be the most interesting thing revealed in the course of these conversations. The attitude is surprising not merely in its substance but in its ramifications, which can hardly be called logical but which have an eccentric consistency to them. He has two preoccupations concerning sex: it is contemptible except insofar as it depends on the love of a Predestined Woman; and it is a primordial means of liberation from the grip of traditional morality.

The first of these preoccupations leads him to condemn the notion of desire as such: "I've been absolutely unable to conceive of making love with a woman I merely desired"; "I have never so to speak experienced sexual 'pleasure'"; "Impossible to sleep with a woman I don't love or think I love." So libertinism is rejected as "a taste for pleasure for its own sake." The absolute supremacy in sexual matters of the psychic mystery of love leads him to reject all mechanistic or physiological justifications of behavior (Breton calls them "materialist": in discussing sexual experiences during sleep, he asks, "Would Queneau give any credence to what I think are deplorable theories which claim that the rubbing of a sheet, or some other physical cause, can produce orgasm?") He claims not to "see any difference between the encrusted shit of the woman one loves and her eyes." He is "completely against" physical love taking place between a man and two women. Prostitution is rejected ("under no circumstances" would he consent to sleep with a woman he paid). And "I have the lowest opinion of erotic literature (for me, Sade and Louÿs are not erotic literature)." More intimately, he declares that physical failures "can only happen with a woman one loves." He is "appalled" at the idea of hearing a woman fart (which makes his remark about "encrusted shit" sound passably theoretical). What excites him in a woman is her eyes and breasts. His primordial vision of having amorous relations with a woman was of "the face. This took shape very late (seventeen or eighteen years old) in connection with the paintings of Gustave Moreau (a face, a look). Absolutely ideal love." (This sentiment touches me because it expresses what were once my own feelings, albeit at a considerably earlier age.)

In contrast to this absolute, rather austere romanticism, Breton's second preoccupation—the power of sex in undermining bourgeois morality—leads to his adopting views that while of a different tone are no less dogmatic:

> *Pierre Eluard*:   How do you reconcile your love for the woman and your taste for sodomy? . . .
>
> *André Breton*:   [The question of] reconciliation doesn't arise. I prefer sodomy first and foremost for moral reasons, principally non-conformism. No child with a woman one doesn't love. With a woman I love, her self-abandon seems to me infinitely more moving in this form.

Paul Eluard:	Why?
André Breton:	From a materialist angle, in the case of the woman I love, it is infinitely more pessimistic (law of shit) and consequently more poetic.
Paul Eluard:	Why, for example, does the idea of conception through coitus not seem to you more pessimistic than shit?
André Breton:	Because it conforms to the idea of becoming which for me is indistinguishable from the idea of good.

Non-conformism and denying the positivist notion of the good is what gives Breton his "taste for sodomy": elsewhere he says, ". . . it is sodomy which seems to me to have the greatest possibilities, although I don't like it." It appeals to him because it outrages the accepted view of what is natural, and especially the centerpiece of society that is the family. For the same reasons, and never out of sensual inclination, Breton encourages not only masturbation but "depravity," although he often seems to be forcing himself in this direction and has in fact a hard time saying what he means by the word.

Breton's two preoccupations inevitably get in each other's way. He is all in favor of female homosexuality, but male homosexuality clearly disgusts him, although in a society that reveres procreation it should earn high marks for disruptive potential. Queneau and Aragon rightly lambast him for hypocrisy on this score, but Breton on each occasion refuses to discuss the issue at any length, plainly because woman in his eyes must be enshrined as the supreme erotic power. (Even masturbation "must be accompanied by feminine images"—an assertion he sticks to despite disagreement from his fellow participants.) Aragon is also the first, after Queneau and others say that for them ejaculation is not necessarily accompanied by orgasm, to nail Breton for a more general and no less surprising tendency on Breton's part:

André Breton:	These can only be pathological cases.
Louis Aragon:	I must point out that for the first time during the discussion the word "pathological" has been brought up. That seems to suggest that some of us believe in the idea of the normal man. I object to this idea.

Aragon's observation is supported throughout the exchanges. Breton has already dismissed the notion of congress with animals as a joke (we can only hope he pays attention to Baldensperger's later testimony); in the fifth session he denounces Ernst's statement that "orgasm precedes ejaculation" as "personal [and] subjective"; he cannot imagine that the clitoris may play a central role in a woman's pleasure (seventh session); he will not even accept the possibility that Duhamel and Prévert can both be excited by women wearing slippers. He does indeed seem to be inhabited by the idea not only of the normal man but of a normative pattern of sexual behavior.

André Breton turns out to be something of a prude. His two preoccupations do after all have one thing in common: whether he is going to bed with the woman he loves or doing his best to commit depravities to the detriment of bourgeois society, he is not acting out of pleasure. He is a mental sexualist. Adopting such an attitude is not necessarily silly: even without help from Freud, it may issue from a healthy revulsion from a frivolous libertinism that, if not universal in France, was more easily accepted there than elsewhere and so played a part in the social system Breton despised. It seems surprising, nevertheless, that with such a lack of interest in sexuality per se he should have cared so much about defining and advocating it.

Why, more particularly, did he take the trouble to instigate and pursue the lengthy inquiry that fills *Investigating Sex*?

A hypothetical answer has been proposed by Mark Polizzotti, author of a forthcoming biography of Breton. In 1928 Breton was still married to Simone Kahn, with whom he enjoyed a close but less than passionate relationship. Passion had recently appeared in his life, however, in the shape of Suzanne Muzard: she was, apparently, the first intensely sexual woman he had loved, and in a sense he began discovering through her the unguessed depth and power of sexual experience. He was elated, then despondent, and in any case confused; and it was to clarify this confusion that he organised his group's investigation of a subject that he couldn't master on his own. (Breton's habit of declaring his personal concerns to be important topics for the surrealists became something of a joke: after leaving the group, one member observed that if André Breton developed a taste for pig's trotters, his comrades would soon learn that pig's trotters were of great revolutionary significance.)

lived in furnished flats, changing his address frequently but never leaving the neighborhood of the *grands boulevards* and the Bourse. In 1868 a first version of the opening canto of *Les Chants de Maldoror* was published anonymously and, like all of Ducasse's work, at the author's expense. The following year the complete Maldoror was printed and bound in Belgium, the author being identified as the "Comte de Lautréamont"; fearing trouble with the imperial censorship, the publisher declined to distribute the book in France. In 1870 both parts of the *Poésies* were published, with his own name on the title page. Isidore Ducasse died during the siege of Paris on November 24th of the same year.

From even so spare a summary, one can understand the fascination that Ducasse's life has exercised on his readers. His origins both cosmopolitan and provincial, his mother's early and unexplained death, the precocity of his output, his own early death provide promising materials for a legend. There is no point, where its facts are beyond dispute, in trying to exclude the author's life from consideration of his work. An example of its relevance is François Caradec's observation that Ducasse "spoke with a Gascon accent" and that many of his misspellings and turns of phrase reflect the speech of Bigorre. But the biographical lure that has sidetracked so many critics arises from underdocumented events in his life. The problem, as Caradec points out in his own excellent biography,[2] is not that we know so little about him but that we know too much; and the personal tone of his writings prompts us to eke out deductions from them in order fill in the tantalizing gaps. The procedure is notoriously unreliable. All the same, the lure remains, and I myself have been tempted by it. Simple curiosity about the man makes me want to know what sort of a relationship he had with his father; how his mother's death affected him (according to one recollection, when confronted with a cow's rotting carcass, he is said to have asked, "Do humans stink like that when they die? . . . And Mama too?"); how he spent his time during the Paris years; whether he was homosexual; what sexual experiences he had. Other anecdotes are more directly pertinent to the work. A report that at the beach Ducasse "swam like a fish" seems relevant to Maldoror's aquatic coupling with the shark. Another account claims that "he wrote only at night, seated at his piano. He worked out his sentences by declaiming them, punctuating his recitation with chords." This method, "the despair of the other tenants," suggests a "body language" that would have delighted Roland Barthes. If Ducasse was indeed nicknamed "The Vampire" at school, can this shed light on the recurrent figure of the vampire in Maldoror? When he died, books by Poe and Eugène Sue were supposedly found on his bedside table. Might this indicate that Poe was as great an influence on Ducasse as Sue?

Plausible as they may seem, and accurate as they may actually be, these are not facts: they are either recollections noted long after the event or second- and third-hand reports, likely to remain unsubstantiated food for speculation. The category includes a particularly irritating item. Why is the author's name on the first complete edition of Maldoror given as "le Comte de Lautréamont"? It seems likely, but only likely, that the name was derived from the Latréaumont who is the protagonist of a novel by Eugène Sue. Did Ducasse choose the pseudonym? He had certainly read Sue, and Caradec emphasizes the appeal to the creator of the "diabolical" Maldoror of Latréaumont the character ("a kind of cruel clown, a moral and physical monstrosity"). Or was the name proposed by Lacroix, Sue's publisher as well as Ducasse's, simply as a way of protecting the author from probable prosecution (this is the explanation ventured by Jean-Luc Steinmetz, a recent editor of Ducasse's work[3])? Lykiard, who as usual reviews the answers perceptively and succinctly, raises an intriguing point when he asks, "Does this self-conferred nobility, Comte de Lautréamont, purposely link the writer with the Marquis de Sade and Lord Byron in an aristocratic elite of the intellect?" We shall probably, once again, never know. If I find the question irritating, it is because the author has come to be universally referred to by a name that appears only once in his work, that he never refers to in his letters, and that may have been no more than a temporary legal expedient. No doubt there is little point in defying a usage so entrenched; on the other hand, did Lautréamont write the *Poésies*, signed "Isidore Ducasse"?

The best escape from these uncertainties lies in the work. Once we begin reading, they are overridden by questions even more unanswerable and far more exciting, questions that address not historical details but the cultural and intellectual assumptions that govern the way we read and, in reading, think and feel. We still speculate, indeed we are condemned by the work to virtually infinite speculation because the questions confronting us have no answers except provisional ones. Whatever the relevance of Ducasse's biography to what he wrote, his writing has a life all its own, and all his own: and this is the life that matters.

2

Besides "Lautréamont," another name has provoked speculation of a more interesting sort among Ducasse's commentators: that of Maldoror, the character who overwhelmingly dominates the author's first work. Other characters appear, but all, including God, are subordinate to him. A first-person narrator is also present; but Maldoror often assumes the narrator's role himself, and while one can often distinguish the two voices, they are frequently confounded. (For instance, in the brothel scene in Canto III we do not know before the final sentence which "I" we have been listening to.)

What may the name Maldoror signify? Since the character claims to be devoted to evil, the *mal* apparently presents no problem. The word as a whole has a Spanish ring to it, which suggests *mal d(e) horror*, the "evil of horror," as a possible, not inappropriate interpretation. A great many other readings have been derived from French or Spanish features of the name. Perhaps none of them are "wrong." After all, the author has at no point felt obliged to explain a word resonant with suggestiveness and almost a provocation to decipherment. Suggestiveness, allowing implications to vary from scene to scene and keeping a sonorous enigma hovering over the entire text, undoubtedly served his ends better than clarification. Ducasse has in fact introduced in the title of his book a first sample of the uncertainty, ambiguity, and unease that will color its every aspect.

I hasten to add that, being no less susceptible than the next reader, I too prefer a particular interpretation of Maldoror, which is *mal d'aurore*. This is no discovery of mine; however, the reading is usually taken to mean "dawn's evil," whereas I understand *mal* as it figures in the expression *être en mal de quelque chose*, "to miss or long for or be deprived of something" *(être en mal de tendresse, être en mal d'amour)*. Maldoror would then be someone "longing for dawn" or "deprived of dawn." An obvious vindication of this reading is that Maldoror has renounced sleep and spends his nights arduously fighting it off; each dawn represents a liberation from his daily struggle. But I have a more general reason for my preference.

If Maldoror is a unique personage in literature, he nevertheless has his forerunners: Byron's Manfred and Milton's Satan, to mention only familiar English prototypes. In spite of his self-proclaimed baseness, he frequently wins our sympathy, for instance in his role as an irreverent latter-day Prometheus. Speaking to the abject Creator, he warns him,

> I shall hit your hollow carcass so hard that I guarantee to rout out the remaining scraps of intelligence which you did not want me to give to man, because you would have been jealous had you made him your equal, and which you had brazenly hidden in your bowels, wily villain, as though you did not know I would have eventually espied them with my ever-open eye, filched them from you, and shared them with my fellow men. (Canto II, p. 63)

Mostly, however, he compels our attention as an eloquent villain who like Richard III surpasses our expectations in the extravagance of his misdeeds and has the wit to mock himself as he does so. Maldoror claims to be bad as bad can be. He equates himself with the female shark that, after a shipwreck whose possible survivors he has killed when they approach shore, massacres her own kind as it feasts on the drowning and drowned. Maldoror plunges into the water to join her:

> . . . They fell upon each other . . . in a hug as tender as a brother's or sister's. Carnal desires soon followed this demonstration of affection. . . . The foamy wave their nuptial couch . . . they rolled over and over towards the unknown depths of the briny abyss and came together in a long, chaste, hideous coupling! . . . At last I had found someone who

resembled me! . . . From now on I was no longer alone in life! . . . She
had the same ideas as I! . . . I was facing my first love! (Canto II, p. 99)

"A long, chaste, and hideous coupling": is it possible to react single-
mindedly to this phrase, any more than to the entire scene, at once appalling, magnificent and preposterous? The preposterousness sets the
speaker's declared passion beyond credence; but as in other horrific forms
of science-fiction, we are entranced by some other passion that precedes
our disbelief. "A long, hideous coupling" would not have surprised us. It
is "chaste" that is unexpected. It not only reinforces the element of incest
in the scene (which as a result colors the following "hideous") but reveals at a most unlikely moment one of Maldoror's basic obsessions: his
exaltation of purity.

As in Sade's tales, the crimes Maldoror commits or witnesses—murder,
rape, and torture—are performed on innocents. Some, like the shipwreck
victims, are merely undeserving of their fate; most are innocent in the sense
of being guileless—an unsuspecting little girl, a sweetly hopeful schoolboy,
an angelic youth. Maldoror, unlike Sade's tormentors, both worships and
despises purity. He worships it for its humanity and despises it for its blindness to humanity's fate. The one being he absolutely admires and loves is
the hermaphrodite of Canto II, whose saintly abstinence stems from knowledge, not ignorance, of depravity. The evil of which Maldoror constantly
speaks lies less in the crimes he boasts of than in the illusion that purity is
the jewel of human nature. His vindictive rage is directed to destroying that
illusion. The youth abused by God in the brothel epitomizes innocence and
its just desserts:

> He was literally flayed alive from head to foot; along the flagstones of
> that room he dragged his hide turned inside out. He kept saying to him-
> self that his disposition was full of goodness, that he liked to believe his
> fellow men good too; for this reason he had acquiesced in the wish of
> the distinguished stranger who had called him to approach, but never,
> never, had he expected to be tortured by an executioner. . . . Without
> abandoning his skin, which might still be of use to him, if only as a
> cloak, he tried to leave this cutthroat's den. . . . (Canto III, p. 124f.)

Ignorance of corruptibility is unforgivable. Innocence calls out for punishment as a revenge for the delusion it creates. Mervyn's fate in Canto VI is the parable of this lesson that must be taught; it must be taught because cruelty is not a matter of choice but inherent in the human condition. Maldoror apostrophizes humanity: "'Fear naught, my children, I do not wish to curse you. The evil you have done me, the wrong I have done you, is too great, too great to be spontaneous *(volontaire)'*" (Canto I, p. 44). The "sacrilegious" abuses of the image of the mother (Canto V, p. 161; Canto III, p. 129) confirm Maldoror's belief that human savagery is innate, that it is his destiny to wreak, as it were, this knowledge on the world, in spite of his veneration of purity and his bitter love of humankind. He is the incarnation of the Baudelairean post-romantic. No new dawn of hope is possible, although he might wish otherwise: he is condemned to remain perpetually *en mal d'aurore.*

3

Such is Maldoror's view of the world. Its consequences are related in six cantos, each of which consists of a varying number of "stanzas." Every stanza has its own internal unity; but if the succession of stanzas undeniably creates a dramatic continuity, it does not produce a story or even a chronology. The one exception comes in the final canto, where Maldoror's encounter with Mervyn takes the form of an extended parable, which the author calls a "novel." This tale gives the work an ironically conventional conclusion, and an aesthetically satisfying one in which the reassuring ordinariness of the narrative method leaves the by now familiar extravagances of cruelty and obsession intact. Elsewhere, the succession of stanzas is invariably non-linear, a fact that suggests, at least to this reader, that not only in personae like Manfred but in the mosaic-like, digression-packed construction of *Don Juan* Byron should be considered a primary influence on the work.

The voice we hear throughout *Maldoror* is clear, consistent, authoritative, emphatic, and recognizable on every page; and yet, as a succession of recent scholars has shown, it exploits sources of remarkable diversity. It assumes many tones: that of the Homeric bard (1830 version), the scientist, the schoolmaster, the Gothic novelist, the introspective Romantic poet, the blasé memorialist; and there is no foreseeing when one tone will yield to another. The originality of the voice lies in their seamless (if unsettling) fusion:

> It is time to curb my imagination and to pause a while along the way, as when one looks at a woman's vagina. It is good to inspect the course already run, and then, limbs rested, to dart forward with an impetuous bound. (Canto II, p. 105)

Nor is appropriation limited to styles: actual texts are repeatedly plagiarized and parodied, not only literary works from the Bible to Baudelaire but encyclopedias, scientific publications, and current press items. Their documentation makes fascinating reading, but it seems ultimately irrelevant to what the author makes of them. In any case, as Steinmetz says, the reader quickly senses that other texts are everywhere looming beyond the immediate words. (The very opening, "May it please heaven . . ." is the contemporary equivalent of the classical invocation of the Muse.) Ghosts of many hues are summoned and infused with new life; it's enough to sense the ghostly presence and devote our attention to what they have now become.

Ducasse was obviously not the first successful plagiarist. (It seems fitting that a frequent object of his pillage is Maturin, who in Melmoth incorporated the entire narrative of Diderot's *La Réligieuse*.) But no one before him put plagiarism and imitation to such nimble and sustained use in creating a poetic identity—an achievement that distinguishes *Maldoror* as the primordial exemplar of such later collages as *The Waste Land, The Cantos, Finnegans Wake*, and *Life A User's Manual*. This role of precursor differs radically from the one assigned Ducasse by the surrealists, who saw in Maldoror above all a triumph of inspired automatic writing: coordinating a multitude of texts and styles plainly demands a most conscious exercise of intelligence. Lykiard aptly comments that "it is surely doubtful if a work as complex as the *Chants* could have been written at great speed," an assumption the surrealists were by no means alone in making.

When a stylistic manner is crossed with material from another context, surprises are sure to come. In the following passage, Homeric simile, a frequent ornament of the work, exploits elements from two technical treatises:

> The Virginian eagle-owl, lovely as a thesis on the curve described by a dog running after its master, swooped down into the crevices of a ruined convent. The lamb-eating vulture, lovely as the law of arrest of development in the chests of adults whose propensity for growth is not consonant with the quantity of molecules assimilated by their organism, was lost in the upper strata of the atmosphere. (Canto V, p. 166)

The first comparison is bewildering but somehow accessible; the second verges on the hilarious. Humor in fact plays a recurrent and wily role in discomfiting the assumptions we keep making as we read. It must be emphasized that the humor in Maldoror is strenuously deadpan, never declaring itself as such: like that of Kafka and Queneau, it is the inevitable product of a rigorous "logic" applied to material that does not quite fit (the logic here issuing, perhaps, precisely from the axiom that all the components of our culture are equal and omnipresent). Maldoror himself claims to be incapable of laughter. One of his several comments on the subject illustrates his feint and the actual effect of his words:

> "I often happen to state, solemnly, the most clownish propositions. . . . I do not find that that provides a peremptorily sufficient reason for expanding the mouth! 'I cannot help laughing,' you will answer me; I accept the absurd explanation, but let it be a melancholy laugh, then. Laugh, but weep at the same time. If you cannot weep with your eyes, weep with your mouth. If this is still impossible, urinate. But I warn you, some sort of liquid is needed here to attenuate the aridity which laughter, with her rear-split features, carries in her womb. . . ." (Canto IV, p. 136)

Its humor aside, this passage raises a question that can be asked again and again as we read *Maldoror:* what is the speaker actually saying? The words clearly cannot be taken at face value—what exactly is their face value?

If they are meant ironically, how far do they diverge from their intended sense? What is the relation here of the author to his creature? These questions have no simple answers. A more useful point to consider is that Maldoror's words (and his uttering of them) are not in their reading unclear. They have the eloquent reality of a theatrical event, one which carries us forcefully on to whatever comes next. This suggests that the work's "sense" should be looked for in its continuity rather than in any privileged moments that might reveal some central, unifying point. It must also be said that Maldoror's incessant ongoingness makes a point of each moment: since there is no center to turn to, the scene we are reading becomes central. Funny moments are funny, gruesome ones gruesome; and through the rejection of all reasonableness, as illustrated in the preceding quotation, the whole becomes not only a preposterous fantasy but a nightmarish one. Maldoror exclaims that "human beings . . . have rejected so indescribably the realm of reason in order to let in—in place of this dethroned queen— nothing but savage revenge!" (Canto IV, p. 142). His words recall the title of one of Goya's *Caprichos*, "The dream of reason produces monsters," and there are unquestionably late-Goyesque horrors in Maldoror, seriously rendered in their intermittent, almost casual appearances:

> Not finding what I sought I raised my dismayed gaze higher, still higher, until I caught sight of a throne fashioned of human excrement and gold upon which, with idiotic pride, body swathed in a shroud made of unwashed hospital sheets, sat he who calls himself the Creator! He held in his hand a corpse's decaying torso and bore it in turn from eyes to nose, from nose to mouth: once in his mouth one can guess what he did with it. . . . (Canto II, p. 76)

The grim visions are perfectly consistent with the rest of the world that the work describes: a world in which language, and with it thought and feeling, has been sundered from the absolutes that had underpinned its use for centuries; a world, remarkably like our own where, for those who resist falling asleep, there is no way out.

4

How written language is unmoored from an ordered reality is demonstrated in a very different way in *Poésies I* and *II*, Ducasse's next, last, pithy, and equally provocative work. Because most of the material it draws on comes from French literature, notably Pascal and Vauvenargues, it is harder going for foreign readers (the translator's copious annotations help greatly, even if, curiously, he has left source texts in the original). But the *Poésies* are no less original than *Maldoror* and well worth studying. They signally lack their predecessor's drama, in fact they are deliberately cast in a laconic, didactic style that seems a negation of *Maldoror*'s exuberance.

The *Poésies* consist mainly of aphorisms and short dogmatic assertions. What we customarily ask of an aphorism is that it ring true, that it clinch a point, sometimes new but necessarily self-evident, with succinct elegance. We quickly learn that Ducasse's aphorisms will not satisfy such expectations. Reading "Goodness, thy name is man" or "No reasoner believes contrary to his reason," we must assume either that the author has turned into Candide or a hypocritical liar or that he is pulling our leg. Other specimens leave us bewildered: "I can accept Euripides and Sophocles, but I do not accept Aeschylus"; "I shall leave no Memoirs." Points are evidently being made, but we cannot tell what or why. Aphorisms and doctrinaire proclamations are being put to some new use.

That use is making explicit a proposition latent in *Maldoror:* never believe what you read, because written language can be made to say anything. The *Poésies* in their entirety are a serious and sustained experiment in duplicity. Statement upon statement is made, each one more or less askew, and their succession cumulates in the giddy impression that making statements is madness clothed in reasonableness.

The work starts undermining itself in its title: except for a few Maldororian asides (subversions in their own right), the *Poésies* are as unpoetic as writing can get. The process continues in the text, which is presented as a defense of goodness, a claim made ridiculous by such declarations as: "A fifth-form teacher who says to himself 'I should not wish to have written novels like

those of Balzac and Alexandre Dumas,' for that alone is more intelligent
that Alexandre Dumas and Balzac"; that "The masterpieces of the French
language are school prize-giving speeches and academic writings"; that
"Judgment is infallible." The potentially subversive procedure of translating
statements of illustrious predecessors into their opposites ("correcting soph-
isms") is itself subverted by instances where the statements are left intact,
barely modified or tamely paraphrased. At one point, after allowing himself
(and us) the pleasure of a full page's worth of supposed abominations, the
author claims that he "blushes to name them" (p. 224f.). It would be tedious to detail Ducasse's many ways of turning his supposedly optimistic
harangue into a mockery of itself. Not that a pessimistic harangue would be
any "truer": the ultimate effect is that one cannot write definitive conclusions about experience, whatever their content. Furthermore, once our
necessary skepticism about the affirmations in the *Poésies* is established, we
can begin interpreting them as the objects of speculative ambiguity they are
intended to be. "Nothing is incomprehensible" no longer need simply mean
"no thing is incomprehensible" but suggests that the concept "nothing" (and
by analogy all similar concepts) is beyond definition. "I know no obstacle
that surpasses the strength of the human mind, except truth" is transformed
from a bow to piety into an insinuation that, if truth lies beyond our capaci-
ties, what is being said here cannot be true, that the truth can never be said.
The following paragraph is particularly stimulating. The first two sentences
leave Pascal's words unchanged; the last two contradict him:

> A number of certainties are contradicted. A number of falsehoods are
> uncontradicted. Contradiction is the sign of falsity. Non-contradiction is
> the sign of certitude. (p. 244)

This puzzle can serve as a synopsis of the work.

Out of respect for my own illustrious predecessors, I should mention
that many of them have accepted Ducasse's claims—in letters to publish-
ers and his father's remittance man as well as in the *Poésies* themselves—
that his second book represented a change of heart and that, having
sung the glories of evil in *Maldoror,* he was now determined to praise the

good. Interpretations based on such unquestioning acceptance of Ducasse's words fail, I think, to explain the text and its "inconsistencies"; but readers should know they exist and are held by respectable critics. I feel happier in the company of those such as Lykiard when he writes, "All opinions, Ducasse is saying in the *Poésies*, can be attacked and reversed, just as all words can be rearranged. Nothing is fixed or static. Stasis is death."

It should also be acknowledged that, fascinating as the *Poésies* may be, without knowing *Maldoror* many readers would not devote so much attention to them or be so concerned with "justifying" them. These thirty pages are nevertheless packed with their own odd brilliance and power. They confirm, incidentally, that the author of *Maldoror* possessed a deliberate, witty and stubborn mind, and that *Maldoror* is the product of that mind and not, in the words of one distinguished and not untypical enthusiast, a "volcanic phenomenon . . . an outpouring of lava from incandescent inner magma." Views like this imply the simplistic notion of a Lautréamont/Ducasse duality derived from the patent differences between the author's two books. Caradec rightly exclaims, "What an about-face [the *Poésies*] require of the reader of *Maldoror*!," and no less rightly refrains from extending his observation to the author. For Ducasse, there need not have been any about-face at all.[4]

Maldoror and the *Poésies* are complementary works. The first is a long melodrama written in mock-epic style, the second a short homiletic compilation written in mock-aphoristic style. Both are, except locally, non-sequential. Both are permeated by the awareness that the written word functions not as a neutral transmitter of pre-existing ideas, facts, perceptions or feelings but as an agent of ambiguity and uncertainty. Ducasse had already demonstrated in *Maldoror* the didactic method he would use throughout the *Poésies*. Here is one example of many. God, the *"Grand-Tout,"* who has already been portrayed as a self-indulgent monster and who has just returned to the brothel where he has indulged in sordid sexual commerce and vicious sadism, now admonishes mankind:

> "Drive evil from your dwellings and let the cloak of virtue enter your abode. . . . May modesty thrive within your cottages and be safe in the shadow of your fields. Thus shall your sons wax fair and obey their

parents with gratitude; otherwise, puny and stunted like the parchment in libraries, and led by revolt, they shall march with great strides against the day of their birth and the clitoris of their impure mother. . . ." (Canto III, p. 129)

This "good" advice is obviously made contemptible by its context; otherwise, the concluding image aside, it would not be out of place in the *Poésies*. In any event, drawing ethical conclusions from it seems out of the question.

We might say that *Maldoror* is a duplicitous defense of the unreasonable and the *Poésies* a duplicitous defense of the reasonable. Mark Polizzotti, in a recently published booklet, recommends reading the two works together "in the perspective of an infinite movement of evasion and disappearance."[5] He also comments that the *Poésies* "protect *Maldoror* (and the entire opus) from being reappropriated by the distributors of meaning," referring not only to professional critics but to the "distributor of meaning" latent in each of us. We are all everlastingly tempted by the comfort of pinning down what and whom we read. We should remember that as soon as we put an author into a cosy nutshell, we start missing what is exceptional in the writing. With Ducasse, we shall miss everything—not least, the extravaganza of our own bad dreams.

5

The English painter Trevor Winkfield told me recently that what he most admired in Ducasse was that no definitive reading of his work was possible. As a corollary, I can add that, starting with my first simple-minded encounter with the *Poésies,* no two readings of my own have been alike. This is a predictable consequence of Ducasse's mastery. In a sense he was too clever for his own good: like Kafka, he invalidated himself (except at the price of earnest misreadings) as a future Eminent Classic, an author who could in venerated monumentality represent a period, a tradition, a movement, a philosophical or political position. He relentlessly evaded the finalities that even minor monuments require. As Polizzotti points out, he wrote with an infallible determination to disrupt our longing for classification, for the "logic of meaning" that imposes clear distinctions between poetry and fiction, sense and nonsense, good and evil, truth and falsehood.

The truth, the *Poésies* tell us, surpasses the strength of the mind: it is not something that can be straight-forwardly written down. Reality cannot be identified as this or that; it's more something like "not this" and "not that" in a state of perpetual flux, the direction of the flux being nowhere in particular. Nothing is stable but change; nothing is certain but ambiguity. Nor should these statements themselves be trusted.

Meaning cannot be classified, except provisionally: it exists only as the movement through which conclusive events are shown not to exist. Ducasse's writing corroborates Nietzsche's view that our knowledge of the nature of an event cannot extend beyond the time and place of its occurrence. The next event creates a new context and needs new terms to be apprehended. Meaning happens in between.

So we are left with the unpredictable experience of reading and the consciousness of that experience. Perhaps, while we read, that is what matters, and we have not given up anything of importance. A passage in *Maldoror* suggests that this is so, that we do not have to spend a lifetime finding the right answers. The narrator is addressing the reader:

> . . . I do not wish to put your well-known passion for riddles to a severe test. Suffice you to know the mildest punishment which I can inflict upon you is still to make you realize that this mystery will not be revealed to you (it will be revealed to you) until later, at the close of your life, when you and your death-throes open philosophical discussions by your bedside—and perhaps at the end of this stanza. (Canto V, p. 163)

But here as elsewhere, it may be foolish to draw any sort of conclusion from what we read. The passage may not mean anything at all.

"Yet everything that happened was real, that summer evening."

NOTES

1. *Maldoror & the Complete Works of the Comte de Lautréamont*, translated by Alexis Lykiard (Cambridge, Massachusetts: Exact Change, 1994). All page citations refer to this edition.
2. François Caradec, *Isidore Ducasse, Comte de Lautréamont* (Paris: Gallimard, Collection Idées, 1975).
3. Isidore Ducasse, le Comte de Lautréamont, *Les Chants de Maldoror, Poésies I et II*, édition établie par Jean-Luc Steinmetz (Paris: GF-Flammarion, 1990).
4. Curiously enough, even those who do not agree with a "naive" reading have often used tags from *Poésies* as literal justifications of their own purposes; for instance, the Surrealists ("Nothing is incomprehensible" as title of a section in *L'immaculée conception*), the editors of *Locus Solus* ("Poetry must be made by all. Not by one" as epigraph for an issue of collaborative work), and the editors of *Action Poétique* ("Poetry must have as its aim practical truth" as epigraph for many of their early issues).
5. Mark Polizzotti, *Lautréamont Nomad* (Paris and London: Alyscamps Press, 1994).

A VALENTINE FOR ELENA

Early in my reading of Edmund White's *Forgetting Elena,* I began drawing conclusions: Elena embodied the incestuous family attachment that blocks individual growth; the weird ways of island society replicated the scary world a child finds outside his home. I soon came to mistrust such insights. Matters were not so simple; matters—cards of identity included—had been dealt double.

I had at first believed what I was reading, assuming that the book and the narrator's story were one. I learned that the book is a mirror reflecting the narrative for our benefit; our listening to the narrator tells us another story. After expecting a tale of discovery and rebirth, I was discovering one of repression and death. Under the social comedy lay not initiation but tragedy.

These realizations came in time. At the beginning, I went on reading because of the elegant oddness of the situation and, mostly, because of the sympathy I felt for the narrator.

Why did I sympathize with the narrator, a young man surrounded by trivial people and assailed by trivial doubts? He is not even "bad," merely confused. He does not know what he is supposed to do; he does not know where he is; he can't remember *who* he is. We sympathize with him, we "suffer with" him because we too are confused:

> Then [Herbert] looked at all of us and slowly pushed his chin forward, like a pianist embarking on a new phrase. "As to your question, 'Why

do we put up with Bob?,' I should have thought that nothing would be easier to do. He's a charming young man. We are all equals now."

Herbert's closing words, delivered almost inaudibly, arose as unexpectedly out of the drift of his argument as a human arm out of the waves at night. (5)*

The "closing words" leave us as mystified as the narrator. We share his predicament; we're with him. Unlike him, however, we do not forget. Book and narrative here start to diverge.

The narrator is also knowledgeable and alert; we do not ally ourselves with a hapless idiot. And the trivialities reveal only one side of his character. Elena will describe his double nature thus: on the one hand, "He could reflect other people's excitement, but when he was alone he was no one at all"; on the other hand, "he [could] set himself an independent course and seldom tacked" (74). If he were merely the impressionable nobody, we wouldn't care what happened to him. As an independently minded man, he is worthy of our interest.

Forgetting Elena begins, "I am the first person in the house to awaken, but I am unsure of the implications."

"I am the first person," the first and only: the world never exists outside the narrator's anxious perceptions of it; "but I am unsure," as if to say, " 'I' is the first person," a grammatical cipher as yet unsubstantiated. There is at first only an impressionable nobody uttering variations of this "I am unsure" ("I can't be absolutely certain," "I doubt," "I have no way of knowing," "I wonder," all in the first eighteen lines).

The narrator would like to know what he is—he wonders "if I am even an islander" (33). Like a child, he worries about urination and constipation; Elena will describe him as "a child, born again" (171). His state resembles that of Neoplatonic reminiscence: he recognizes things, but he has to re-learn what they signify. He is a child of about thirty, and there is nothing childish about his observations:

---

*Page numbers refer to *Forgetting Elena* (New York: Ballantine, 1990).

One bush, or tree, particularly interests me because it has three different leaf shapes, one that looks like an elm's, another with three lobes and a third that resembles a mitten. This plant has arched over to touch a holly bush, creating a dark tunnel of waxy greenery and a grill of shadows. (27)

But what he notices serves egocentric immediacy: What is happening to me, how am I to respond?

Other people are at first nameless: "The men . . . burst into laughter," "Everyone urged . . . ," "Someone asked. . . ." The awareness of others invariably precedes their identification. They are unspecified presences impacting on consciousness when and as they appear.

The exception is Herbert, who is always recognized, remembered, and named. Herbert is a person of authority, a kind of surrogate father whom the narrator respects to the point of fear: "I certainly don't want to give Herbert or any of my superiors grounds for complaint" (32). We deduce that Herbert is training the narrator in proper conduct: for instance, he makes him write a conventional spontaneous poem during their first visit to the island's hotel. If Herbert does not lessen the narrator's anxiety towards his surroundings, he provides them with an unwavering point of reference.

Otherwise the narrator's reactions are as helpless as a child's or an amnesiac's—"I have no way of knowing." When instructed by Herbert to clear an isolated hillside of its pine needles, the narrator spends his solitary hours behaving like an unsupervised schoolboy, making up silly games, cheating, feeling sorry for himself, playing with his penis, and as usual wondering what it's all about. His forgetfulness does not yet concern him, although earlier "an image, or perhaps a memory, had flashed" through his mind of being with a silent woman on the palace steps (11); he lets it go. He accepts his amnesiac state, if that is what it is. The first series of events he relates has actually occurred on the preceding evening, and the narrator has no difficulty recalling what happened then. This should make us start suspecting his version of himself.

In the course of this remembered evening we learn that an apparently important event in island life is the solemn arrival by boat of the prince.

Presumably the accession of a prince follows on the death of his predecessor. We later are told that Herbert is regent.

We never learn the narrator's first name, possibly because "I" remains such
a precarious entity. What is certain is that naming and not naming in this
society follow rules both whimsical and strict. Herbert at one point sighs for
the past, when "There were names for everything" (134). At that time the
Old Code, now superseded, still applied. It was a time when a family called
Valentine flourished—perhaps established names, such as theirs, are associated with the discredited Code. (The narrator will offhandedly reveal that
his own name is Valentine.) At present names are improvised, for people
(as with the youth the narrator baptizes the Pale Stranger) and more conspicuously for events—for *all* events. An early instance occurs when Herbert,
having shared an observation with the narrator, asks, "shall I call it 'the
clavicle'?" (14). Other names include "the yawning syndrome," "The Closer
Look," "The Fire Viewing," "the Little Stroll"—ad hoc labels that stick until
the events themselves are forgotten.

Speech, like names, is whimsically used. Some words come into fashion,
others are discarded. The narrator learns "'back' was the latest way of saying 'thoroughly' at the hotel" (4), whereas *attractive* is "a word we find absurd" (48) (while *absurd* is anything but that, especially if pronounced *ab-
zurd*). There is no such thing as plain assertion of fact or feeling. Just as the
Pale Stranger brackets a word in quotation marks, as if it were on probation
("This, believe it or not, is my first 'snack'" [60]), the narrator distances his
statements from his intentions:

> "Yes, read us this 'history of the Valentines,' " I tell her sarcastically. . . .
> I was sarcastic simply because I wanted to hear those words coming
> from my own lips. . . . How else could I justify lingering over what must
> be a perfectly common phrase? (69f.)

The narrator claims to flounder amid these caprices of language yet often
he triumphs: his banal remark, "Not adorable" (64), becomes the mot of
the day.

As for the written word, the New Code has no visible use for it outside the spontaneous poem. Like the improvised name, a poem accompanies events great and small, private or public; it does not commemorate them but transforms them into allusively arcane fragments. The ab-zurdity of the custom is epitomized, not without poignance, when Herbert and the narrator exchange "dawn poems" (135). Each of their texts happens to consist of the same word, *love*. But Herbert arrives at his result after uncharacteristic, embarrassed hesitations; while the narrator's is (so he says) the product of trivial word play. The two texts are identical; their authors remain far apart.

Elena the renegade hates spontaneous poems and has put writing to other uses in an autobiographical account of an ended love affair—a true memorial. Although she speaks of it with fashionable disparagement, her *having* written—as well as what she has written—threatens the narrator's supposed amnesia: she has inscribed the memory that he disclaims. The prospect of listening to her read her work out loud plunges him into a "curious horror," where his powers of observation desert him and, frighteningly, his mind is "investing objects and sounds with a significance devoid of meaning" (68). When she starts to read, he "can scarcely breathe" (71). Elena fares little better: "She's chained to that text, which was composed long ago, in solitude"—unwelcome fare for an era given over to the "adjustable amoeba" of noncommittal conversation. "Books," the narrator comments, "overexplain and . . . too slowly to be understood" (69).

Like the purple-and-gold book of ceremonials, this archive of memory nevertheless retains its power. For two days the narrator will at all times carry Elena's manuscript with him, like a suitcase of nuclear codes, although he only reads it when it is too late, when the bomb has been detonated and Elena is gone. It is clear by the time it ends that the narrator's own tale is no such memorial. It is an inner soliloquy, not a book—not a book, that is, that *he* will read. His own language is beyond recall; he forgets everything and learns nothing. Given the speech practiced around him, he may not be entirely to blame, although he has seen that speech can be surpassed, by laughter, for instance, and—Elena's preference—by silence:

> "I love it when we don't say anything," she murmured. . . . "Then I
> can imagine what you must be thinking. . . . I can invent your thoughts,
> invent all sorts of wonderful thoughts for you." (153)

Elena continues:

> "I can imagine our . . . [b]ecoming different people. Forgetting all codes,
> old and new. Walking out of a room in simple, natural fashion instead of
> *recessing*. No more arch comments. No more mystification. We all pass
> judgments on one another. . . . It's the easiest way to be witty. But if we
> didn't?" (153)

The capricious word reflects a capricious society that is both fantastic and
disconcertingly familiar. It combines elements of (say) an enlightened European principality in the wake of the French Revolution, Fire Island, and
colonial life in Kenya. Because it is a society in flux between regimes, it has
to extemporize many of its social rituals, and behavior, like expression, is
arbitrarily and sternly codified. The *recessing* scorned by Elena is a code word
for a code act.

Under the New Code, lesser codes of behavior are unstable and perpetually redefined. There are always rules in play, but no one is sure what they
are. Not only the amnesiac narrator struggles to decipher how to act in his
beach house (amnesiac or not, he knows there *is* a code to decipher): his
fellows also labor to improve their social styles—a neighbor supplies a revealing report on their posturings in the bathroom mirror. (Even Herbert is
caught out: "you will be amused to learn that he does the most . . . *ridiculous*
isometric exercise for the 'character' lines below his nose" [99].) It is hard to
predict what will be approved or condemned. It's enough for the narrator
to declare, "I've decided to be eccentric" (105), to justify the bathing suit
and woman's robe he wears to the hotel.

The Old and New Codes themselves are not much help. The Old Code
has become irrelevant except for the Valentines and their ilk, who continue in their traditional ways. And while those now in power act forcefully and even violently against the traditional upper class, dismissing its
members from positions of influence, burning down houses deemed

sumptuarily offensive, the New Code has merely enveloped old ways in a democratic gloss. At least that is Elena's view:

> "Under the New Code the islanders, forbidden to ridicule people for their low birth or humble position, have resorted to rejecting their inferiors for some supposed insensitivity to beauty or for some social blunder. But it all amounts to the same thing. The good people are automatically considered creative and tactful . . . ; the wrong sort . . . are always found to be bores." (170)

What has survived intact is the "island's cult of beauty," which Elena places "at the heart of its vapidity. . . . [W]e had been trained to thread subtleties and spout verses and deflate enemies" (170). Because the morality of the island is aesthetic, that is, one of appearances, its inhabitants ceremonialize events. This is done less through stereotyped performances (like that of the *fatalia* singers) as in instantaneous stylizations of the unforeseen. During the first evening, "a voice from the top of the hotel shouts 'Fire! Fire!'"; the cry is straightaway appropriated by those on the dance floor, who use it (as a "slightly bored, certainly stylized chant of 'Fire fire'") to invent a new dance step (20). By the next day the dance has become a standard number. The real fire is at once removed from its causes and consequences and made into an aesthetic object. It is, typically, dehumanized. The narrator later remarks, as he watches a watchful cat, "Movements must be small and inhuman and nervous to awaken a cat's interest, or mine. We're both poets of phantom inconsequence" (116); and the narrator, whatever doubts he may have, is very much an islander.

Claiming to see island society as an uninformed stranger, the narrator discovers a world whose only principle is beauty—the avoidance of ab-zurdity at any cost. He learns to see not who people are but how they look and sound. That is why others are nameless presences before they become identities. On two instances the same grotesque old man is anonymously described before turning into "Jason" (22, 143). Even "the woman" takes most of the book to become Elena. People's effect on others is what matters. And so everybody keeps wondering, how do *I* look?

Mirrors abound. The narrator runs into the bathroom to rediscover his own "friendly face" (29) or reminds himself to "practice a shrug in the mirror" (57). Maria, Elena's black servant and companion, uses a hand mirror to inspect a perfectly visible shrimp placed on her naked belly. Herbert and his household rehearse in their mirror. The mirror, the rehearsal space for performing in front of others, yields inconclusive results because those others are not present. They are the mirror that counts—they alone can validate or censure the *representations* that on the island constitute behavior. As a result, everyone is watching everyone else all the time to see not just others but themselves. Only the responsive gaze of others certifies an individual's existence.

But when others become our mirrors we can no longer understand them or communicate with them. The narrator sees and hears but cannot look or listen; he sees only people seeing *him.* When Elena's "eyes pass over me as though she didn't see me" (158), or, at the very end, Maria "won't look at me" (181), the narrator's "I" empties like an unplugged sink. Part of what precipitates the first of these collapses—Herbert's exposition of his "sexual meta-etiquette" (150), nominally addressed to bystanders but intended for the narrator—totally escapes him; the poison of the words he registers flows into him without his grasping what is being done to him; nor is he any more conscious of the subsequent betrayal of Elena that the words incite. He is committed to appearances and pays no attention to motive or feeling in himself or others.

The narrator has some justification for wearing such blinkers. When on the previous evening he performs his solo dance at the hotel, he acts with bizarre originality and sincerity. The dance is hardly more outrageous than the costume he is wearing, but to the others it is literally "unimaginable"— it lies outside the scope of known decorum—and the result is a scandal. Even open-minded Billy fails to understand it, and it leads Herbert and Doris (a senior Valentine) to reconcile their differences, forget Codes Old and New, and create a sinister New *Order.*

Only in Elena's company does the narrator ignore the gaze of those around him. He is otherwise assailed by uncertainty, above all the uncertainty of who he is. In this state of precariousness he sometimes turns for reassurance to material phenomena, such as landscape and music: their identities at least are fixed: "Bubbles topping one shred of foam glower red and green in the late afternoon sunlight and then break, one after another, like small eyes winking shut" (46). This reassurance is only an illusory attempt to keep the world under control; whenever the narrator's factitious integrity is undone, the phenomena he has appropriated escape him and turn against him. In these states of "curious horror" a deck chair takes on "a pure attitude of exclusion," two "pines are full of reproach" (68), urinals, sinks, and toilets become "blanched, vitrified persons" (121), and whole landscapes disintegrate in raucous madness. In his paranoia he intuits an indecipherable network of hidden connections underlying the visible world:

> Yes, even the most innocent and insignificant thing, like a particular leaf of grass, may serve as a template for all natural and human configurations and events, and if I could only pick out which leaf, which pebble, which shadow cast at what hour, which lowering of bamboo blinds, which combination of colors, exactly which crossing and uncrossing of whose legs was the ruling impulse, then, magically, all else would fall into place. (55)

Such speculation cannot bring the knowledge he craves: that knowledge lies in his past, in memory, "awakening old hopes or troubling their sleep" (130). But he has "no heart to pursue a memory" (139), because "I don't remember. I'm innocent" (159). Forgetfulness is the condition of the innocence without which, it seems, he cannot survive and for which he is willing to renounce his humanity and the sense of his own reality.

In Elena's company the narrator ignores the gaze of those around him. When she first catches sight of him, she kisses him on the cheek and pronounces one word, "Darling." Since he cannot acknowledge motives or feelings in others or himself, he describes his reaction as if it were that of an imaginary listener who "repeats the word to himself, or rather plays back the remembered, still vivid sounds," until the word "becomes a meaning powerful enough to elicit tears (if tears could be elicited from such a guarded listener) . . . able to arouse in the poor, hopeful, relieved listener such studious attention, my darling, my darling!" (43). But in an instant the narrator recovers the rudiments of independence. He does not forget Herbert—he promptly defies him and goes off with Elena (and with Billy, who accompanies her).

Elena is Herbert's antagonist. She has ridiculed him and soon pours scorn on his beloved spontaneous poems: "It's true Herbert and his ilk are always sending for that blasted paper and ink, and *he* is a formidable power—but could even he stand up to our ridicule?" (45). "Perhaps he could" is Billy's response; later, although solidly in Herbert's camp, Billy will actually admire the narrator's new freedom: "I rather like it. Do you imagine that it's always been like this. . . . That no one has ever followed the rules?" (119). The narrator is not yet entirely free: encountering Herbert, he is terrified. But seeing that Herbert is flabbergasted, he recovers his poise and sticks with Elena. (Herbert, clever as he is, joins their "Little Stroll" and even manages to have their group photographed with himself in a central role.) But immense as the effect of Elena's presence on him may be, at no point during the first hours they spend together does the narrator admit to knowing her. He will not remember her.

His amnesiac stance is sustained through their first sexual encounter. Such are the demands of innocence that he not only tells himself that he has never made love with Elena but that he does not know what lovemaking entails. Yet by now he has learned that Elena is a Valentine and that her autobiographical pages concern the two of them. Be that as it may, she leads him expertly and almost wordlessly out of innocence into a fury of orgasm that shatters his brittle self-control.

Later that evening, he discovers her as a "woman in gray" sitting at a hotel table with other Valentines. When they belittle the narrator ("he responds to the latest stimulus, the nearest voice"), the "lady in gray stands—it's the woman! My woman, my sister, my Valentine, my love" and passionately defends him. This dual recognition propels him into near recklessness:

he filches food from the deserted table and, when he learns that Herbert has observed him, confidently retorts with his cleverest impromptu poem. After a spell of despondency, his struggle with his demons leads to his creating social havoc on the dance floor and reaches a climax in his solo dance.

Later still, alone on a beach, he comes upon Elena once again. Now a murky figure of varied grays, she responds to his approaches silently and disappears into the landscape, a "dim garden goddess" (133). The next morning he unhesitatingly quits Herbert to go off with her. Then, after a day of lovemaking, he realizes that "When I'm with Herbert again, I'll attune my harmonies to his. I'll forget the woman. . . . An hour or two ago an attack of impatience overcame me, annoyance at being touched. *Mauled* is the word that sprang to mind, although she did nothing more than rest candidly by my side" (140).

Elena's candor is too much for him. He prefers the little codes. When she takes him to Jason's party—it is the eve of the prince's arrival—he deserts her. It is on this occasion that we at last hear her name.

The narrator, too, claims to have just learned Elena's name. He is lying.

He is lying to no one but himself—the narrative is pure soliloquy—but lying all the same. He has been lying with an insistence desperate enough to shut reality out except for a few occasional chinks, such as the slip he makes after noticing a perfume in Elena's bedroom—a casual shocker that should make us gasp: "Our mother may have worn it when we were children; it's barbarous and musky enough to suit the Valentines" (86). He claims to remember nothing; he knows everything.

Elena describes the aftermath of their first intimacy: "He forgot me. He became more and more eccentric, crafty and at the same time more innocent; he met my eyes with enormous innocence; he was a child, born again, all memories erased" (171). The narrator himself says, "I remember nothing. Nothing clearly, nothing precise: nothing. In that way I differ from everyone else" (130) and, more revealingly, "Of course I am innocent. I don't remember" (140; virtually the same words are repeated on 159). Why this desperate insistence?

By making him responsible for knowing who he is (someone half-inde-pendently minded, half-impressionable nobody), how he feels (without hiding behind imaginary listeners), what his motives are, and how others feel and what their motives are, remembering would impose on him the recognition of uncertainty. The narrator prefers what he calls innocence, meaning safety, the control of appearances, the reassurance of satisfying others. He has taken literally to heart the admonition, "In the struggle be-tween yourself and the world, back the world."

The world around him is regulated by Herbert, not only because he is "a formidable power" but because the narrator's father has given him that power by naming him regent. He is very much this father's surrogate: "Herbert put posthumous words in his mouth ('Your father wouldn't have wanted you to . . .')" (178). He is the father's never-seen (or forgotten?) face, at times the narrator's very own face: "A full-length mirror hangs on the far wall and I watch my reflection approach me—no, it's Herbert, it's not a mirror. I had forgotten what I look like" (120)—a surrogate identity. The narrator does not forget Herbert—he *never* forgets him.

The narrator forgets Elena. Elena is memory itself: the knowledge of life as uncertainty, possibility, questioning, the knowledge that shows up innocence as a delusion. The narrator lies in order to maintain the fiction that Elena has never existed because he is committed to that delusion whatever the cost.

The cost is being unable to look or listen, only watch and endure, even if the "curious horrors" that ensue lead him to the brink of insanity. The cost includes his humanity: in a moment of bitter lucidity, the narrator admits as much—"I'm an islander, and as Elena said in her book, Herbert's island-ers can't accept the paucity of the possible emotions. . . . [T]hey want to appear *not quite human*" (169). Of course the cost includes Elena herself, whom he "innocently" destroys. As he pitifully confronts the inner conse-quences of what has happened, hiding behind another imaginary stand-in, he says, "I hate the way these phantom things are starting to play around with the grief in the air. They should contain themselves and let the man who's grieved feel the grief, should he know what he's feeling and should that happen to be grief" (168). Yet for two days he has lugged Elena's book around with him like a repressed memory, in which now, too late, he reads "and you'll return only for a night or two or three and then leave me again. If that should happen, I don't think I could go on living" (168).

On the same day an exceptional hiatus occurs in the narrator's obduracy. The two sides of his existence are reconciled. The visible world he fears acknowledges him in overwhelming fashion ("the entire population of the island sinks slowly to its knees") and he becomes what he was always destined to be: "a prince, *the* prince" (176). He can let go; in the palace, memory, truth, and reality come flooding back. He recognizes everyone, he remembers everything, including his early trysts with Elena, "as if I'd known this all along." And he *has* known it all along. When he remarks, "As I walk barefoot down the dark corridor my muscles remember to sidestep a loose strip of parquet" (178), we are taken back to the start of his solo dance— performed to music from the palace—when he reflects, "I don't know the proper steps"; however, "They're still within me, stored within my muscles" (125)—another chink in his burnished armor.

The return of reality doesn't last long. At the symbolic burial that follows each prince's arrival, confronted by Maria's refusal to look at him and by a coffin whose inmate Herbert names, the narrator returns to his oblivion: "I remember nothing." For the first time, he forgets who Herbert is.

Forgetting Elena ends: "Am I a newcomer to the island? I remember nothing. Who is Elena?" The reader understands the double impact of the words: what the narrator thinks they mean and what they tell us about him. The title of the work becomes a brilliantly suitable, even necessary link between narrative and book: the reader understands the title, while the narrator is beyond imagining the appropriateness of the active gerund *forgetting*. He can say of himself, "I remember" or "I have forgotten," not "I am forgetting," still less, "What I'm now doing is forgetting Elena."

The book we read is not the narrator's. He could never have *written* his narrative. It is a moment-to-moment recording of his perceptions, set entirely in the present tense (except for two flashbacks, a first lengthy one shrewdly placed at the start, and a shorter one following the Little Stroll). Two

other lapses from the present, momentary but telling, are associated, naturally enough, with memorable Elena. One, encapsulated in the single word
vanished after a string of eight present participles, accompanies the initial recollection of a "silent woman" (11). The other, close to the end, happens while
the narrator is recalling an Italian song Elena sang to him in their palace days:

> "A visit to *this* room?" I ask him. . . .
> *Pioveva, piangevo.* That song always seemed so glamorous to me. . . .
> It was about a man who'd loved a girl years ago but they'd parted
> (*"Non mi ricordo perché"*), then he finds himself one day standing beside
> her under an awning. (180)

No more than that; but this unprepared intrusion of the "normal" grammatical past is as final as the "yellow note" of *1984* or the gentle reprise of
the title song at the end of the movie *Brazil.*

As usual, the narrator does not grasp what he has expressed. The text of
Forgetting Elena is always double, an inner soliloquy and our reading of it.
Nor is our reading univocal: in surroundings we decipher only gradually, it
shifts between possible interpretations of the narrator's role; it's not until
the final lines that we fully accept the omnipotence of his obsession. Many
characters in literature, from antiquity to the present, have embodied such
extravagant "humors," all-too-human traits carried to inhuman lengths,
although not until the romantics and modernists do these monomaniacs
appear as full-fledged narrators. Like *The Good Soldier*'s, the protagonist of
Forgetting Elena is an exemplar of the type.

As so often in works like these, the narrator suffers from what might be
called a comic flaw. When the narrator asks Elena after their first lovemaking,
"Who am I?," she replies, "My darling, you have the oddest sense of humor" (94), and we see what she means. His failing memory would be hilarious if he didn't hang on to it so compulsively. But its consequences are
serious, fatally so, and social comedy forces its way into tragedy. (Or at least
into tragic parable. The book is like a grown-up fairy tale—a make-believe
world of aristocracy and opulence—spiked with futuristic elements, the
elsewhereness of *Erewhon* and its progeny that recurs in such details as the

"sheets of edible silver leaf" covering the Valentines' meat [115]. By disarming us, the exoticism sharpens the point of the tale.)

Ultimately the substance and the genius of *Forgetting Elena* lie in its telling. The elaborate social and psychological constructs provide matter and context for a most economical dramatic progress. Carefully alternated episodes of a few types of experience—in nature, in society, with Herbert, with Elena—are knitted together in a tough, resplendent mesh of language to reveal, bit by tantalizing bit, the fabric of island life, the role of the narrator, the narrator's dissimulation, the narrator's identity. This slow sequence of revelations marks the stages of the drama—*our* drama, since it is we, not the narrator, who learn what is happening—and the stages of our participation in the narrator's tragedy. The much-admired "beauty of the writing" provides us with more than incidental pleasure; it enamels the sequence of cockeyed events with a glassy, repercussive surface over which we follow the narrator in his unwitting skid while glimpsing through the chinks of its disparities all that he tries to hide. We are smitten at the end of our entertainments with a most classic pity and terror at the sight of the abyss separating what he tells himself and what we see he has become. Exquisiteness, revealed as poetic eloquence, has lured us out of a skeptical contemplation of decadence into tragic reality.

In this brilliant mesh of language, colors provide a conspicuous skein. They bespangle the text with subdued glitter: "Black hair passes in front of an amber gel and stray wisps glow like sun flares. A diamond earplug facets scarlet and orange, then moves and projects blues and greens" (148). The colors are rarely symbolic (purple is predictably royal): they play another kind of role, to which the preceding quotation points. Of the six colors named, only *amber* is faintly rare; the other five could be found in a children's book. In the entire work there are only three words denoting nuances *(aquamarine, heliotrope, Kelly green)*, three metaphorical terms *(Mercurochrome, flesh-colored, sherry-colored)*, and five material colors (like *amber*); used again and again, the rest are plainest *gray, purple, scarlet, pink, blue, brown, red, orange, green, yellow,* and *crimson.*

How can such plainness be reconciled with the narrator's visual precision? Why should his blue be deprived of *periwinkle* or *turquoise?* The names
he uses may be simple, their effect is not; unless simplicity is understood,
once again, as innocence: the deft accumulation of childish colors in fact
reflects the narrator's affectation of it. In terms of the book, the expertly
placed simplicities create a substratum of lustrous preciosity. The author
turns the narrator's affectation to his own advantage: Why blur the enamel
of the text's surface with shadows of *fuchsia, taupe,* or *amaranthine?* Precision hardly depends on them ("Bubbles topping one shred of foam glower
red and green in the afternoon sunlight and then break" [46]).

Black and white, the two "colorless" colors, together appear almost as
often as the rest, and for good reason: they have their own roles to play,
emblematic if not symbolic—black, as we know, of the Valentines, white of
the new prince. One significance of black and white is thus political and
historical, a dimension that takes on a sinister cast when we learn from the
official palace book that "the Arrival once recalled the royal family's con-
quest of the indigenous black population" (166). Since the only blacks now
to be seen are Elena's Maria and a solitary naked "black native," it seems
probable that the island principality, like most of the world's societies, conceals a past of genocidal repression. It is not surprising that Elena, Valentine
though she may be, is associated not with black but gray (neither black nor
white); as Doris says, "Elena is not one of us" (155). Alone of the islanders,
she lives with a black companion.

The prince wears white for his Arrival; the narrator wears white from
the start. The clothes he finds waiting for him are revealed in "a blaze of
anonymous white" (11), the adjective suggesting that we wear clothes like
names. *White* in any case shines fleetingly from page after page of *Forgetting
Elena* until at last, when the prince arrives, we learn why those clothes fit
the narrator so well. The word of course also appears on the book's title
page—a discreet insinuation by the author that he, or we, might easily be
wearing those very same clothes. There was little point in adding that his
own middle name is Valentine.

Review of Contemporary Fiction, 1996

CHARITY BEGINS AT HOME

Each time I read a novel by Raymond Queneau I remind myself that I have yet to do my homework: the author's acknowledged spiritual masters—the Gnostics, Hegel, and Kojève (whose lectures on Hegel were compiled by Queneau himself)—remain on my shelves unread. Planning to read Hegel has in fact come to typify for me the well-meaning New Year's resolution that will never be fulfilled. My road to death, if not to hell, is decidedly paved with such good intentions, and I shall no doubt depart this world ignorant of Hegel and the Gnostics, self-deprived not only of what I might learn from them but also of the tools I need to penetrate to the kernel of Queneau's thought. In each of his books I sense mysteries, which I suspect to be Gnostic and Hegelian, nourishing each delicious mundanity. As I stare into the tantalizing background, the promising shadows vanish, and again I curse my sloth. If only I knew!

On the other hand, perhaps not. My fellow Oulipians, who are the Queneau enthusiasts I know best, had read Hegel before their majority and the Gnostics not much later. Strangely enough, they too find Queneau's novels mysterious. It seems that the main difference between us is that they have richer materials from which to concoct their mysteries. Even with their superior knowledge they speculate as unremittingly as I do in my ignorance.

The fact is that no one has ever completely deciphered any one of Queneau's novels, and my suspicion is that no one ever will. Perhaps that's part of their point. Perhaps novels, these no more than any other, aren't meant to be deciphered but to provide grist for endless deciphering, which suggests that the process of deciphering may be more rewarding than its completion. Certainly, when reading Queneau, unresolved residues of meaning do not detract from our pleasure, quite the contrary: they make us pay particular attention to what he does, since we know that explanations will not be served to us on a platter. The author himself wrote somewhere that only trivial literature provides answers, whereas serious literature raises questions.

The Skin of Dreams (Loin de Rueil), published in 1944, certainly qualifies as serious literature; it also exploits a quantity of trivia that would normally bore us beyond all patience and that instead induces only delighted curiosity. Body lice, to take one example, play a prominent role in the text. Countless references are devoted to them, as well as several pages of dialogue scattered here and there through the book. This dialogue is peculiar: when people talk about lice, whether at home, in cafés, or in proper society, they always say more or less the same not very interesting things; and this variable litany, in addition to whatever it may tell us about the relationship between humanity and the louse, by its very recurrence comes to play a role in the book that can be called musical. We greet its reappearance with the same satisfaction we take in the return of a bizarre theme in, say, *Til Eulenspiegel* or *Petrushka;* we furthermore sense that merely by assuming this musical role the apparently trivial subject of lice has assumed at least formal significance.

It has another significance. The recurrence of the topic of lice suggests that it is a very concrete universal of human experience; more exactly, that it is treated as a universal at moments of small talk. But the use to which people in *The Skin of Dreams* put conversation suggests that there is little else, that all talk is small talk. Is this necessarily so, and if so, why?

An interesting feature of this novel is that it virtually concludes with its own summary. The story ends as it began in Rueil, a sleepy suburb of Paris, where a talking film starring and directed by James Charity is being shown. The film's opening is set in France, in the last years of the silent movie. A little boy called James Charity, who is watching a Western with William Hart, suddenly climbs out of the audience and into the film, where he assumes the remainder of the hero's role before at last returning to his seat. Growing older, James goes on living in similar fantasies. We see him in turn playing the part of explorer, inventor, artist, boxer, and thief. His dreams lead him at times into dubious situations.

In one farcical episode he joins a provincial touring company. By chance he goes on to play bit roles, including some in films. We see him gaining prominence. He is cast as an explorer, an inventor, an artist, a thief. He spends time among the Borgeiro Indians, a tribe noted for its savagery. In San Culebra del Porco he meets Lulu L'Aumône and goes with her to Hollywood to try their luck. Fame and success await them. They marry. In the final take, as he kisses Lulu on the mouth, he signs with his free hand a fabulous contract for a multilingual film called *The Skin of Dreams*, the very film now being shown.

And the very book we have just read. Readers know, as the spectators do not, that James Charity began life as Jacques L'Aumône (*aumône* = charity) and Lulu L'Aumône as Lulu Doumer; readers also recognize something familiar in "The Ramon Curnough Company presents . . ." of the production credits. We are aware of witnessing a double transformation: Jacques L'Aumône has turned his story and his identity into a movie, and Ramon Curnough has turned his book into an imaginary version of itself. Which of course it always was; but usually such facts are not advertised. Here the revelation is so satisfying it strikes us as not only right but inevitably so. To put it more simply, we feel that there can be no other way out.

The written summary of the cinematic summary of the written book attains a peculiar significance by appearing as an *event* in the narrative, indeed as a climactic one: the narrative from the start has been composed of tangible occurrences and the imaginary occurrences that proceed from them, the two sorts existing side by side with one another in a state of perpetual, unstable exchange. Two apparently incompatible worlds seem to be present in human activity, neatly contrasted in the title of the final film, *The Skin of Dreams*, and the name of a winning horse Jacques has played much earlier in the story, Skin of a Louse. The omnipresent louse infests the tangible world as dreams do the other. The tangible or louse world might be described as the world of materiality and our direct perception of it; the other world is the realm of dreams and fantasies. It would be convenient to say that the material world is real and the fantasy world illusory, but this turns out not to be the case: *both* are illusory—a fact that the fantasy world acknowledges and the material world does not.

On the face of it, the material world would seem to be anything but illusory. The mechanism of cause and effect, its sovereign law, governs its human subjects ruthlessly: in Jacques L'Aumône's life, his demonstration of a movie kiss to the immature Camille Magnin is paid for years later by a painful love affair with her; the pleasure of pinching Suzanne as she brushes against him leads to fatherhood and an unsatisfactory marriage. Furthermore, nothing, absolutely nothing, can become manifest in the world without acquiring a material form; even Jacques's fantasies only become "real" as a movie. Given this unyielding presence, how, in *The Skin of Dreams*, can the material world be considered an illusion?

For one thing, material forms are transient: everything we perceive is doomed to become something else and is as we perceive it already a prey to change. The memento mori emanating from Offroir's discussion of the agents of posthumous putrefaction only crystallizes what has been happening throughout the book: identities and appearances incessantly dissolve, nothing is left as it first so solidly appeared to be. Early on, Jacques chances upon the blabbering senile husband of his concierge, healthy several days before, whose gift of speech has now been reduced to a repeated "Everything's okey-dokey-doke, everything's okey-doke": Jacques identifies himself at once, and intensely, with this image of the transience of flesh, bone, and brain.

But the illusory nature of materiality is revealed more tellingly in the plight of those who must cater to its laws; more exactly, of those who look to the material world for the satisfaction of their imaginary longings. *The Skin of Dreams* is essentially an account of Jacques L'Aumône's struggle to achieve a synthesis between two irreconcilable worlds.

Characters neither blessed nor afflicted with immaterial fantasies live comfortably enough within the bounds of materiality: Jacques's parents; the entomologist Offroir; Suzanne, Jacques's wife; and the veterinarian

It isn't surprising that Jacques's fantasies disarm him for material success. His visions always bring him to the achieved status of king, pope, or inventor, never to the paths that might get him there. He is, for instance, a talented boxer; but when it is suggested he train for the championship, he soon quits because he has at once "experienced" not only being champion but the life that might follow such success. At one point he bitterly admits that, young as he is, his future is already behind him (as his father has so sententiously told him), and he thereupon recites a glorious page-long list of all the achievements he has "unrealized." He says that he has no use for specialization, and while he makes the remark contemptuously, it is a pertinent one. Specialization means submitting to the process of becoming, to materiality in its inextricable succession of illusory stages (the last of which is death). What Jacques wants is pure, unmediated being.

But in the material world no such thing as pure being exists. So Jacques must suffer, and suffer failure, as a dreamer as well. Either actively or through observation, he explores a variety of human activities that might bring him freedom, all of which sink him lower in his despair. After boxing, he dabbles in gambling and a pathetically low form of confidence racket. His indulgence in sexual pleasure leads him into a domestic prison in which he is an indifferent father and cuckolded husband. He endeavors to get his hands on a chemical invention that will make him rich; his own ill-prepared efforts produce eccentricities at best, and when he approaches the pharmacist Linaire, who has actually found a cure for ontalgia, he not only is turned away by him but learns that the capacity for making such an extraordinary discovery has not freed its possessor from the bonds of the sensuous world. Jacques then turns to love to make his own escape. He pursues in turn the two Magnin sisters he had known as a boy. Camille, now Rojana Pontez, throws him out after ridiculing his childhood dreams. Dominique, married to a tycoon, hypocritically indulges his idealized passion without yielding to him. Each woman exemplifies in her way the mediocrity that follows submission to the material life, Rojana by her more sympathetic but bitterly narrow-minded pursuit of theatrical career, Dominique by her voluntary confinement in the world of wealth that Jacques had once dreamed of and that now disgusts him.

This disgust fuels Jacques's ultimate attempt to transcend the world, although it is initiated by his frustrations in love. His aim, both ludicrous and touching, is to attain humility, sainthood, and "nothingness." He achieves only humiliation, absurdity, and more fantasies, which now of course center on the glories of ascesis. He still does not understand that, even through denial, materiality allows no way out of itself. Whether Jacques strives after fortune, love, or holiness, he can only find more transience and more unreality. The louse is everywhere.

It isn't that the louse represents the inexorable dominance of materiality in human life. That view is more the received opinion of those (virtually everyone) who discuss the subject. The louse may or may not be a universal of human experience; it unquestionably is one of human conversation; and this suggests a more interesting connection with materiality, that of language, that is to say, language as we currently use it *not* to say anything to one another. (The author on one occasion mentions the pitfalls to which "knowledge of human language" can lead.) It would seem that people are condemned not so much to abide the louse as to talk about it, forever repeating a round of clichés (the women complaining that louse ointment makes for dirty pillows, the men recalling the incursions of lice in army life). The conversational louse extends the intractability of the material world beyond such unsurprising domains as money and ambition into the realm of speech and consequently of thought, where it contaminates the abstract topics we resort to in our contemplation of the human condition, not excluding such grandiose ones as love and death.

It is des Cigales's comparison of the death of the louse with that of the individual that brings on his first ontological seizure, during which he reflects, as he struggles for survival, that man is no greater than a louse—an image that occurs to Jacques L'Aumône at the start of his first movie fantasy (much later, in his ascetic period, he will associate the dissection of a louse with that of his own body); it is in speaking to Jacques that des Cigales vividly connects the doom of true love to this fragile mortality: "That is not love. You shall see later. One day. It squeezes your heart like a vice and it tears it for you crrac! and afterwards it bleeds, it bleeds. A whole lifetime." Less nobly, the louse also infiltrates the nest of love in the guise of *phthyrium pubis,* vulgarly known as the crab: Linaire in the blindness of his obsession with the adolescent Pierrette cannot refrain from mentioning it to her, and Jacques provocatively refers to it just before his illusions concerning Dominique's chastity are rudely shattered.

Jacques, it should be said, takes an interest in the louse that verges on affection. He declines filling the parental socks so as to do research on lice; he knocks a man down for saying only a fool could bet on a horse called Skin of a Louse (he confesses to an actual fondness for the name); and while working in Baponot's laboratory, he devotes time to developing a strain of giant lice. Jacques (it should also be said) is more than an ineffectual dreamer, and throughout his misadventures he displays considerable wit, originality, and a great if confused enthusiasm for life. It therefore hardly surprises us that he plans to raise giant lice, nor does the choice seem haphazard: it rather suggests that he is aware of the absurdity of the task of reconciling boundless imagination with the constraints of the tangible world. His "dream" lice would have embodied his quandary in aptly grotesque form.

The giant lice, even had they existed, would clearly have been a "reconciliation" of the two worlds that belonged less to the material than to the imaginary one: the potential giant-louse circus that seems to excite the interest of *le Tonton* (rediscovered in San Culebra) is already theater: that is, halfway to the absolute dream-domains of poetry, where des Cigales modestly flourishes, and film, where Jacques will ultimately triumph. The point to be made is this: there is no escape from materiality except one, which is to accept that there is no escape, that contingency and transience are the stuff of the world and of our lives. It then becomes possible to choose to imagine—to dream—exactly such a world, and in imagining it to transform it into an object of play. You declare yourself the world's inventor—an inventor on a scale that even Jacques had never contemplated—and do what you like with your invention. If you cannot materially be the pope without going through the process of becoming the pope, you can play being pope or anyone else anytime you feel like it. For this it is not necessary to be an actor: any one of the lively arts will provide the terrain and rules for such

games. It is not even necessary to be a lunatic; being a lover or poet will do—
such inspired folk all make things up, assign them names of their choosing,
and call them true. This is not how schools teach us to behave; but neither
are we taught that we have been born into a world where a dutiful pursuit
of reasonableness promises nothing but a deluded struggle for survival.

This in any event is the path Jacques chooses for his way out, or in. Even
before he comes to San Culebra del Porco, the battering he has undergone
(mostly self-inflicted) has so diminished his resources that things can hardly
get worse, and his lively nature has begun to reassert itself. Almost involuntarily he recovers his pugnacity; he experiences some professional success;
he takes up with Martine, who is smart and affectionate. One evening his
frustration with the virtuous Dominique abruptly impels him to leave town.
On the train to the coast he meets a boyhood chum. This man, who has also
rediscovered Dominique, has found her not only attractive but available.
His enlightening statement, "And so, that's the way it turned out: she got
laid," concludes the chapter and middle section of the book. We skip straight
to Jacques's arrival in San Culebra del Porco. The documentary on the
Borgeiro Indians that he had just filmed has subjected him to extraordinary
hardship, and disreputable San Culebra is the last stop at the end of all lines.
It can be assumed that the material world has no illusions left for him. It is
here, among other fugitives from Rueil, that Jacques meets Lulu Doumer
and sets off with her to Hollywood. Interestingly enough, we learn of his
subsequent life only through a newspaper interview read out loud by des
Cigales to Jacques's parents, wife, and son, who have no inkling who "James
Charity" might be. The interview is written in a systematically inflated style
that sounds neither like Jacques nor anyone else of this world, and this is
quite appropriate, since the "real" Jacques and Lulu have disappeared. The
final paragraph of the San Culebra chapter contains one sentence, "They go
out together," and not only from the Saint James Infirmary Bar but from
the book and from the material world. They have been translated into purest stardom. The question of their happiness is left unresolved; happiness
belongs to the reader. Jacques's disappearance from the world of lice into
the world of dreams may or may not bring his ascesis to a desirable end, but

pression "had been" raises the question of what, in these circumstances, "being" may signify. Still within the domain of subject matter, Jacques's penchant for identifying himself with others, "less in order to discover the other than to try him on for a few minutes," suggests the extension of moviegoing habits to everyday life. But the presence of film is most telling in its visual and dramatic use. The very opening of the book is cinematographic: a close-up of garbage tumbling out of a can, the camera dollying backward to reveal the can and the arm holding it (it belongs to des Cigales) and then panning to include the arrival of Lulu Doumer. At the end of the first chapter, dialogue from the next scene intrudes unexpectedly into a conversation des Cigales is having at a café: the effect strikingly resembles that of sound track and image overlapping (its conspicuousness is fully justified; it is at this moment that Jacques enters the scene). There are many similar straight cuts, and they never fail to bewilder and then delight. My favorite occurs when Jacques, returning by riverboat from Rueil to Paris, unfolds the latest *Paris-Sport* (a racing paper). One line later we hear an acquaintance saying he'd never have put money on a horse with a name like that. We thus know how Jacques has found out that, much advice to the contrary, in Skin of a Louse he has backed a winner.

Although less demonstrably cinematic, other moments appear to be at least partially derived from film. At the Saint James Infirmary Bar, Jacques, after talking to one of the B-girls for a while, asks what her name is: "Lulu Doumer" is the reply, which means nothing to Jacques, who has never laid eyes on her, but for us rings a loudly familiar bell; and to accommodate, as it were, its reverberation, a striking (a *visually* striking) event ensues: one of the nightclub performers devours a live lobster, shell and all. This seems rather like showing fireworks in the wake of a movie embrace (of course it's a lot less corny). The incident also suggests less atmospheric meanings, such as the dissolution of the tangible in the "impossible." If this were the case, the eating of the lobster would not only reflect the significance of Jacques's and Lulu's encounter but point forward to Jacques's final "appearance" in which he, with Lulu at his side, disappears like the lobster into his own story—one which the Ramon Curnough Film Company has now made ours.

There is, I should add, a "happy" coda to the happy epilogue. Des Cigales, with whom in his affliction the novel began, and who from the start has shown himself to be an expert movie fantasist, now starts finding content-ment in his poetic oeuvre. As we leave him, he is about to go to bed with Suzanne, Jacques's first and most-material wife. He is leading her toward *the bedding,* which is, fittingly, the last word and the last object in the book—the original and incomparable field of dreams. At this moment I am looking forward to my very own bed, and looking forward to dreaming in it, per-haps hoping that I may some day even manage to dream about Hegel and the mysterious Gnostics. Last night, curiously enough, just after finishing a draft of this article, I was visited in my sleep by a man called Valentine—but surely he is a character from another novel?—and was solemnly asked this question by him: To which class of mankind did I think I rightly belonged, the material, the psychic, or the spiritual? He no less solemnly warned me that all matter is evil, that only the spirit is good. He told me that salvation can only be attained through the possession of esoteric knowledge, and that such knowledge cannot be learned: it must be revealed. I then in-quired of him if he might not pronounce a few first words to start me on the path toward illumination. He acquiesced at once, saying with perfect grav-ity, "And so, that's the way it turned out: she got laid."

Review of Contemporary Fiction, 1997

IV

GEORGES PEREC

Italo Calvino once wrote of Georges Perec that he was "so singular a literary personality that he bears absolutely no resemblance to anyone else." Perec was not only original; as with Kafka and Raymond Roussel, his originality cannot be defined, or even suggested, through comparison with other writers. In his work there are many traces—references, even direct quotations—of the authors he admired, among them Kafka and Roussel; but it is difficult to find passages that can be described as Kafkaesque or Roussellian, and no easier to identify traits that might allow us to recognize in Perec the disciple of Melville or Nabokov, of Lowry or Thomas Mann, or even of Raymond Queneau, all of whom he held in the highest esteem. If Flaubert is undeniably present throughout Perec's first novel, *Les Choses (Things)*, the exception is only apparent: Flaubert here is not an influence but a deliberately chosen object of imitation, the results of which are put to unquestionably original use.

Perec's two most highly acclaimed books, *Les Choses* and *La Vie mode d'emploi (Life A User's Manual)*, earned him the reputation of being an almost scientific observer of contemporary society; but his work is essentially intimate. Still other writings—*La Disparition (A Void)* and the texts he produced as a member of the Oulipo—led many observers to think of him as a verbal acrobat, an impression belied by the candor of every page he wrote, even the most formally complex. Both misinterpretations are perhaps inevitable consequences of Perec's originality, an originality that is to be found neither in his subject matter nor in his style nor even in his renewal of available traditions and forms, but that lies rather in his primordial approach to his art. What Perec did was to reimagine and reinvent the act of writing itself. How radical his approach was can be seen in the extraordinary role played in his work by that basic unit, the letter: not only in *La Disparition* but in such works as *W (W or The Memory of Childhood)* and *La Vie mode d'emploi* it is used in a variety of formal and narrative ways to express the emptiness, the absence, the sense of death that lie at the center of Perec's literary enterprise.

Perec was the offspring of one of the greatest disasters in history (*"L'Histoire avec sa grande hache,"* as he said—History with its capital ache): the attempt at genocide that produced the concentration camps of the forties. It was in reacting to the personal consequences of this disaster that Perec discovered his originality. Deprived of a family and a community he could call his own, he found in literature a medium where he could literally recreate his origins. Of a book reread many times during his adolescence he wrote: "I began using it almost as an individual past—it was a source of things to remember, of things to keep thinking about, of things I could count on." Of his parents he said: "If I write, it is because they left their indelible mark on me, whose sign is the written word: writing is the remembrance of their death and the affirmation of my life." Elsewhere he speaks of writing as "a scrupulous attempt to preserve something, to make something last. . . ."

There is little point in separating Perec's writings into what is autobiographical and what is nominally fictitious. His work is of one piece—the transcription of a rare intelligence and sensibility united in the crafty and straightforward attempt to refashion a world where nothing could be relied on by assembling and disassembling those things of the world that we call letters and words, poems and books.

"I HAVE NO CHILDHOOD MEMORIES. . . ."

Georges Perec was born in Paris on March 7, 1936. His parents were Jews who had emigrated from Poland ten years earlier. He was orphaned young:

his father was killed during the Battle of France in June, 1940; his mother was arrested in 1942 and died in a concentration camp, perhaps Auschwitz. From 1942 to 1945 Perec lived with relatives who had taken refuge in the French Alps near Grenoble; after the war, he returned with them to Paris. He was admitted to the Sorbonne nine years later; his studies were irregular. He began earning his living as a public-opinion analyst. Later, he was hired by the Centre National de Recherche Scientifique as a research librarian specializing in neurophysiology, a position he held until 1979, when the success of *La Vie mode d'emploi* encouraged him to live entirely by his pen.

Writing had attracted Perec early. By 1955 he was contributing reviews and commentary to literary magazines. His public career as a novelist began in 1965 with the appearance of *Les Choses*, which was hailed as a masterpiece and won the Prix Renaudot. Many other works were to follow, even more remarkable for their variety than for their abundance: six novels, several plays and collections of poetry, autobiographical works, and a book-length essay. With the film *Un Homme qui dort* (Prix Jean Vigo, 1974), adapted from one of his novels and directed by himself and Bernard Queysanne, Perec initiated a second career. He was also a celebrated compiler of crossword puzzles, and in that capacity he was, after 1976, on the staff of the weekly magazine *Le Point*. His last published work was "L'Éternité," a poem printed in a limited edition in 1982.

THE EARLY NOVELS

With *Les Choses*, Perec made a spectacular appearance on the literary scene. The reputation of the book has survived its initial success: it has been reprinted and translated many times; extracts appear regularly in school and university textbooks. Those honors are based partly on a misunderstanding.

The book concerns the difficulties of a young couple, Jérôme and Sylvie, in the Paris of the early sixties. After graduation, they eke out a marginal life in the midst of a world obsessed with material well-being; more exactly, it is they who become obsessed with the objects of elegance and luxury (the *Things* of the title) that the world offers them. They yearn to possess these things, and at the same time they refuse to submit to the time-consuming demands of professional careers. Finding their situation impossible, they try to escape it by leaving France and settling in Tunisia, where they end up leading unsatisfactory lives in a postcolonial small town.

Les Choses has often been read as a sociological case history, almost as a tract denouncing consumer society; to some extent that interpretation gave the book its fame. But from the outset *Les Choses* also impressed readers by its structure and style. Its use of time and tense typically illustrates Perec's artistic powers. The first chapter, the description of a fashionably "perfect" city apartment, is written entirely in the conditional tense; the last chapter, an epilogue in which Jérôme and Sylvie hypothetically return to Paris, is entirely in the future. Between those two "unreal" time zones, the bulk of the story is related in the past definite and the imperfect in sentences of such Flaubertian inexorability as to exclude all possible alternatives. Because the grammatical structure corresponds to the situation in which Jérôme and Sylvie find themselves, it transforms a detached, apparently cold story into a touching personal drama. Perec says of his two characters, "Nothing human was unknown to them." Jérôme and Sylvie are the incarnations of a basic human dilemma (of which consumer society is merely a particular context): they desire a world they cannot accept because it has been imposed on them.

We find in *Les Choses* traits that were to become typical of Perec's style, notably an almost compulsive penchant for accumulation. In his next work, *Quel petit vélo à guidon chromé au fond de la cour? (Which Moped with Chrome-plated Handlebars at the Back of the Yard?)*, a rambunctious account of the efforts of some more or less bohemian Parisians to keep a drafted friend from being sent to Algeria, Perec introduces two new techniques: the exhaustive application to everyday language of a corpus of rhetorical forms (inspired by one of Roland Barthes's courses and also, no doubt, by the newspaper chapter in *Ulysses*), and a systematic repetition of words, phrases, and sentences that provides a lively counterpoint to the narrative. For all its charm, *Quel petit vélo* . . . remains a minor work, but Perec's use of repetition was to acquire an extraordinary resonance in the major work that followed, *Un Homme qui dort (A Man Asleep)*. That book tells the story—the absent story—of a student who drops out of not only college but life. In order to escape the tyranny of time and space, he gives up family and friends and fills his days and nights with indifferent acts, wandering through the streets, going to movies he does not bother to choose, playing game after game of solitaire. By pretending that nothing in his life is of any importance, he tries to deny the very fact of having been born into the world. Perec renders his protagonist's attempt to immerse himself in emptiness by meticulously re-counting the moments he spends between sleep and waking (moments when his will can no longer protect him) as well as by detailing his futile activities: out of their almost stagnant repetition, a slow, hallucinatory mu-sic evolves, until finally, recoiling from the nightmare into which his ex-periment has led him, the young man turns back toward life. What follows is neither a triumph nor a rebirth, only the plain acceptance of his existence among others—a moment at once flat, poignant, and serene.

THE OULIPO

Un Homme qui dort was published in 1967. That same year, Perec started what was to be his most perplexing work, *La Disparition*, a novel written entirely without the letter *e*. (The frequency of *e* is even greater in French than in English.) A written work that excludes one or more letters is an ancient form called a lipogram. Perec's interest in such rare and difficult modes led to his election, in 1967, to the Ouvroir de Littérature Potentielle, or Oulipo. The event was for him a capital one; he was to declare years later that he considered himself "an offspring of the Oulipo." The Oulipo was founded in 1961 by François LeLionnais and Raymond Queneau; it is a small group of writers and mathematically oriented scientists devoted to invent-ing and rediscovering "constrictive forms," procedures and structures so pe-remptory in their demands that no one using them can avoid subordinating his personal predilections to them. (It is impossible for anyone avoiding the letter *e*, for instance, to say what he normally says the way he normally says it.) The Oulipo provided Perec with an ideal context in his search for new and complex tools: an amiable laboratory where ingenuity, rigor and game playing are encouraged. The consummation of his Oulipian exploration was to come ten years later with the completion of the monumental *La Vie mode d'emploi.*

" W OU LE SOUVENIR D'ENFANCE"

In the meantime, Perec abandoned the novel (with the exception of *Les Revenentes (The Exeter Text: Jewels, Secrets, Sex)*, a work complementing *La Disparition* in that *e* is the *only* vowel used). He published a series of autobiographical works: *La Boutique obscure* (The Dark Shop), the record of his dreams over a three year period; *Espèces d'espaces (Species of Spaces)*, an essay on the notion of space, starting with the written page, proceeding thence from bed to room to the world at large; *W ou le souvenir d'enfance;* and *Je me souviens* (I Remember) (suggested by Joe Brainard's *I Remember* series), a captivating compendium of facts that once were common knowledge but have since been largely forgotten. (Perec's first poems date from this period; the most remarkable collection of them, *La Clôture* (The Enclosure), is also autobiographical.) Of those works *W* is doubtless the most considerable. It is part fiction, part autobiography: Perec sets the resources of imagination against those of factual reconstitution so as to invoke through their repercussion an excruciating, literally unspeakable subject. A strange tale—at first of mystery, then of pseudo satire and finally of visionary horror—alternates with the painstaking and often painful reconstitution of the author's early years. The tale, whose apparent subject is a utopian society grotesquely dedicated to the ideals of Olympic competition, and the autobiographical chronicle, which centers on the loss of the author's parents, move toward a point of intersection that is never quite reached: the product of capitalism gone mad that was the Nazi concentration camp. The relation between the two strands is never made explicit; it is no less heartrendingly expressed.

"LA VIE MODE D'EMPLOI"

Perec's longest and most ambitious novel was, like *Les Choses*, acclaimed upon its appearance (it was awarded the Prix Médicis). Nine years passed between the conception and completion of *La Vie mode d'emploi*. Perec had mentioned his project in *Espèces d'espaces:* "I have imagined a building . . . that has had its façade removed . . . so that from ground floor to roof all its rooms on the street side are instantaneously and simultaneously visible." Elsewhere he wrote, "The entire book was conceived as a house whose rooms would fit together like the pieces of a puzzle." In the novel, the rooms are those of a Parisian apartment building; associated with them are the lives of their present and former tenants. The book thus assembles a multitude of biographies, alternately touching, peculiar, silly, and tragic; critics have compared it to Balzac's *Comédie humaine*.

The puzzle not only played a role in the conception of the book; it also appears in the central story around which the other narratives revolve. Percival Bartlebooth, a rich eccentric who has spent years traveling around the world solely to complete a series of five hundred watercolors, has commissioned Gaspard Winckler, a skilled craftsman, to transform the paintings into jigsaw puzzles; Bartlebooth will subsequently reassemble them. Serge Valène, a painter who has closely followed the activities of the other two, is engaged in working out a puzzle of his own, one that bears a striking resemblance to *La Vie mode d'emploi:* he is painting the building in which he lives, without its façade, so as to portray what is happening in each room.

In these three characters Perec presents us with a complex portrait of the artist, as well as of man in his social and economic roles. There is first of all Bartlebooth, the inventor of elaborate and difficult procedures, the one who gives orders, a generous, distant, obsessively organized man; then Winckler, who must submit to the procedures in order to execute them, the subordinate whose genius transforms five hundred puzzles into a single grand design, someone obsessed, because of his subordinate condition, with thoughts of vengeance and death; and finally Valène, compassionate, solitary, like Bartlebooth an inventor of demanding forms but one who assumes them freely. Crystallized around these three lives, the book in all its profusion becomes a masterly demonstration of the origins and consequences of the creative act.

The artisan of absence

After *La Vie mode d'emploi,* Perec published only two book-length works in prose: *Un Cabinet d'amateur (A Gallery Portrait),* a novella about a collection of doubly fictitious paintings, and *Récits d'Ellis Island (Ellis Island),* a voice-over commentary for a film by Robert Bober in which, for the first time, Perec discusses his Jewishness. He left an unfinished novel, *"53 Jours" ("53 Days").*

Two things about Perec's work strike us when we consider it as a whole: its abundance and its dependence on exceptionally strict procedures. It is essential to realize that the strictness makes the abundance possible. Every writer who confronts a world without meaning and undertakes to transform it through language must answer the questions: Where do I begin? What right have I to speak at all? Perec's circumstances gave these questions special urgency. He was an orphan, and a Jew for whom Jewishness meant not a community of language or tradition but "silence, absence, doubt, instability, anxiety. . . ." Being Jewish meant "owing one's life entirely to chance and exile." Faced with such deprivation, Perec was forced to invent a place to start from: what he chose was the autonomy of complex structures, later subsumed in the Oulipian notion of constrictive form. (It is worth pointing out that Perec's early works are as formally exacting as his post-Oulipian ones; the procedures are only harder to describe.) The choice freed him from the agonizing problem of self-expression. (How can you express yourself when history has confiscated your voice?) Constrictive forms speak for themselves: they bring their own justification with them; there is no limit to what they can say. In *La Disparition* (a book crucial to Perec's achievement in its demonstration of the productive power of deprivation), he explains: "To my mind you can find in it a Law for writing today: and to gain insight into a thrust of imagination that has no limit, nourishing its own growth in colossal outcroppings, you must (you must only) submit to using no word gratuitously . . . to having, contrarily, all words function as products of a constraint, of a canon that is in total command!"

The abundance of Perec's work is itself a "colossal outcropping"; the expression also reminds us of his habit of repetition and collection. Clearly the goal of that habit is not gratuitous accumulation but rather inclusion: it expresses Perec's desire to expand his world as he creates it. Such a goal conforms to the proliferation of stories in *La Vie mode d'emploi,* and we can see how it could lead as well to the extravagant visions that in certain of his books take us to the brink of delirium—the Gargantuan mirages of *Les Choses,* the invasion of the freaks in *Un Homme qui dort,* the erotic explosion of *Les Revenentes,* or the subterranean world imagined in *La Vie mode d'emploi.*

These visions, which almost burst the fabric of Perec's fiction, remind us how fragile that fiction is. Perec knew perfectly well that even if he committed himself utterly to remaking the world through writing, his new world would be no less doomed than the one into which he had been born; and he leaves the reader with no illusions on that score. His books end in emptiness. The final pages of *La Vie mode d'emploi* are perhaps the most shattering of all: we learn that the entire novel has taken place during the moment of Bartlebooth's death, and the book turns to dust in our hands (everything that has passed is only fiction; fiction is no more than what is past). The canvas painted by Valène, the author's counterpart, remains empty. The concluding paragraph of *Un Cabinet d'amateur,* his last work of fiction, similarly undoes everything that has gone before: "Thoroughgoing inspections soon revealed that the majority of pictures in the collection . . . were indeed false, no less false than the majority of details in this chronicle, conceived merely for the pleasure, merely for the pang, of make-believe."

After an illness of several months, Georges Perec died of lung cancer on March 3, 1982, in a hospital in the suburbs of Paris.

Grand Street, 1983

VANISHING POINT

The reissuing in 1980 of Georges Perec's fourth novel *La Disparition* (1969) rescued a very intriguing work from the shades of unavailability. The book tells a funny, mysterious, bafflingly complex tale, in the course of which all the main characters disappear one by one. First to go is the Parisian bachelor Anton Voyl, whose obsession with an enigmatic motif in a rug he owns propels him into hallucination, insomnia, a life of fantasies, even a desperate resort to surgery, at the end of which he vanishes without a trace. Several friends and two detectives begin examining the circumstances of his disappearance. All eventually gather in Agincourt, in a chateau belonging to a certain Augustus B. Clifford, and there uncover a concatenation of accidents, plots, and crimes stemming from a terrible curse, of which they themselves have been designated as future victims. As the malediction works itself out, we learn about curious laws of primogeniture that are practiced in Ankara, the love of an Albanian bandit for a beautiful Hollywood star, and other exotic matters; but the tangle of stories is unraveled at Agincourt itself, where in the final chapter the last disappearance occurs, leaving only one survivor—the author himself, or at least his stand-in. . . .

The final sentence of *La Disparition* reads: "Dying marks this book's conclusion." The novel begins:

> Four cardinals, a rabbi, a Masonic admiral, a trio of insignificant politicos in thrall to an Anglo-Saxon multinational inform inhabitants by radio and by mural displays that all risk dying for want of food.

These two sentences share a peculiarity, one which remains constant through the book's three hundred pages: they lack the letter of the alphabet that occurs most frequently in French as in English, the vowel *e*. Perec's novel is an example of the lipogram, a procedure, dating back to classical times, by which a writer voluntarily excludes one or more letters from his resources. Whatever the point of using such a procedure in the past, it seems natural to ask why, in our day, a novelist would want to forego all the words in the language containing an *e*. (Such a step would exclude, for example, all but one word in the opening sentence of *A la recherche du temps perdu*, as well as the three main words of its title.)

A first clue to Perec's intentions is his membership in the Ouvroir de Littérature Potentielle, or Oulipo. Founded in 1961 by Raymond Queneau and François LeLionnais, both of whom wanted to combine mathematics and experimental writing, this Paris-based group is dedicated to the creation and recreation of constrictive literary structures—that is, of forms and procedures so impervious that no writer using them can avoid (at least initially) subordinating his personal predilections to their requirements. The difference between constrictive and ordinary forms (such as rhyme and meter) is essentially one of degree. Composing a good sonnet may be as difficult as ever, but not because of the sonnet form itself. On the other hand, writing a series of ten sonnets all of whose first lines are interchangeable (this gives a possible total of 10 x 10 sonnets), whose second lines are no less interchangeable (multiply by another 10), and where such interchangeability is maintained throughout the fourteen lines of the ten original poems, thus creating the cosmic potential of 10^{14} sonnets in all, is a task in which the formal act itself acquires an inescapable primacy. It was the realization of this very task—Queneau's *One Hundred Thousand Billion Poems*—that precipitated the founding of the Oulipo.

Another early and somewhat notorious Oulipian procedure was the poet Jean Lescure's "N plus 7." In this method—like a number of others, it requires a preexisting text to function—*N* stands for "noun," and "plus 7" means: at each *N* in your text, pick the seventh noun following it in the dictionary of your choice, then replace *N* with it. (Using the pocket American Heritage Dictionary, "Mighty oaks from little acorns grow" becomes "Mighty oaths from little acrimonies grow.") The device is entertaining, apparently mechanical, apparently unpredictable. With others like it, it earned the Oulipo a reputation of being not only frivolous but addicted to chance operations. The points are pertinent ones and worth examining.

An easily overlooked fact is that the Oulipo is not a literary school. It produces no literary works; it does not claim that constrictive structures are the writer's salvation. It proposes such structures only for the sake of their *potentiality.* The name of the group means "workshop of potential literature," but an *ouvroir* was also a place where devoted ladies gathered to knit woolens for the needy. In isolating new or neglected structures in experimental conditions, the Oulipo's aim is to provide methods that writers can use according to their needs. To the Oulipo, the value of a structure is its ability to produce results, not the quality of those results, which will be demonstrated elsewhere, if at all. The most the Oulipo ever does is supply one or a few examples of each structure, to show that it works. These examples are usually lighthearted: they are meant to avoid prejudicing the structure's future yield; no one should be able to mistake them for models. Queneau put it in other words when he said that the work of the Oulipo was naive, in the manner of "naive" mathematics, which develops problems for their own sake, without a preestablished point to make.

Queneau also observed that the Oulipo's work constituted an *anti-hasard,* an anti-chance. In mathematics, chance does not exist; and Queneau the mathematician felt that whenever a writer resorted to chance—either directly or by relying on such notions as automatism, spontaneity, or inspiration—he risked trapping himself in systems of "low-level regularity." (By analogy, Queneau said that when you try and think up an irregular series of numbers out of your head, it invariably turns out to follow a rather ordinary pattern.) For the Oulipians, even an apparently mechanical structure will, when it is deliberately chosen, offer an escape from the "low-level" systems that impose themselves on us without our knowing it; and it is true that in practice even "N plus 7" turns out to be more fertile than we might expect.

If the Oulipo itself creates no true works of literature, it would be surprising if those of its members who are practicing writers did not sometimes test the group's discoveries in their own undertakings. It was, after all, the existence of Queneau's *One Hundred Thousand Billion Poems* that inspired the Oulipo at its beginnings. The most notable of such works are probably Jacques Roubaud's **∈** in poetry, and in prose (aside from *La Disparition* itself) Italo Calvino's *The Castle of Crossed Destinies* and Perec's monumental *La Vie mode d'emploi*. (There are of course Oulipian works by writers *not* in the group, such as Walter Abish's *Alphabetical Africa*, not to mention *The Divine Comedy*. . . .) *La Disparition*, in which Perec creates a book-length work of fiction out of a particularly unpromising and arduous constrictive procedure, is a fascinating example of the poetic functioning of Oulipian ideas.

Jacques Roubaud says that constrictive form has three effects: it defines the way a text is to be written; it supplies the mechanism that enables the text to proliferate; ultimately, it gives that text its meaning. His statement reads like a summary of Perec's approach to *La Disparition*. His problem was: Having reduced my vocabulary this viciously, what do I do now? There is no value inherent in the product of a constrictive form, except one: being unable to say what you normally would, you must say what you normally wouldn't. Without *e*, what has become unsayable and what remains to be said? Perec's genius was to make this question the subject of his fiction; to make it his fiction. Instead of trying to inhibit the inhibiting constriction, he expanded it into absolute law. In Oulipian terms, he transformed a syntactic construction into a semantic one.

The first disappearance in the novel is one imagined by Anton Voyl. A captain in mufti goes into a bar and orders a porto flip. The barman refuses to make one. The captain insists. After desperate protestations, the barman dies, because he has no . . .

To make a porto flip, you need eggs: the word the barman cannot speak is *oeufs*, which to a French ear sounds the same as the letter *e*. An *e* is not only a forbidden letter but a forbidden egg; not only an egg but a bird (born from an egg). *E* is the number 3 (because of the three bars in *E*) and the number 5 (*e* is the fifth letter of the alphabet; there is no chapter 5). *E* is, of course, *The Purloined Letter. E* is absence, in many ways, not only all manner of holes and voids but *le blanc,* meaning blank, also meaning white: and *e* through this whiteness becomes not only Moby Dick but (via the Latin *albus*) Albion and Albania. (If white *e* is Moby Dick, three-pronged *E* is a fish spear.) Finally, because in this book *e* decides matters of life and death, *e* becomes king (a "white, dead king"), the Pied Piper, the vengeful father— the terrible Bearded Man who in his ultimate incarnation is none other than the author.

Perec has drawn from his constrictive procedure not only the material but the dynamic of his story. It isn't (for example) merely that Augustus *B. Clifford's* son Douglas *Haig* (the last name in its French pronunciation sound- ing like *egg*) meets his doom when, playing the Commendatore in *Don Giovanni,* he is costumed in white plaster to become his own egglike self (furthermore committing the lamentable transgression of singing *mi*): all the characters in the book are in flight from a similar doom. Every event concerning them involves the agency of an Enigma that will destroy them *whether it is resolved or not.* One protagonist describes this enigma with her dying breath as *la maldiction—malediction* minus its *e* becoming "ill-speech." An onlooker comments: evil is incarnate in the act of speech; the more we say, the more we become victims of what we can't say; salvation can only mean enunciating one word that would dissolve our problem along with our existence, and that word is taboo. There is no way out. In the last chap- ter, a character confronted with a text that is a double lipogram (without *a* or *e*) says: "Not only no *a*'s but no—" and immediately, on the verge of this impossible truthtelling, swells like a balloon and explodes. He leaves be- hind him only a minute pile of gray ash.

Those ashes are the book we have been reading: a gray of black vanish- ing into white; and they are The Book. By the end of *La Disparition, e* has become whatever is unspoken or cannot be spoken—the unconscious, the reality outside the written work that determines it and that it can neither escape nor master. *E* has become what animates the writing of fiction; it is the fiction of fiction. What began as an apparently sterile and arbitrary de- vice has turned into a dramatic enactment of our inescapable, paradoxical, hopeless struggle with language. The bearded Perec knows that, even as Author, he cannot escape his own law, which decrees that once his children are dead, the father must die.

In a postscript to his story, Perec says that he began writing *La Disparition* on a bet, that after becoming entertained and then fascinated by his project, he decided to try and make a useful contribution to the creating of fiction. Starting from the current notion that the signifier has absolute primacy, he would attempt to expand the writer's knowledge of the nature of his materials. The seriousness and brilliance with which he realized his ambition produced a book that is not only funny, stimulating, and, in its prodigious digressions on the duplicity of language, extraordinarily moving, but one that must remain untranslated: not because of the technical obstacle (not all that hard a one), but because an indissoluble unity determines every facet of the book (even, on occasion, its punctuation). The novel could only be re-created in a foreign language by inventing new characters, new events, new texture; by writing a brand-new book. In this, too, *La Disparition* can serve as provocation and exemplar.

American Book Review, 1981

"THAT EPHEMERAL THING"

Nearly ten years after its publication in Paris, Georges Perec's monumental *La Vie mode d'emploi* has at last been published in this country as *Life A User's Manual* in David Bellos's elegant translation. Where for the French the novel came as the culmination of a distinguished twenty-year career, for most Americans it coincides with their discovery of its author. They could hardly pick a better place to start; although I must, at the outset, declare my opinions in this matter altogether partial. Two chapters of this translation of *Life* are my doing; Perec and I were close friends—I am biased in favor of his work simply because it is his. I hope that the familiarity underlying this bias will make it possible for me to provide useful information for Perec's English-speaking readers.

Autobiography, or at least concern with autobiography, underlies much of Perec's writing, even in those works in which it is least obvious. (The obvious instances—Perec was a public-opinion analyst like the young couple in *Les Choses;* tried to stop a friend's transfer to Algeria like the gang in *Quel petit vélo* . . . ; became a total dropout like the protagonist of *Un Homme qui dort*—are at best examples of how a novelist transforms firsthand materials into imaginary narratives.) Although *La Disparition* and *Life A User's Manual* are not overtly autobiographical, I think they can be read, among other ways, as products of Perec's preoccupation with autobiography or, perhaps more accurately, of his obsession with the autobiography he felt he could never write.

Two passages in which Perec writes about himself may help to explain what I mean. The first, from *W*, describes how his lost and ever-present parents inform his writing:

> I do not know if I have nothing to say; I know that I say nothing. I do not know if what I might have to say remains unsaid because it is unspeakable (the unspeakable is not ensconced in writing, it is what instigated it long before). I know that what I say is blank and neutral, a sign for all time of an annihilation for all time . . .

> That is what I say, that is what I write, and nothing else is to be found in the words I inscribe. . . . It would do me no good to track down my slips (for example, I wrote "I committed" instead of "I made" concerning my mistakes in the transcription of my mother's name) or to daydream for two hours about the length of my father's greatcoat. . . . I shall never find anything . . . besides the last reflection of a speech absent from the written word, the outrage of their silence and my silence. I do not write in order to say that I will say nothing, I do not write in order to say that I have nothing to say. I write. I write because we lived together, because I was one among them, a shadow among their shadows, a body next to their bodies. I write because they left in me their indelible mark, whose trace is writing. In writing their memory is dead. Writing is the remembrance of their death and the affirmation of my life.

Perec once said that he had been deprived not only of his mother and father but of their deaths. They had been taken away from him behind his back.

Perec considered his Jewishness as another condition of deprivation. In the commentary he wrote to the film *Chronicles of Ellis Island*, he contrasts his attitude with that of the director, Robert Bober, to whom being Jewish "means continuing to reaffirm one's place in a tradition, a language, and a community":

> What I find present [on Ellis Island] can in no way be called references or roots or remnants, rather their opposite: something shapeless, on the outer edge of what is sayable, something that might be called closure, or cleavage, or severance, something which in my mind is linked in a most intimate and confused way with the very fact of being a Jew. . . .

[Being a Jew] isn't a sign of belonging. . . . It seems closer to a kind of silence, emptiness, to being a question, a questioning, a dubiousness, an uneasiness, an uneasy certainty, and looming beyond that, another certainty . . . : that of having been labeled a Jew, Jew therefore victim, and so beholden for being alive to exile and luck. . . .

In some way I'm estranged from myself; in some way I'm "different"—not different from others but from "my own people": I don't speak the language my parents spoke, I don't share whatever memories they had. Something that was theirs and made them what they are—their culture, their experience, their hope—was not handed down to me.

The pretexts of writing, for Perec, are "silence," emptiness, and death: "I know that I do not say anything" means not "I have nothing to say" but rather "nothingness cannot be said." But if silence and emptiness seem a reasonable response to the historical deprivation to which Perec found himself condemned, how then explain the abundance of his output? Why did he become a writer in the first place?

A partial answer to the last question can be found in another passage in *W*, in which he describes his experience as an adolescent reader. Speaking of Dumas's *Vingt ans après,* he tells of reading it over and over again to make sure all its familiar details are still in place. "I not only felt that I had always known them but that they had almost provided me with my own story: [they were the] source of unfathomable memory, of perpetual renewal, of certainty." As an adult, he finds in rereading the books he loves the joy of "complicity and, beyond even that, of kinship restored at last."

Many of us who are not orphans have had the experience of literature as "family," even if we can only guess at its intensity in Perec's case. However, the experience not only partially explains Perec's attraction to literature but, once he felt the urge to write, how he dealt with his particular quandaries: since the sense of loss and of being lost is inexpressible, what can you say in its place? How can you say anything at all?

Instead of struggling to find an answer to these questions, Perec sidestepped them, by becoming what used to be called a formalist, ignoring history, looking for things to do inside language, inside writing. Instead of trying to find words to describe the world, he tried to invent interesting ways to use words in their own right. He set himself "precious" tasks. In *Les Choses*, for instance, he methodically explored Flaubert's method of using syntax for stylistic purposes (Perec's opening chapter is written entirely in the conditional tense, the final one in the future tense), using the advertising pages of glossy magazines as his subject matter. The book was read as a realistic commentary on the perils of the consumer society. There is no denying the vividness and authenticity of *Les Choses;* but it must also be said that the subject of the book became "real" as it was invented in the arbitrary tasks the author set himself, without which he might not have written the book at all.

Perec's approach to writing was conveniently codified when, in the mid-sixties, he became, as later did Italo Calvino and the present writer, a member of the Oulipo. Albert Mobilio neatly described Oulipian activity in a recent article in the *Village Voice:*

> Unabashedly arbitrary in conception, Oulipian constructions nonetheless adhere to an internal logic. Formal constraints spur the imagination to thrive within strict limits similar to those of sonnets and sestinas. Of course, language presents its own brick wall of rules: grammar and available vocabulary. Self-contained and ingeniously coherent, Oulipian subsystems derange the grid and impose a fresh, idiosyncratic order that mirrors language's own arbitrary nature.

Perec distinguished himself at many levels of Oulipian experiment, which has ranged from the trivial (spoonerisms) to high art (Calvino's reader-writer chapters in *If on a Winter's Night a Traveler*). Such difficult abstract procedures appealed to him as a writer of fiction because, I suggest, they take formalism to its extreme limit in providing ways of composing that are empty, autonomous, and self-propagating. Empty in that they presuppose no particular content, thus finessing the question of what to say, of how to deal with history; autonomous in that they require no justification beyond obedience to their rules; self-propagating in that, through a simple application of those rules, works are almost automatically generated. Oulipian procedures offer a clear escape from the paralysis of writer's block, or, in Perec's case, a deep sense of historical displacement. More positively, the procedures can become tasks as inspiring as the creation of any hero or heroine. Several years ago in another context the composer David Del Tredici declared: "For whatever reason, you emotionally embrace a technical process because it excites you, and the restriction really is a way of defining your personality. You have to fill the severity with a lot of passion."

How Perec filled his "severities" is typically illustrated by *La Disparition*, his most purely Oulipian novel. The book is written without any word containing the letter *e*, a procedure even harder in French than in English (although in English, whenever I try it, hard enough for me to glue an upturned thumbtack on the *e* key of my typewriter). Perec took this absurdly confining idea and made of it a way of creating incident, situation, and plot. Eggs *(oeufs)* are declared to be taboo because they sound like *e*. And so a barman drops dead when asked to concoct a porto flip, a cocktail requiring port wine and eggs:

> Voix du gars, s'attablant (air bourru, sinon martial): Garçon!
> Voix du barman (qui connaît son chaland): Bonjour, mon Commandant.
> Voix du Commandant (satisfait qu'on l'ait compris, quoiqu'il soit pour l'instant civil): Bonjour, mon garçon, bonjour!
> Voix du barman (qui jadis apprit l'anglais dans un cours du soir): What can I do for you?
> Vox du Commandant (salivant): Fais-moi un porto-flip.
> Voix du barman (soudain chagrin): Quoi? Un porto-flip!
> Voix du Commandant (affirmatif): Mais oui, un porto-flip!
> Voix du barman (qui paraît souffrir): On . . . n'a . . . pas . . . ça . . . ici . . .
> Voix du Commandant (bondissant): Quoi! Mais j'ai bu trois porto-flips ici il y a moins d'un an!
> Voix du barman (tout à fait faiblard): Il n'y a plus . . . Il n'y a plus . . .
> Voix du Commandant (furibond): Allons, tu as du porto, non?
> Voix du barman (agonisant): Oui . . . mais . . .
> Voix du Commandant (fulminant): Alors? Alors? Il y a aussi . . .

Voix du barman (mourant tout à fait): Aaaaaaah!! Chut!! Chut!!
Mort du barman.
Voix du Commandant (constantant): Rigor mortis.*

Since birds are born of eggs, they too are outlawed, or more exactly
become dangerous outlaws; so does the number five (*e* is the fifth vowel);
so does whiteness because of the blank *(blanc)* left by *e*'s disappearance; and
so therefore does Moby Dick (so also the three-pronged, *e*-shaped harpoon).

The central story tells of the disappearance one by one of all its main
characters, victims of a nameless, terrible power that threatens at any moment to destroy everything in sight—a power that ultimately takes the shape
of a bearded king who devours his offspring (resembling not only Saturn
but the author himself) and that is at one point defined as an "enigma that
will destroy us whether it is solved or not." In the world of *La Disparition*,
threatened by the absent but ever-menacing *e*, people can neither speak
nor remain silent: it might be said that in this plot that combines elements
of a detective story, a tale of adventure, and a Marx Brothers movie, Perec

---

*Man (sitting down, looking not only churlish but almost martial): Bar-
man!

Barman (who knows this guy): Good morning, Captain.

Captain (happy, although in mufti, for this nod to his status): Good
morning, my lad, good morning.

Barman (who has had a flirtation with Italian at night school): Posso
far qualcosa?

Captain (licking his lips): How about a porto flip?

Barman (downcast): What? A porto flip?

Captain (insisting): What do you think I said? Naturally, a porto flip.

Barman (visibly paling): No . . . such . . . thing . . . at *this* bar.

Captain (irritably): What? I drank porto flips at *this* bar last January,
May, and August.

Barman (totally sunk): But not now . . . Not now . . .

Captain (furious): You got port, right?

Barman (actually dying): OK, but . . .

Captain (fulminating): So? So? You also got—

Barman (last gasp): Aaaargh! Stop! Stop! (Barman falls to floor, kaput).

Captain (judiciously noting): Rigor mortis.

has also replicated his historical situation—the sense of historical loss—without even mentioning it.

No such simple procedure characterizes *Life A User's Manual*. *La Disparition* wears its torn-out heart on its sleeve; Perec's later and longer work depends on multiple artifices, some of them mathematically complex, all of them virtually invisible. The importance of abstract procedures nevertheless remains the same: they enable the author to choose and organize his material, and in this case to produce an almost Balzacian "world" teeming with characters and events. But I think the time has come to forget about Oulipian structures, and Perec would probably agree: he repeatedly compared the devices used in writing *Life* to the scaffolding of a building, something to be discarded once the work was completed. *Life* is not a puzzle, or else it is one that the author has already solved, leaving every piece in place. It presents with almost nonchalant transparency a prodigious variety of objects and of both ordinary and exotic characters.

The narrative conceit of *Life A User's Manual*, originally suggested by a Saul Steinberg drawing, is to imagine a nine-story, turn-of-the-century Parisian apartment building from which the façade has been removed. Each chapter of the novel corresponds to one of the streetside rooms thus revealed and describes the objects it contains, the present occupants of the room or of the apartment to which it belongs, sometimes the former occupants. The conceit might seem likely to produce no more than a catalog of lives and things; and *Life* often seems to present such a catalog, replete with accounts of kitchen equipment, bric-a-brac, and undistinguished works of art, all detailed in meticulous and neutral terms. But this is only pretense, an elaborate display of hyperrealism veiling the reality of what we slowly and almost unwittingly learn as we wend our distractible way from room to room.

Among the thirty-odd characters whose stories are told at length, three are soon recognized as central: Bartlebooth, Winckler, and Valène. As his name implies, compounded as it is from Valery Larbaud's Barnabooth and Melville's Bartleby, Percival Bartlebooth is an Englishman endowed with the virtually unlimited wealth of the first and with the second's enduring conviction of the pointlessness of human existence. To fill up the vain time ahead of him, in his youth he conceives a preposterously demanding and altogether gratuitous scheme that will require several decades to carry out. First, he will master the technique of painting watercolors. He will then travel around the world to paint views of five hundred widely scattered seaports, at the rate of two a month. The watercolors will then be transformed into jigsaw puzzles that Bartlebooth, once his travels are over, will reassemble, after which each will be dispatched to the place where it was painted, there to be destroyed. Gaspard Winckler, a craftsman of genius, is hired by Bartlebooth to turn the watercolors into puzzles. Serge Valène is a painter who teaches Bartlebooth the skills he needs.

At the start of the book, Bartlebooth's scheme is nearing its conclusion. The watercolors have all been made into puzzles, and Bartlebooth has almost completed the 439th of them. Winckler has died after a life of disillusion and heartache; Valène and Bartlebooth by now are old men. Valène is engaged in a project of his own, which resembles that of Perec's novel. He is painting the building in which he, Bartlebooth, and Winckler have lived, with the façade removed so that each room behind it lies open to view. An intensely compassionate man, Valène is obsessed by a sense of the transience of things and of human life. Bartlebooth, the kind and courteous if distant gentleman, has withdrawn into solitude, alone with the puzzles that Winckler has left him, each designed to baffle and frustrate him with their unpredictable and ever more difficult configurations.

As a background to these three lives we are told a multitude of stories about the other inhabitants of the building. One can hardly say that these lives remind us of the three principal ones, except in one respect. Like Bartlebooth with his insane scheme, Winckler with the revenge he has plotted against his employer through his five hundred puzzles, and Valène with his gigantic painting project, most of the secondary characters are dominated by some obsession. Henri Fresnel sacrifices his family and his career in his determination to become an actor. His wife devotes her life to waiting for him so that she can throw him out when he comes back. The ethnographer Appenzzell wastes away, haunted by the memory of an elusive primitive tribe. Bartlebooth's uncle,

James Sherwood, squanders a fortune because of his mania for collecting *unica* (one-of-a-kind objects). Sven Ericsson spends many years and most of his money in order to murder the accidental agent of his child's death. The entire youth of Léon Marcia is consumed in a compulsive reading binge. Then there is the case of Cinoc,

> who . . . pursued a curious profession. As he said himself, he was a "word-killer": he worked at keeping Larousse dictionaries up to date. But whilst other compilers sought out new words and meanings, his job was to make room for them by eliminating all the words and meanings that had fallen into disuse.
>
> When he retired in nineteen sixty-five, after fifty-three years of scrupulous service, he had disposed of hundreds and thousands of tools, techniques, customs, beliefs, sayings, dishes, games, nicknames, weights and measures; he had wiped dozens of islands, hundreds of cities and rivers, and thousands of townships off the map; he had returned to taxonomic anonymity hundreds of varieties of cattle, species of birds, insects, and snakes, rather special sorts of fish, kinds of crustaceans, slightly dissimilar plants and particular breeds of vegetables and fruits; and cohorts of geographers, missionaries, entomologists, Church Fathers, men of letters, generals, Gods & Demons had been swept by his hand into eternal obscurity.

The accumulation of such stories, together with that of the three main characters, produces an effect of inevitability, of fatality, almost of futility: less that these obsessive human lives allow no room for choice than that knowledge and self-knowledge not only do not modify fatality but confirm it. It is as if no possibility existed outside a single narrative possibility, as if human life was confined by a syntax as unyielding as language itself, as if life were the outcome of some arbitrary, abstract, formal constraint.

The relations of Bartlebooth, Winckler, and Valène underscore this sense of fatality. It is tempting to describe the three men in Marxist terms (Perec after all was a socialist): Bartlebooth the capitalist, the master; Winckler the exploited laborer condemned to work at the production of goods he will never use; Valène the sympathetic but expendable parasite, full of petit-bourgeois sensibility. Although such an account would be absurdly reductive, it does suggest something of Perec's view of fatality and choice, with respect to a particular form of production, that of the artist, especially the writer.

If we look at our triumvirate as a composite portrait of the artist, we can identify Bartlebooth as the passionless inventor of abstract and gratuitous formal procedures; Winckler as the rebellious agent who nevertheless submits to such procedures; Valène as the compassionate witness who freely invents his own forms. Each of the three depends on the others: Valène and Winckler are both employed by Bartlebooth, who of course cannot carry out his scheme without them. Naturally Valène's position strikes us as the most enviable: if you have to adopt demanding forms, you are surely better off choosing your own. But the events of *Life* do not confirm our bias. Valène barely manages to begin his great painting. Bartlebooth will never solve the remaining puzzles. Only Winckler, bitter and resentful, succeeds, by creating (in a Proustian cork-lined room) his own unforeseen and hermetic strategy of revenge while executing the years-long task that has been imposed on him. So choice—at least the kind of choice that produces results—lies not in the unconstrained will but in the circumstances of fatality itself, as though choice and fatality were anything but opposites.

Life does not have a conclusion. It only comes to an end with the disappearance of its two surviving protagonists. The final pages proceed toward a last image of the dying Bartlebooth bent over a puzzle of which every segment is in place but one. We realize that everything that has taken place so far is shown to be only a prelude to this moment, an elaborate and elusive preparation. The abundance of stories, the multiplicity of lives, have brought us to a conclusion empty of life and possibility; all we have read now collapses in a hopeless finality. The effect is of "something," in Perec's words, "that might be called closure, or cleavage, or severance." We are left, as the author elsewhere remarked, with nothing "except this object you have shut, a few images, blank shadows or dark ghosts that have flitted through your head and mine."

One of the transient inhabitants of Perec's apartment building, Emilio Grifalconi, "a cabinet-maker from Verona," gives Valène an unusual object in appreciation of a family portrait the artist has painted for him. The object resembles "a large cluster of coral," and it has been produced by the solidification of a liquid mixture Grifalconi once injected into the tangle of minute tunnels that termites had bored inside the base of an antique wooden table. Even reinforced, the base proves too fragile to support the table top and has to be replaced; but Grifalconi salvages

> the fabulous arborescence within, this exact record of the worms' life inside the wooden mass: a static, mineral accumulation of all the movements that had constituted their blind existence, their undeviating single-mindedness, their obstinate itineraries; the faithful materialisation of all they had eaten and digested as they forced from their dense surroundings the invisible elements needed for their survival, the explicit, visible, immeasurably disturbing image of the endless progressions that had reduced the hardest of woods to an impalpable network of crumbling galleries.

Since the object is referred to at one point as a *réseau de vers*, which can mean a network not only of worms but of verses, we can claim it for literature; most usefully, for this very book. The novel is certainly a "record of life" in all its "obstinate itineraries," at least as it has manifested itself in a particular place during a longish time. The book's pretext of methodically reviewing the inhabitants of a variously populated apartment house guarantees as much. But as I have suggested, this pretext does not necessarily correspond to what actually happens. Perec's deliberate cataloging enables him to reinforce his personal narrative with an apparently authoritative objectivity. For example, when in chapter seventeen the logical sequence of his investigation lands him "On the Stairs," we find there—not by chance and not by rote—the Perec-like Valène engaged in melancholy reflection:

> The stairs, for him, were, on each floor, a memory, an emotion, something ancient and impalpable, something palpitating somewhere in the guttering flame of his memory: a gesture, a noise, a flicker, a young woman singing operatic arias to her own piano accompaniment, the clumsy clickety-clack of a typewriter . . . or, on the sixth floor right, the

persistent droning hum of Gaspard Winckler's jigsaw, to which, three
floors lower, on the third floor left, there was now by way of response
only a continuing, and intolerable, silence.

Here as elsewhere, Perec has used his systems to discover exactly what he
needs to say as a novelist—in this case, to confront us through his counterpart with a vision of the evanescence of things past and present. Such visions recur throughout the novel, and they are what to me make Grifalconi's
salvaged arborescence such an appropriate emblem of the book: life, and
lives, leave nothing behind them but a faint or ossified residue. Once gone,
they "mean" no more than these traces. And writing, like Grifalconi's sculp-
ture, sometimes is such a trace.

I wrote that *Life A User's Manual* might be read as part of Perec's preoccupation with the autobiography he could never write since, in his case, the
"historical" pretext of writing was a dumbfounding sense of emptiness and
death. But if the novel ends in the fatal, futile "closure" of its protagonists'
careers, we reach that point only after exploring a prodigiously varied universe of high and low life:

> One day, well before his fatal hibernation had gripped him, [Grégoire
> Simpson] had told Morrelet how as a little boy he had played drum
> major with the *Matagassiers* on mid-Lent Sunday. His mother, a dress-
> maker, made the traditional costume herself: the red-and-white-squared
> trousers, the loose blue blouse, the white cotton bonnet with a tassel;
> and his father had bought him, in a fine circular box decorated with
> arabesques, the cardboard mask which looked like a cat's head. As proud
> as Punch and as grave as a judge, he ran through the streets of the old
> town along with the procession, from Place du Château to Porte des
> Allinges, and from Porte de Rives to Rue Saint-Sébastien, before going
> up into the high town, to the Belvedères, to stuff himself with juniper-
> roast ham and to slake his thirst with great gulps of Ripaille, that white
> wine as light as glacier water, as dry as gunflint.

It hardly matters if this episode comes from observation, memory, or another book. Its value, that of a small item from a large repertory, can perhaps

be best discerned through one of Perec's definitions of his aims as a writer: "to pluck meticulous fragments from the deepening void, to leave somewhere or other a furrow, a trace." Just as in the novel James Sherwood collects *unica*, Perec gathered many such fragments and assembled them into a replica of his most treasured *unicum* of all. Death may come first and last; in between we find life: Perec has embedded his account of decay and loss in a painstaking and generous rendering of *"cette chose éphémère qu'est la vie."*

New York Review of Books, 1988

Appendix
Practical Illustrations

MATHEWS'S ALGORITHM

From the reader's point of view, the existence in literature of potentiality in its Oulipian sense has the charm of introducing duplicity into all written texts, whether Oulipian or not. It isn't merely a sonnet in Queneau's *One Hundred Thousand Billion Poems* on which doubt is cast by the horde of alternatives waiting to take its place: the most practical work of prose, no matter how sturdy it may seem in its apparent uniqueness, will prove just as fragile as soon as one thinks of subjecting it to the procedures of N + 7 or Semo-Definitional Literature.[1] Beyond the words being read, others lie in wait to subvert and perhaps surpass them. Nothing any longer can be taken for granted; every word has become a banana peel. The fine surface unity that a piece of writing proposes is belied and beleaguered; behind it, in the realm of potentiality, a dialectic has emerged.

The algorithm here discussed is a new means of tracking down this otherness hidden in language (and, perhaps, in what language talks about). It is one more way of saying two things at once. It has its particular attractions. First of all, it's a simple mechanism into which complex materials can be introduced. If these materials require a certain amount of care in their presentation to form an algorithmic table, their potential duplicity is realized through means that are virtually automatic. The algorithm can make use of existing material as well as of material specially invented for it (a point that will be abundantly demonstrated later on). Its creative potentiality can manifest itself either in the actual construction of the table or in its subsequent solution. It can be used both to decompose (or analyze) texts or to compose (or invent) them. Last, the algorithm can be applied to every one of the rows of Queneau's Table, semantic as well as syntactic. (And why stop there? The limitations adopted here—which run from letters to rudimentary semantic elements—define only a small part of what the algorithm can handle. It is capable of dealing with fragments of letters, either graphic or phonetic, as well as *their* component parts, not to mention amoebas, molecules, and quarks. It can juggle not only episodes of fiction, as will be shown later, but entire books, indeed entire literatures and civilizations, planets, solar systems, galaxies—anything in fact that can be manipulated either in its material or its symbolic form. . . .)

So: how does it work?

Here is what you do.

I. Materials

Several—at least two—sets of heterogeneous elements are required.

Comment: The heterogeneity can sometimes be minimal, but it is nonetheless essential for the proper functioning of the algorithm. The less it is respected, the more likely the machine will simply reproduce replicas of the original sets. In theory, to avoid any chance of this happening, the rule is that in a table of n elements, $n^2 - (n - 2)$ elements must be different. (Example: In a table of 4 sets of 4 elements, 14 of the 16 elements must differ.) In practice, however, it is often possible to lower this level of heterogeneity.

II. Arrangement

1. All sets must contain the same number of elements.
2. Each element in a set must have a function equivalent to or consistent with the corresponding elements of the other sets. (If, for instance, the elements are words, the equivalence will be one of grammatical function.) In other words, the elements of each set must be arranged in the same order (not $a_1b_1c_1d_1$ and $c_2a_2d_2b_2$ but $a_1b_1c_1d_1$ and $a_2b_2c_2d_2$).
3. The sets are superimposed one above the other to form a table consisting of rows (the sets) and columns (the corresponding elements). Here is a table of 4 sets of 4 elements:

$$
\begin{array}{c c c c c}
1 & a_1 & b_1 & c_1 & d_1 \\
2 & a_2 & b_2 & c_2 & d_2 \\
3 & a_3 & b_3 & c_3 & d_3 \\
4 & a_4 & b_4 & c_4 & d_4
\end{array}
$$

Comment: In all the examples, the number of elements in each set equals the number of sets. This is a convenience, not a requirement.

III. Operation

1. Shift each set n – 1 places left. (In other words, shift the second set one place left, the third two places, etc.)

$$
\begin{array}{c c c c c}
1 & \mathbf{a_1} & b_1 & c_1 & d_1 \\
2 & b_2 & c_2 & d_2 & \mathbf{a_2} \\
3 & c_3 & d_3 & \mathbf{a_3} & b_3 \\
4 & d_4 & \mathbf{a_4} & b_4 & c_4
\end{array}
$$

2. Read the columns downward starting with the initial elements *(a)* of
    the sets. Four new sets result:

$$\begin{array}{llll} \mathbf{a_1} & \mathbf{b_2} & \mathbf{c_3} & \mathbf{d_4} \\ \mathbf{a_2} & \mathbf{b_1} & \mathbf{c_2} & \mathbf{d_3} \\ \mathbf{a_3} & \mathbf{b_4} & \mathbf{c_1} & \mathbf{d_2} \\ \mathbf{a_4} & \mathbf{b_3} & \mathbf{c_4} & \mathbf{d_1} \end{array}$$

3. Perform the same manipulation with a shift *right:*

$$\begin{array}{lllll} 1 & \mathbf{a_1} & \mathbf{b_1} & \mathbf{c_1} & \mathbf{d_1} \\ 2 & \mathbf{d_2} & \mathbf{a_2} & \mathbf{b_2} & \mathbf{c_2} \\ 3 & \mathbf{c_3} & \mathbf{d_3} & \mathbf{a_3} & \mathbf{b_3} \\ 4 & \mathbf{b_4} & \mathbf{c_4} & \mathbf{d_4} & \mathbf{a_4} \end{array}$$

4. Read the results upward, still beginning with the initial elements *(a)* of
    the original sets:

$$\begin{array}{llll} \mathbf{a_1} & \mathbf{b_4} & \mathbf{c_3} & \mathbf{d_2} \\ \mathbf{a_2} & \mathbf{b_1} & \mathbf{c_4} & \mathbf{d_3} \\ \mathbf{a_3} & \mathbf{b_2} & \mathbf{c_1} & \mathbf{d_4} \\ \mathbf{a_4} & \mathbf{b_3} & \mathbf{c_2} & \mathbf{d_1} \end{array}$$

In this way, from *n* sets *2n* new sets can be obtained.

IV. Uses

The applications *of* the algorithm considered here are classified according to
the *elements* forming the sets: *a, b, c,* and so on will be, in turn, letters,
words, word groups, groups of word groups, and finally, semantic elements.

At every stage, two examples will be given, one involving existing material, the other new material.

1. Letters

(a) Using existing material: here, the words of all known languages, living or dead. From English:

$$
\begin{array}{cccc}
\mathbf{T} & I & N & E \\
\mathbf{S} & A & L & E \\
\mathbf{M} & A & L & E \\
\mathbf{V} & I & N & E \\
\end{array}
$$

After a shift left:

$$
\begin{array}{cccc}
\mathbf{T} & I & N & E \\
A & L & E & \mathbf{S} \\
L & E & \mathbf{M} & A \\
E & \mathbf{V} & I & N \\
\end{array}
$$

(tale, vile, mine, sane)

After a shift right:

$$
\begin{array}{cccc}
\mathbf{T} & I & N & E \\
E & \mathbf{S} & A & L \\
L & E & \mathbf{M} & A \\
I & N & E & \mathbf{V} \\
\end{array}
$$

(tile, sine, mane, vale)

(b) Using new material, i.e., words that do not yet exist, in known or imaginary languages.

This example is drawn from the dialect of a Montagnard tribe in Pan-Nam (cf. H. Mathews, *The Sinking of the Odradek Stadium*) that uses a vocabulary at once spontaneous and combinatorial:

B	A	G	O
K	E	D	U
F	E	S	I
L	O	M	I

After a shift left:

B	A	G	O
E	D	U	**K**
S	I	**F**	E
I	**L**	O	M

(besi, ladi, fogu, kemo)

After a shift right:

B	A	G	O
U	**K**	E	D
S	I	**F**	E
O	M	I	**L**

(bosu, kami, fegi, ledo)

2. Words

Here the rule of equivalence (II,2) becomes obligatory. Sets of words[2] must be arranged in identical grammatical sequence.

(a) Using existing material: Take the first lines of four well-known sonnets of Shakespeare:

> Shall I compare thee to a summer's day?
> Music to hear, why hear'st thou music sadly?
> That time of year thou may'st in me behold . . .
> Farewell! thou art too dear for my possessing . . .

Arrangement: Reduce each line to four main words (the remaining words will be considered as their auxiliaries):

I, compare, summer, day	(shall, thee, to a)
music, hear, thou, music	(why, sadly)
time, year, thou, behold	(that, of, in me)
farewell, thou, art (dear), possessing	(too, for my)

Align these four sets according to corresponding parts of speech:

I	summer	day	compare	(shall, thee, to a)
thou	music	music	hear	(why, sadly)
thou	time	year	behold	(that, of, in me)
thou	farewell	possessing	art (dear)	(too, for my)

Apply a shift left to this table. The results will read:

I	summer	day	compare
music	music	hear	thou
year	behold	thou	time
art (dear)	thou	farewell	possessing

Reintroducing the auxiliaries, compose four new lines in blank verse (the openings of four undiscovered Shakespearean sonnets):

> The music of the years, too dear for me . . .
> The summer's music sadly thou beholdest . . .
> Today thou may'st in me hear the farewell . . .
> Possessing thee, why doth my Time compare . . .

Similarly, after a shift right:

> Shall I, sadly hearing the year's farewell . . .
> Possessing me, thou hast beheld my summer . . .
> Too dear a music for a day thou art . . .
> Music thou art of Time, that doth compare thee . . .

(b) Using new material: In the following example, where words are taken one by one, four propositions are arranged according to the rules of the algorithm:

Truth	left	him	cold.
Wealth	made	her	glad.
Work	turned	you	sour.
Love	kept	me	free.

After a shift left:

Truth	made	you	free.
Love	left	her	sour.
Work	kept	him	glad.
Wealth	turned	me	cold.

After a shift right:

Truth	kept	you	glad.
Wealth	left	me	sour.
Work	made	him	free.
Love	turned	her	cold.

Extending the notion of word to include auxiliaries (Cf. IV, 2, a), we can move on to a more elaborate table:

Frustrated members	of the Cabinet	were found conspiring in	local massage parlors.
Drivers	from the Sanitation Department	will go on strike against	the new garbage helicopters
Six terrorists	of the Keep Kids Kleen Klub	have planted bombs in	sexually integrated restrooms.
Female impersonators	not licensed by their union	are not allowed into	nursing schools.

After a shift left we read:

Frustrated members	from the Sanitation Department	have planted bombs in	nursing schools.
Female impersonators	of the Cabinet	will go on strike against	sexually integrated restrooms.
Six terrorists	not licensed by their union	were found conspiring in	the new garbage helicopters.
Drivers	of the Keep Kids Kleen Klub	are not allowed into	local massage parlors.

And after a shift to the right:

Frustrated members	not licensed by their union	have planted bombs in	the new garbage helicopters.
Drivers	of the Cabinet	are not allowed into	sexually integrated restrooms.
Six terrorists	from the Sanitation Department	were found conspiring in	nursing schools.
Female imper-sonators	of the Keep Kids Kleen Klub	will go on strike against	local massage parlors.

3. Word groups (verses, sentences)

(a) Using existing material: Returning to Shakespeare, take fourteen of his best known sonnets, arrange the verses of each sonnet horizontally so as to form a set, and superimpose the sets. After a shift left, here is the first of the fourteen possible readings (slightly edited as to punctuation):

> Shall I compare thee to a summer's day
> And dig deep trenches in thy beauty's field?
> Why lov'st thou that which thou receiv'st not gladly,
> Bare ruin'd choirs where late the sweet birds sang?
> Anon permit the basest clouds to ride
> And do what'er thou wilt, swift-footed Time:
> Nor Mars his sword, nor war's quick fire, shall burn
> Even such a beauty as you master now.
> Love's not Time's fool, though rosy lips and cheeks
> (When other petty griefs have done their spite,
> And heavily) from woe to woe tell o'er
> That Time will come and take my love away;
> For thy sweet love remembered such wealth brings
> As any she belied beyond compare.

Comment: It is perhaps at this point that the analytic potential of the algorithm clearly manifests itself. The new poem throws light on the structure and movement of the Shakespearean sonnet.

(b) Using new material: The following example demonstrates a table made up of three sets of three sentences. Each sentence refers to an event concerning three different characters.

The conductor wanted his orchestra to produce an utterly muffled sound.	He declared, "If we keep everything low key, perhaps we can work out a satisfactory arrangement."	He kept insisting: "Please don't strike the drums with anything harder than a sponge!"
The young Laotian chiropodist wandered around New York with his phrase book, which was a fraud—a collection of useless, ridiculous expressions.	He kept repeating his request without ever managing to get what he wanted: an adequate supply of absorbent cotton.	It wasn't until he flashed a fat bankroll that a compassionate saleswoman at last took care of him.
A crafty sheik came to town to buy a wife on favorable terms.	He tried Macy's, Bloomingdale's, and Korvette's without finding what he needed.	Since it was hard to take him seriously, everyone simply ignored his words.

After a shift left:

The conductor wanted his orchestra to produce an utterly muffled sound.	He kept repeating his request without ever managing to get what he wanted: an adequate supply of absorbent cotton.	Since it was hard to take him seriously, everyone simply ignored his words.

The young Laotian
chiropodist wandered
around New York with
his phrase book, which
was a fraud—a collec-
tion of useless,
ridiculous expressions.

He tried Macy's
Bloomingdale's, and
Korvette's without
finding what he
needed.

He kept insisting:
"Please don't strike
the drums with any-
thing harder than a
sponge!"

A crafty sheik came to
town to buy a wife on
favorable terms.

He declared, "If we
keep everything low
key, perhaps we can
work out a satisfactory
arrangement."

It wasn't until he
flashed a fat bankroll
that a compassionate
saleswoman at last
took care of him.

4. Groups of word groups (stanzas, paragraphs, episodes, etc.)

(a) Using existing material: Shakespeare is here joined by George Herbert,
    Ben Jonson, and John Donne. Take four sonnets that follow the
    Shakespearean model and divide them into their four main compo-
    nents: three quatrains and the concluding couplet. Using these compo-
    nents as elements, align those of each poem horizontally to form a set.
    Arrange the sets as a table. Here, after a shift left, is the first of four
    possible readings:

> Farewell! thou art too dear for my possessing,
> And like enough thou know'st thy estimate:
> The charter of thy worth gives thee releasing,
> My bonds in thee are all determinate,
> While mortal love doth all the title gain!
> Which siding with invention, they together
> Bear all the sway, possessing heart and brain
> (Thy workmanship) and give thee share in neither.
> But now thy work is done, if they that view
> The several figures languish in suspense
> To judge which passions false, and which is true,
> Between the doubtful sway of reason and sense;

> That thou remember them, some claim as debt;
> I think it mercy if thou wilt forget.

(b) Using new material: Here a process of condensation can be profitably introduced. Rather than manipulate lengthy paragraphs, it seems more interesting to apply the algorithm directly to more substantial entities. The elements in the following examples are fictional episodes, summed up in one or two sentences:

1. (a) A and B are husband and wife. (b) A is summoned to the bedside of his ailing mother. (c) At this very moment B becomes involved with someone else. (d) On his return, A feels disgust for B, whom he decides to exclude from his life. (e) B has a nervous breakdown.

2. (a) A loves B. B does not love A. (b) When he inherits a fortune, A at first thinks of letting B benefit from it. (c) In the meantime, B, who has fallen on evil days, starts thinking of A as a possible savior. (d) If B now looks on A with fresh eyes, A, absorbed in his new life, is gradually forgetting about B altogether. (e) A and B never see each other again.

3. (a) A owes B a great deal of money. (b) Having decided he must earn financial independence, A settles in a developing country, where he succeeds in amassing a fortune. (c) B's mother gives B an unexpected sum of money. She also tells B of the goal A has set himself. (d) These new circumstances move B to suggest to A that he forget his former obligations. (e) A never forgives B for nullifying the solicitude of so many years.

4. (a) A knows young B well, but he does not know that he is B's father. B is also ignorant of the fact. (b) A accidentally learns that he is the father of a child whom he has never known. He drops everything to look for his offspring. (c) B's mother falls ill; B is notified. (d) B thus finds A at the ailing woman's bedside. B's unexpected appearance is the immediate cause of her death. (e) The relationship between A and B remains unchanged.

5. (a) A and B know each other. A decides to kill B in order to experience an existential "random act." (b) A falls in love with an acquaintance of

B. (c) Quite involuntarily, B becomes violently resentful of this person for taking A away. (d) Furious at B's outrageous behavior, A abandons his plan. But A's anger starts B wondering if he isn't considering murder. (e) B kills A.

After a shift right:

1. (a) A and B are husband and wife. (b) A falls in love with an acquaintance of B. (c) B's mother falls ill; B is notified. (d) These new circumstances move B to suggest to A that he forget his former obligations. (e) A and B never see each other again.

2. (a) A loves B. B does not love A. (b) A is summoned to the bedside of his ailing mother. (c) Quite involuntarily, B becomes furiously resentful of this person for taking A away. (d) B thus finds A at the ailing woman's bedside. B's unexpected appearance is the immediate cause of her death. (e) A never forgives B for nullifying the solicitude of so many years.

3. (a) A owes B a great deal of money. (b) When he inherits a fortune, A at first thinks of letting B benefit from it. (c) At this very moment B becomes involved with someone else. (d) Furious at B's outrageous behavior, A abandons his plan. But A's anger starts B wondering if he isn't considering murder. (e) The relationship between A and B remains unchanged.

4. (a) A knows young B well, but he does not know that he is B's father. B is also ignorant of the fact. (b) Having decided he must earn financial independence, A settles in a developing country, where he succeeds in amassing a fortune. (c) In the meantime, B, who has fallen on evil days, starts thinking of A as a possible savior. (d) On his return, A feels disgust for B, whom he decides to exclude from his life. (e) B kills A.

5. (a) A and B know each other. A decides to kill B in order to experience an existential "random act." (b) A accidentally learns that he is the father of a child whom he has never known. He drops everything to look for his offspring. (c) B's mother gives B an unexpected sum of money. She also tells B of the goal A has set himself. (d) If B now looks on A with fresh eyes, A, absorbed in his new life, is gradually forgetting about B altogether. (e) B has a nervous breakdown.

5. Semantic elements

The Oulipo divides constrictive structures into *syntactic* and *semantic*. The former affect the material aspects of language (letters, words, syntax): the latter affect what language talks about (subject, content, meaning). Obviously, in the last example we have already moved from syntactic to semantic objects. Perhaps it will suffice to speed the algorithm on its course toward the absolute by ending this demonstration with one or two examples in which the semantic factor is even stronger.

(a) Using existing material: in this case, *Hamlet.* We can sum up our perception of the play according to the rules of the algorithm:

1. Having received instructions,	the son	hesitantly	chooses revenge.	Death is the condition of success.
2. Irrepressibly erotic,	the widowed mother	hastily	remarries.	This is a deceptive pleasure.
3. In the clutches of resentment,	the uncle	desperately	indulges a posthumous passion.	Can we possibly approve?
4. Royally willful,	the dead man	obsessively	tries to rewrite history.	Someone has to pay.
5. A prey to this incestuous violence,	Ophelia	faithfully	abandons her reason and her life.	A father's death is also involved.

After a shift to the right:

1. Having received instruc-tions,	Ophelia	obsessively	indulges a posthu-mous passion.	This is a deceptive pleasure.
2. Irrepressi-bly erotic,	the son	faithfully	tries to rewrite history.	Can we possible approve?
3. In the clutches of resentment,	the wid-owed mother	hesitantly	abandons her reason and her life.	Someone has to pay.
4. Royally willful,	the uncle	hastily	chooses revenge.	A father's death is also involved.
5. A prey to this inces-tuous vio-lence,	the dead man	desperately	remarries.	Death is the condi-tion of success.

Here is another way of handling the same subject:

1. With the husband dead,	the mother	marries	the brother-in-law.
2. With the father dead,	the son	chooses	the mother.
3. With Ophelia dead,	reason	takes	a holiday.

4. With the brother dead,	the uncle	falls victim to	the son.

After a shift right:

1. With the husband dead,	the uncle	takes	the mother.
2. With the father dead,	the mother	falls victim to	a holiday.
3. With Ophelia dead,	the son	marries	the son.
4. With the brother dead,	reason	chooses	the brother-in-law.

Comment: It is probably unnecessary to point out that, here as elsewhere, the results yielded by existing works can be used in two ways: either as a means of commenting on those works or as materials for inventing new ones.

(b) Using new material: For this last example, the elements are far more abstract (although the abstraction falls short of actual concept); they represent situations or events that writers have used since the beginning of literature. They have been arranged in patterns of minimal causality.

Given love,	consummation;	therefore resumption.
Given possession,	danger;	therefore flight.
Given victory,	war;	therefore reassessment.

After a shift left:

Given love,	danger;	therefore reassessment.
Given victory,	consummation;	therefore flight.
Given possession,	war;	therefore resumption.

After a shift right:

Given love,	war;	therefore flight.
Given possession,	consummation;	therefore reassessment.
Given victory,	danger;	therefore resumption.

Comment: Perhaps more clearly than the preceding ones, this example shows how the inventiveness of the algorithm (indeed, of Oulipian techniques in general) can be realized in two ways: (1) in the setting up of the constrictive structure and (2) in its solution. In most of the earlier examples, the algorithm has produced its effect by requiring the creation of a table that "works" (cf. what is needed to solve a crossword puzzle). In the last example, on the other hand, one's ingenuity must be exerted to complete or justify the table (cf. what is involved in working out a procedure like Queneau's procedure, "the character x takes y for z"). This last table is a table of *provocation*.

It must be realized that whatever its semantic level, the material of the algorithm must always be manipulated syntactically. (In the examples drawn from *Hamlet,* the elements are *handled* as words or phrases, no matter what their meaning is.) The algorithm can approach abstraction only through simple linguistic systems.

And also, perhaps, through its actual operation: It is here, at any rate, that the "meaning" of the algorithm is to be found. This meaning is nothing new as far as the activity of the Oulipo is concerned. First of all, two other Oulipian structures can be classed as special cases of the algorithm (that is, with sets composed of two elements): the perverbial poem and the equivoque (or "Poem for Möbius Strip"). Furthermore, the algorithm fits in with the Oulipo's general interest in combinatorial literature: the results the algorithm produces are, after all, only segments of the much vaster range of circular permutations that each of its tables implies. The algorithm would thus have as its remote ancestor the *Ars Magna* of Ramon Llull, which inspired Giordano Bruno's admiration, Leibnitz's *Dissertatio de Arte Combinatoria*, and Martin Gardner's genuine, albeit skeptical, interest. In Llull's work, circular permutations are given literal shape in figures consisting of concentric circles. These circles are divided into sections; when turned, each circle can form with its neighbors all the combinations possible between their respective sections. If most of Llull's figures contain only two circles, one of them—the *figura universalis*—has as many as fourteen.

Fourteen concentric circles: wouldn't Llull then become a forerunner of one of the most extraordinary works the Oulipo has produced, the *One Hundred Thousand Billion Poems* of Raymond Queneau? It is perfectly possible to inscribe Queneau's sonnets on the *figura universalis*. Each circle need simply be divided into ten sections. The outermost circle would contain the first verses of the poems, the circle next to it the second verses, and so on. The arrangement would provide as complete a means of reading the work as it finds in book form (and, probably, a more convenient one). The suggestion that this work of Queneau's be assigned to the Llullian combinatorial tradition is made not for the sake of claiming it as a "relative" of the algorithm but in order to set the latter in its proper place among Oulipian structures. By the way they basically function, these structures can be divided into two complementary categories. The first category is that of the proliferation of possibilities; the second is that of their reduction. In the first we find forms like Semo-Definitional Literature, the Lescurian word square, and attempts at "record setting" (Perec's lipogram and palindrome). In the

DORMOUSE POEM

There is no raw material

Late one spring, I caught a dormouse that must have recently become a mother: while visiting the attic of our farmhouse the next day, I heard a small cheeping sound that led me to two hairless pink baby dormice that had emerged from their hidden nest to wriggle blindly across the floor in quest of the sustenance that only their mother could provide.

Let's take a photograph. The babies are dead and gone. The image looks like nothing imaginable and is clearly pretextual.

I encountered my first dormouse when I saw it perched on a hot-water pipe running under the ceiling of the stable that I had made into a living-room in my house in **Lans-en-Vercors.** The pipe formed one end of a dormouse run that led from the entrance to the room on the south side to a wall, perpendicular to the north side, that separated the stable from a cold-storage room; the wall doubtless concealed a **rodent stairway,** or perhaps elevator, to the upper floor and beyond that to the attic. In the living-room, the visible dormouse route included the hot-water pipe

resistants battle in a coal-mining region

row dents: tear weight

wouldn't main chirr?

tissue like late Gothic architecture

Siamese l'ébrécheur de merles sans son, aide à lilas bol y va

the prank and the Pope si mon bock a l'nez gras

composite hip

the greatest flax

the inspired actress- detective

cheering drums

(south), the top of the **wooden manger** (folklorically left in place), the books on the top shelf of a narrow bookcase, and a plastic wiring tube (east), finally another hot-water pipe leading into the **perpendicular wall** (north).

The shelf of books on this dormouse highway held nothing but opera librettos. Not long after their first appearance, the dormice began eating—nibbling, really—a number of librettos, taking extreme care in their selection. Paperbound and slim, the librettos were packed tightly together in chronological order without any consideration of nationality, so that I was surprised to see that the dormice had managed to extract *Thaïs, Les Pêcheurs de Perles, Samson et Dalila,* and *Bolivar* for their exclusive nourishment. Their adroitness as well as their altogether sympathetic patriotism easily persuaded me to tolerate their misdemeanors.

The day nevertheless came when, having found the edges of *Dido and Aeneas* and *Simon Boccanegra* showing familiar mutilations, I knew that the dormice must go. I caught one with a rat trap. I found it, not dead, with its skull cracked and its right eye half out of its socket and left it in the trap for half an hour in a sinkful of water before throwing it on its back in the **compost heap.** Three hours later the dormouse had righted itself and was breathing in hurried gasps. I put it out of its misery, swearing I would never again inflict such suffering on so courageous a creature.

I then acquired two cats, Basta and **Max.** Basta, a talented mouser, proved useless in catching dormice. They continued to look down on us from the hot-water pipe and Basta would look back, his body elongated towards them like a rubber band stretched to the limit, or **Saint Teresa in her ecstacy,** the image of absolute yearning. I meanwhile fell madly in love with the cats, the first I'd ever had.

Having learned of **Have-A-Heart** traps, I decided to try one out: a rectangular wire box with a narrowing entrance at one end that led into a kind of antechamber from which the quarry was then supposed to nose his way under a horizontally hinged lid that closed behind him as he reached the bait (for dormice, **a piece of fruit**). It struck me that even a curious beast would need the user's manual to penetrate all the way to the heart of this contraption. And why would he ever go near it in the first place?

Apis of root

I felt that I could at least mitigate the latter problem; so after baiting the trap with a slice of apple and setting it behind the upright board that crowned the bookcase against the perpendicular wall (the northern hot-water pipe passed through it), I surrounded the cage on every side with broken pieces of **Melba toast,** which for some reason I felt would appeal to dormice and conceivably draw their attention to the trap's existence.

drinking Violetta's health

The day passed. I was alone at the time. After dinner, I sat down at my harpsichord (directly in front of the libretto shelves, with the perpendicular wall at my back). I began sightreading the *Goldberg Variations* and was well into the repeat of the second half of the theme when I heard behind me a rapid crunching sound. Turning round, I beheld a young dormouse, its elbows resting on the library cornice, a fragment of Melba toast in its paws, its **kohl-ringed eyes** staring at me, its ears cocked, its head tilted to one side in the manner of Georges Perec. I dared not move, or even stop playing, and so read on, from time to time glancing around at my ever-attentive audience, until at last its appetite for Bach or for Melba toast diminished and it disappeared. I couldn't of course tell whether it was this or another animal that I found next morning in the trap, possessed by the apparent demons **of terror and furious disbelief** that were soon to become familiar to me.

a justice's deviations

gold rink-dyes

France in the 1790s: unrestrained loss of faith

Since then I have caught hundreds of dormice, at least ten every year and one year as many as fifty-nine. The bay, beep Poons!

the goal-net
needed a bigger
woman

swish annual guy

Delft under
Demeter
the Apostles'
cento prosodies

nocturne alters
itches

fishbait:
parmesan

long after our
death

variation in numbers has less to do with **baby booms** than with the mundane fact of my presence in mid spring, when the dormice awaken from their winter slumber, and mid fall, when they arrive for the next hibernation. Once caught, they are immediately transferred to **a roomier bird cage.** The transfer demands alertness—the animals are as prehensilely agile as monkeys and fast as quail; in fact the only way I ever caught one that got away was while it flew through the air. When there are four or five dormice in the cage I drive across the valley into a forest and release them. Once they realize I am not subjecting them to yet another humiliating trick, they shoot out of the cage and across the ground to the nearest tree, whose far side they climb to a safe height before stopping to peer down at me. According to my **Swiss animal guide,** dormice are sedentary and will not travel more than **twelve hundred meters,** so there is little risk of their invading the nearest farms, and none at all of their returning to mine.

Sometimes after dinner on autumn nights, when Marie and I were reading in the living room, we would hear the dormice beginning to stir in their cage (they are **nocturnal creatures**), I would move the cage nearer to the couch where we sat, and we would abandon our books to watch our captives bustle about their wire walls and aggressively take turns running in the **drum-like wheel** (intended for I know not what pet) that I had fastened to one side of the cage; its contours blurred with the speed of the whirl imparted to it. At the end of the evening, after turning out the lights, we could hear the wheel whirring in the dark late into the night, **late into our sleep.**

Textual intercourse

A. Markers:

slice a single intuition into several simultaneous approaches
take away writing's patent of nobility
the myth of *raw* material
magnetize the filings in a particular direction
the implied stereotype and its proper name
conversely, reread an existing stereotype literally
originality vs/with dehierarchized leveling, plus (above all) efficacy
poetry: infrapersonal static spaces (Baudelaire's *spleen*, Mallarmé's
    azur, etc.)
how to treat Unidentified Verbal Objects with poetic precision
    without freeze-framing them?

B. Explorations

[1. Rhymes:

dormouse	twelve hundred meters
farmhouse	nocturnal creatures
mutilations	crunching sound
Goldberg Variations	turning round

    the variation
    the next hibernation]

[2. Narrative elements omitted:

> the young dormouse behind the bedroom wall-hanging
> the stubborn young dormouse that pried its wire bars apart
> the asbestos fire-gloves used to handle the dormice
> the ineffectual air-pistol]

3.   dormouse   *ruse mood*
        door muse   mode or us
        door: me, us   more do us
        doom ruse   muse rood
        doom user   moor Duse
        doom rues   moor-used
        doom suer   mouse rod
        Duse, Moro   ur Om-dose
        douse ROM   *used room*
        O rum dose!   sour dome
        O use dorm!   sour mode
        our domes   *some dour*
        rouse mod   sue O dorm!

4. Identified verbal objects

> Lans-en-Vercors
> rodent stairway
> wooden manger
> perpendicular wall
> Thaïs
> Samson et Dalila
> Les Pêcheurs de Perles
> Bolivar
> Dido and Aeneas
> Simon Boccanegra

compost heap
Basta and Max
Saint Teresa in her ecstacy
Have-A-Heart traps
a piece of fruit
Melba toast
Goldberg Variations
kohl-ringed eyes
terror and furious disbelief
baby booms
roomier bird cage
Swiss animal guide
twelve hundred meters
nocturnal creatures
drum-like wheel
late into our sleep

5. Use:

Experiment:

Cross two Rousselian procedures—homophony, polysemy

Example:

the verbal object "twelve hundred meters"

through homophony: Delft under Demeter

through polysemy:
The Apostles [twelve] cento [hundred] meters
        [= prosodic measures]

divide and recombine:

> For Demeter, cento meters
> Delft under the Apostles

hence:

> "   . . . At a wedding the
> pertinent goddess approached among prodigious pastiche
>   prosodies."

> "   . . . dusty missionaries
> shunted down corridors of blue-and-white tiles."

Birth [draft]

After the conclusive battle of the sounding horns,
    incense rose towards a resistance of slag heaps.
The accumulated weeping left the gaze of the onlookers absorbed
    by the destructive string of holes pierced in the rock.
Clumsily installed, big drains then buzzed in the champagne flood
    that drenched our domes and anchors. In time they dried; but
then disease afflicted us, a disease that gave outer cells the
    precedence of birth, so that buffoons came to blows over
their likeness, to hammer-beam roofs. One of them was singled out,
    after the plucky judgment of some dour woman in a ruse mood:
"Germans are all Siamese." Others remained silent—the bitch,
    the strong man, the lilac—and in silence they flourished.
Next came the exquisite effacer, chipping the beaks of
    sinful Nymphenburg blackbirds, and "the Latino," throwing
his weight behind the bowl inscribed *Libertador* in the great
    tableware rebellion, and a lady who expired without notice
from the pope, who had been tricked into visiting a beloved
    aunt by some doltish Faust, his mouth black with stein foam.
We read the report of the thigh joint assembled out of odds and
    ends, the slaughter of unharvested hemp, and the lambs
still fairest at the country fair. Deluded by a prankish hussy,
    a sculptor refused to cast his favorite actress-detective
in bronze—he was the typical victim of a reverse-brainstorming
    percussion device that in cheerful mode contracted
rather than expanded mental processes; so instead he developed his great
    potato monument, which had the shape of a cuddly bull.
The usual ladies convened at Violetta's. A health was drunk
    in the digs of a young swell. Through the frozen city
islanders searched for their relative, the judge, uselessly
    tracking down his familiar deviations, beholding in passing
the watery essence under skaters' blades aglow with myriad
    tributary wedding bands—a reminder of Paris in the '90s

in the midst of so much regularisation (the athlete struggling,
     in frantic loss of faith, to pare his beloved discus
down to official dimensions; across the vast natural harbor
     a plethora of boatswains piping, in hierarchical pain,
the abstractionist out to sea on a raft of spars; the
     reformer's throat too sore to utter his door-muse's name;
the guttural goal keeper fined for swearing; dusty missionaries
     shunted down corridors of blue-and-white tiles). There were
hopeful signals, too. Tab, an active gay and town favorite,
     was named "Muslin Man of the Year." At a wedding the
pertinent goddess approached among prodigious pastiche prosodies.
     A sympathetic observer who had contracted hives found relief
in the night-blooming compositions of John Field played by
     a relay of select melancholics. Another citizen survived
torture—he repeated the word "Parmesan" while smothering
     in a bath of live worms and grasshoppers that were
transforming him into "a loathsome coward"—to tell us, "We
     pursue our lives in a used room where the thought
of 'long after' lurks in the closet grasping a red-scare scenario
     of my death. But as we hear the casino wheels whirring late
into the night, late into our sleep, a pink fuse slips towards
     the light (nettle root, red-onion sprout, fur-nestled bud),
towards the light, nakedness, and decisive surprise."

                            Key West, January 20, 1995

Birth

After the conclusive battle of the sounding horns,
      incense rose towards a resistance of slag heaps.
The accumulated weeping left the gaze of the onlookers absorbed
      by the string of hard holes dug out of the rock.
Clumsily restored, big drains then buzzed in a bubbly flood
      that drenched our domes and anchors. In time they dried; but
disease then afflicted us, a disease that gave outer cells the
      precedence of birth, so that buffoons came to blows over
their likeness to old slabs. Some remained silent—the bitch,
      the goon, the lilac—and in silence they flourished.
The exquisite effacer began chipping the beaks of sinful
      Nymphenburg blackbirds; the Unifier threw his weight behind
the bowl inscribed *Libertador* in the great tableware
      rebellion. We read of the thigh joint made of odds and ends,
the razing of unharvested hemp, the lambs
      still fairest at the country fair. A sculptor refused
to cast his favorite actress-detective in bronze and instead
      raised his great potato monument in the shape of a cuddly
bull. The usual ladies convened at Violetta's. A health was drunk
      in the digs of a young swell. Lost islanders searched for a
relative, beholding in passing the scrumble under skaters'
      blades aglow with tributary wedding bands. The desperate
athlete struggled to hammer his discus into humiliatingly
      reduced dimensions. Across the vast natural harbor,
in hierarchical grief, a plethora of boatswains piped
      out to sea an abstractionist lashed to two spars.
The reformer's throat was sore; the guttural goal keeper
      was fined for swearing; dusty missionaries were shunted down
corridors of blue-and-white tiles. There were hopeful signals,
      too. At a wedding the fitting goddess was seen to approach
among impertinent pastiche prosodies. A sympathetic observer who
      had contracted hives found relief in the night-blooming

music of John Field played by relays of select
         melancholics. A citizen survived torture by repeating
the word "Parmesan" as he was smothered in a bath of live worms
         or grasshoppers that was transforming him into "a loathsome
coward." He told us, "We pursue our lives in a drab room where
         the ghost of 'long after' lurks in the closet grasping a
red-scare scenario of my death. But as we hear the casino wheels
         whirring into the night, into our sleep, pink fuses slip
towards the light—nettle root, red-onion sprout, fur-nestled
         worm—towards the light, nakedness, and decisive surprise."

                                        Key West, March 13, 1995

Onward: Contemporary Poetry and Poetics, 1996

SELECTED DALKEY ARCHIVE PAPERBACKS

PIERRE ALBERT-BIROT, *Grabinoulor.*
YUZ ALESHKOVSKY, *Kangaroo.*
FELIPE ALFAU, *Chromos.*
  Locos.
  Sentimental Songs.
ALAN ANSEN, *Contact Highs: Selected Poems 1957-1987.*
DAVID ANTIN, *Talking.*
DJUNA BARNES, *Ladies Almanack.*
  Ryder.
JOHN BARTH, *LETTERS.*
  Sabbatical.
ANDREI BITOV, *Pushkin House.*
LOUIS PAUL BOON, *Chapel Road.*
ROGER BOYLAN, *Killoyle.*
CHRISTINE BROOKE-ROSE, *Amalgamemnon.*
BRIGID BROPHY, *In Transit.*
GERALD L. BRUNS,
  Modern Poetry and the Idea of Language.
GABRIELLE BURTON, *Heartbreak Hotel.*
MICHEL BUTOR,
  Portrait of the Artist as a Young Ape.
JULIETA CAMPOS, *The Fear of Losing Eurydice.*
ANNE CARSON, *Eros the Bittersweet.*
CAMILO JOSÉ CELA, *The Hive.*
LOUIS-FERDINAND CÉLINE, *Castle to Castle.*
  London Bridge.
  North.
  Rigadoon.
HUGO CHARTERIS, *The Tide Is Right.*
JEROME CHARYN, *The Tar Baby.*
MARC CHOLODENKO, *Mordechai Schamz.*
EMILY HOLMES COLEMAN, *The Shutter of Snow.*
ROBERT COOVER, *A Night at the Movies.*
STANLEY CRAWFORD, *Some Instructions to My Wife.*
ROBERT CREELEY, *Collected Prose.*
RENÉ CREVEL, *Putting My Foot in It.*
RALPH CUSACK, *Cadenza.*
SUSAN DAITCH, *L.C.*
  Storytown.
NIGEL DENNIS, *Cards of Identity.*
PETER DIMOCK,
  A Short Rhetoric for Leaving the Family.
COLEMAN DOWELL, *The Houses of Children.*
  Island People.
  Too Much Flesh and Jabez.
RIKKI DUCORNET, *The Complete Butcher's Tales.*
  The Fountains of Neptune.
  The Jade Cabinet.
  Phosphor in Dreamland.
  The Stain.
WILLIAM EASTLAKE, *The Bamboo Bed.*
  Castle Keep.
  Lyric of the Circle Heart.
STANLEY ELKIN, *Boswell: A Modern Comedy.*
  Criers and Kibitzers, Kibitzers and Criers.

  The Dick Gibson Show.
  The Franchiser.
  The MacGuffin.
  The Magic Kingdom.
  Mrs. Ted Bliss.
  The Rabbi of Lud.
  Van Gogh's Room at Arles.
ANNIE ERNAUX, *Cleaned Out.*
LAUREN FAIRBANKS, *Muzzle Thyself.*
  Sister Carrie.
LESLIE A. FIEDLER,
  Love and Death in the American Novel.
FORD MADOX FORD, *The March of Literature.*
JANICE GALLOWAY, *Foreign Parts.*
  The Trick Is to Keep Breathing.
WILLIAM H. GASS, *The Tunnel.*
  Willie Masters' Lonesome Wife.
ETIENNE GILSON, *The Arts of the Beautiful.*
  Forms and Substances in the Arts.
C. S. GISCOMBE, *Giscome Road.*
  Here.
KAREN ELIZABETH GORDON, *The Red Shoes.*
PATRICK GRAINVILLE, *The Cave of Heaven.*
HENRY GREEN, *Blindness.*
  Concluding.
  Doting.
  Nothing.
JIŘÍ GRUŠA, *The Questionnaire.*
JOHN HAWKES, *Whistlejacket.*
AIDAN HIGGINS, *Flotsam and Jetsam.*
ALDOUS HUXLEY, *Antic Hay.*
  Crome Yellow.
  Point Counter Point.
  Those Barren Leaves.
  Time Must Have a Stop.
GERT JONKE, *Geometric Regional Novel.*
DANILO KIŠ, *A Tomb for Boris Davidovich.*
TADEUSZ KONWICKI, *A Minor Apocalypse.*
  The Polish Complex.
ELAINE KRAF, *The Princess of 72nd Street.*
JIM KRUSOE, *Iceland.*
EWA KURYLUK, *Century 21.*
DEBORAH LEVY, *Billy and Girl.*
JOSÉ LEZAMA LIMA, *Paradiso.*
OSMAN LINS, *Avalovara.*
  The Queen of the Prisons of Greece.
ALF MAC LOCHLAINN, *The Corpus in the Library.*
  Out of Focus.
RON LOEWINSOHN, *Magnetic Field(s).*
D. KEITH MANO, *Take Five.*
BEN MARCUS, *The Age of Wire and String.*
WALLACE MARKFIELD, *Teitlebaum's Window.*
  To an Early Grave.
DAVID MARKSON, *Reader's Block.*
  Springer's Progress.
  Wittgenstein's Mistress.

FOR A FULL LIST OF PUBLICATIONS, VISIT:
www.dalkeyarchive.com

SELECTED DALKEY ARCHIVE PAPERBACKS

FOR A FULL LIST OF PUBLICATIONS, VISIT:
www.dalkeyarchive.com